THE CONTESTABLE CHURCH

This well-researched study explores Baptist identity as expressed in multiple theological and cultural approaches to congregational polity. As such, it provides an insightful history of Baptist ecclesiastical faith and practice, unity and disunity, and individual and collective expressions. Schelin's conclusions offer creative options for a Baptist congregational future, and none too soon.

—Bill J. Leonard, founding dean and professor of Divinity emeritus, School of Divinity, Wake Forest University

Taking seriously Baptists' fondness for dissent and democratic practice, Christopher Schelin transforms both into forces for cultivating a deeper sense of the church. In doing so, this book has shown Baptists one of the ways that they can witness to the kingdom of God in an ever-changing world.

—Derek C. Hatch, endowed chair of Baptist Studies, Georgetown College

Christopher Schelin makes a compelling case for a congregational ecclesiology that he aptly describes as a contestable church, where the way of the gospel is not subjected to the most influential voices or adjudicated by intricate procedural guidelines, but is discerned together in community as a matter of shared discipleship through the practices of cooperative reasoning. It is a most welcome contribution to current conversations about congregational ecclesiology in ecumenical perspective.

—Curtis W. Freeman, research professor of theology and director of the Baptist House of Studies, Duke Divinity School; and author of *Contesting Catholicity: Theology for Other Baptists*

In a time and place in which democracy appears to be imperiled, the value of diversity to a pluralistic society is questioned along with the very idea of such a society, the place of religion in public life is hotly contested, and the possibility of constructive dissent seems unimaginable in both society and church, *The Contestable Church* explores the ecclesiology of Baptist dissenters and discovers there a way of being a community of followers of Jesus Christ that can help Christian communities today envision a more faithful common life, as church and as participants in the civil order.

—Steven R. Harmon, professor of Historical Theology, Gardner-Webb University School of Divinity

PERSPECTIVES ON BAPTIST IDENTITIES

The National Association of Baptist Professors of Religion is proud to join with Mercer University Press in the creation of a new academic series. *Perspectives on Baptist Identities* will explore the rapidly evolving questions of identity that press upon those who call themselves Baptist in the twenty-first century: What does it mean to be Baptist? What does the future hold for Baptists? How does the Baptist tradition relate to the global Church and other ecclesial traditions? How does Baptist identity impact Scripture reading and Christian practice? The series hopes to generate significant scholarly research and engender fruitful and lively conversation among various types of Baptists and non-Baptists.

SERIES EDITORS

Dr. João B. Chaves
Assistant Professor of the History of Religion in the Américas
Baylor University

Dr. Kate Hanch
Pastor
United Methodist Church

PUBLISHED TITLES

Ryan Andrew Newson, *Inhabiting the World: Identity, Politics, and Theology in Radical Baptist Perspective*

Mikeal C. Parsons, *Crawford Howell Toy: The Man, the Scholar, the Teacher*

Amy L. Chilton and Steven R. Harmon, ed., *Sources of Light: Resources for Baptist Churches Practicing Theology*

João B. Chaves, *The Global Mission of the Jim Crow South: Southern Baptist Missionaries and the Shaping of Latin American Evangelicalism*

The Contestable Church

Dissent, Democracy, and Baptist Ecclesiology

CHRISTOPHER L. SCHELIN

MERCER UNIVERSITY PRESS
Macon, Georgia

MUP/ P694

© 2024 by Mercer University Press
Published by Mercer University Press
1501 Mercer University Drive
Macon, Georgia 31207
All rights reserved. This book may not be reproduced in whole or in part, including illustrations, in any form (beyond that copying permitted by Sections 107
and 108 of the U.S. Copyright Law and except by reviewers for the public press),
without written permission from the publisher.

28 27 26 25 24   5 4 3 2 1

Books published by Mercer University Press are printed on acid-free paper that
meets the requirements of the American National Standard for Information
Sciences—Permanence of Paper for Printed Library Materials.

Printed and bound in the United States.

This book is set in Adobe Caslon

Cover/jacket design by Burt&Burt.

ISBN   978-0-88146-927-1

CATALOGING-IN-PUBLICATION DATA IS AVAILABLE FROM
THE LIBRARY OF CONGRESS

CONTENTS

Abbreviations	vi
Acknowledgments	vii
Introduction	1
1: Baptist Democracy in Thought and Practice	25
2: Soul Competency and the Artistic Self	72
3: Receptive Generosity and Interdependent Personhood	113
4: Authority and Tradition	167
Conclusion	220
Bibliography	229
Index	245

ABBREVIATIONS

BGP   *Beyond Gated Politics*

BWA   Baptist World Alliance

CBF   Cooperative Baptist Fellowship

CGM   Church Growth Movement

CF   *The Coming Faith*

IAF   Industrial Areas Foundation

PO   *Priests to Each Other*

RG   *Rethinking Generosity and the Politics of Caritas*

RP   *Recovery of the Person*

SBC   Southern Baptist Convention

SNCC   Student Nonviolent Coordinating Committee

SPO   *Self/Power/Other*

ACKNOWLEDGMENTS

It is clear to me that, despite our best-laid plans, life is shaped most decisively by chance encounters, surprising interventions, and perhaps on certain occasions, acts of Providence. The path toward writing this book has been cleared by several fortuitous circumstances and the grace of companionship. If it is possible to name a distinct beginning to this journey, I attribute it to a conversation with my Duke Divinity School classmate Joel Goza, who shared his experience of the course co-taught by Romand Coles and Stanley Hauerwas. Several months after graduation, I began reading Coles and discovered resonances with Baptist ways of being church that now form the basis of my argument in the following pages.

The present work is adapted from my dissertation, completed at the International Baptist Theological Study Centre and Vrije Universiteit Amsterdam. I enrolled with the intent of studying another topic altogether, but the positive response to my initial paper encouraged me to change course. I extend my deepest appreciation to the entire learning community of IBTS faculty and peers for strengthening my argument with their questions and insights. I am especially grateful to my supervisors Keith Jones, Parush Parushev, and Eddy Van der Borght, as well as Tim and Ivana Noble and Nancey Murphy, for their feedback on my research presentations.

The tangible support of the communities where I have served professionally was essential to this project. I am grateful to the community of Roxboro Baptist Church for all the joys that came with being their associate pastor for several years, of which the study leaves and scholarship funds that enabled my research were just a small part. I offer special thanks to Rev. DuPre Sanders, a superb mentor in pastoral ministry, and Jack Hester, who chaired the scholarship committee. After moving to California and joining the staff of Starr King School for the Ministry, I benefited from further study leaves as well as a brief writing sabbatical. Thank you to the president, Rosemary Bray McNatt, and the dean of faculty, Gabriella Lettini, for giving me your unwavering support and trust.

Because I have been a firsthand witness to conflict among Baptists in its most destructive form, I very nearly abandoned my native tradition for what appeared to be greener theological pastures. My reaffirmation of this corner of the church catholic depends on many colleagues, friends, and congregations who have shared a vision worth claiming and advancing. I have especially learned so much from Curtis Freeman, whom in partial jest I call the most interesting Baptist theologian in the world, and Steven Harmon, who suggested that I publish in this book series and who provided guidance during the proposal process.

To my parents, thank you for loving me at every step along the way, and for faithfully representing the commitment to embody Christ's church as a community of mutual care and discipleship.

This work is dedicated to my wife, Kelly, my most welcome companion in all the planned and unplanned journeys of life, and to our children, Emma and Isaac, the theologians in residence who call forth the greatest wonder and praise.

MERCER UNIVERSITY PRESS

Endowed by

TOM WATSON BROWN
and
THE WATSON-BROWN FOUNDATION, INC.

INTRODUCTION

On May 9, 1963, the messengers assembled in Kansas City, Missouri, for the annual meeting of the Southern Baptist Convention voted to approve a revision to that denomination's confession of faith, the *Baptist Faith and Message*. One of the many changed sections was the article elaborating the Southern Baptist definition of a church, to which an addition was as follows: "The church is an autonomous body operating through democratic processes under the Lordship of Jesus Christ. In such a congregation, members are equally responsible."[1] Baptist confessions of faith are traditionally nonbinding, in that individual adherents are not required to give their assent, but if nothing more they are supposed to be representative of the prevalent convictions shared within the body. With this statement, Southern Baptists—the largest group of Baptists in the world and the largest Protestant denomination in the United States—declared a measure of affinity between their pattern of church government and that of their country's civil government. Their churches are, in some peculiar manner, democracies.

Is the ascription of democracy to congregational decision-making valid? The resemblances may be obvious to anyone possessed of at least a passing familiarity with both Baptist polity and democratic governance. The equivalence of these patterns for social organization has long been acknowledged by internal and external observers alike. Nevertheless, the application of democratic terminology has not sat comfortably with theologians who consider such rhetoric to be a categorical mistake that occludes the Church's distinctiveness from the world. This reticence to correlate congregational polity with democracy may be encapsulated in two major arguments. The first concerns the theologically appropriate understanding of authority. In his ecclesiological project, British Baptist Nigel Wright distinguishes congregationalism from empire-influenced ecclesial structures grouped under his concept of "sacred power," which is principally defined by a clerical elite who employ juridical coercion and even violence to enforce orthodox prescriptions.[2] Congregationalism wrests final decision-making authority away from the few and grants it to gathered

[1] Article VI, *Baptist Faith and Message* (1963), available at "Comparison Chart."
[2] Wright, *Free Church, Free State*, xvii–xix.

communities of believers who have affirmed one another's salvation. In place of the command structure of hierarchical systems and a portrait of God as despotic sovereign, the Baptist vision proposes mutual discernment and a God who invites obedience through persuasive love. Although the practical form of ecclesial self-governance resembles civil democracy, it cannot be so denoted because the exercise of Christ's rule is still the intended aim. Churches possess a restricted authority "under Christ as witnessed to by the Scriptures and interpreted by the Spirit."[3] A Baptist congregation may lack formal, external checks on exercising the "will of the people," but it still stands under normative judgment when it enacts collective choices that stray from Christian faithfulness.

The second objection strives to counter the adoption of procedural methodologies and affective dispositions that undercut the moral commitments of disciples to one another. Democracy in the civil sphere frequently manifests as an adversarial contest between competing interests that jockey for power in order to establish their agendas in law and policy. Democratic systems manage this perpetual conflict through institutionalized, legitimating protocols for allocating and limiting power, such as representational government, voting, and constitutional rights. Several other British Baptist theologians name the problematic implications of associating congregational self-governance with the secular paradigm. Paul Fiddes stresses the responsibility of churches to seek unity in Christ and maintain mutual love in the midst of disagreements. If congregational governance devolves to the exercise of "people power" in majority voting, then the bonds of Christian communion are broken as the concerns of a dissenting minority are summarily excluded.[4] Relatedly, Brian Haymes, Ruth Gouldbourne, and Anthony Cross find danger in identifying with democracy if doing so entails relying on parliamentary procedures that reduce communal discernment to "efficient" determinations of outcome while encouraging partisanship. Such methods displace reliance on the mind of Christ made known through the Spirit, a process of authorization that works through the cooperative practices of prayer and patient listening, with combative practices of determining winners and losers.[5]

These are important objections, but I do not consider them decisive

---

[3] Ibid., 122–25.

[4] Fiddes, *Tracks and Traces*, 86.

[5] Haymes, Gouldbourne, and Cross, *On Being the Church*, 41–42, 51.

Introduction

for undermining the theoretical and practical value of comparing Baptist ecclesiology with political democracy. Before I justify maintaining the conceptual connection between these organizational forms, I will step back to review the historical origins and characteristics of Baptist congregationalism and identify how the term "democracy" embraces a semantic range that opens possibilities for interdisciplinary engagement between ecclesiology and political theory.

The Origins and Features of Baptist Congregationalism

Baptists emerged in the matrix of sixteenth- to seventeenth-century religious dissidents who rejected the Elizabethan Settlement in the Church of England, forming the movements we now know as the Puritans and the Separatists.[6] The latter tended toward congregationalism for good, practical reasons: the continuance of the Reformation would have to be conducted by willing individuals without the support of the state; indeed, persecution by that very state limited the abilities of churches to coordinate their efforts. Congregationalism also received theological justification from the seminal work of the Separatist leader Robert Browne, *A Treatise of Reformation without Tarrying for Any* (1582). Browne argued that a true church is a gathering of Christians who consent to live under the authority of Christ together. Browne's understanding of the church was taken up by the Baptists who emerged within the Puritan-Separatist milieu.[7]

Baptists represent one distinct movement within a larger family of Christian traditions that arose from efforts to radicalize Protestant reform in various contexts. Two classic labels are the "Free Church" or the "Believers' Church." The former may designate one or more of the following "freedoms": a congregational polity free from authoritarianism of the few, the freedom of the church when it is disentangled from the state, and a certain freedom to discern what is right and true apart from rigid creedal adherence.[8] The latter term indicates a theology of the church as a voluntary fellowship of persons who willfully confess Jesus Christ as Lord and covenant to give one another mutual support in the journey of discipleship.[9] A more recent designator is "baptist," coined by Baptist theologian

[6] See Pearse, *Great Restoration*, 155–78.
[7] Haykin, "Some Historical Roots of Congregationalism," 29.
[8] Durnbaugh, *Believers' Church*, 4–8.
[9] Ibid., 32f.

James William McClendon Jr. McClendon's referent is primarily a specific hermeneutical approach to the Bible exemplified by the radical Protestant communities: the "baptist vision" that reads Scripture according to the "plain sense" and from a standpoint that the Church in the present is the same kind of community as both the original followers of Jesus and the "Church Triumphant" at the end of time.[10] The present concern is with the political order of such communities, so the three labels will be used interchangeably to refer to Baptists and other Christians who worship in and witness from voluntary communities of mutual accountability, governed by congregational polity.

Stephen J. Wellum and Kirk Wellum identify five characteristic traits of congregationalist church governance.[11] First, the ultimate authority in every gathered body is the risen Jesus Christ, who is directly accessible to the community and to each member through the Holy Spirit. Questions of policy, practice, and doctrine are to be decided, therefore, by discerning how the church will express its fidelity to Christ as Lord. Second, because each church is fully "the church," with Christ as its head, it bears the responsibility of self-governance without submission to an external, juridical authority. Third, such communities as a whole, not their designated leadership, possess final decision-making authority. Fourth, therefore, the leaders of a church (pastors, elders, and deacons) exercise a form of persuasive authority in that they seek to guide the church toward greater faithfulness through their example and teaching. Theirs is a "weighted" voice in the communal discernment process, but not one that commands or vetoes. Finally, as the repeated use of the word "authority" in this summary has implied, Wellum and Wellum contend that congregationalism requires great care in harmonizing the roles of Christ, the leaders, and the entire membership.[12]

[10] McClendon Jr., *Ethics*, 19f, 26–34.

[11] S. J. Wellum and K. Wellum, "Biblical and Theological Case for Congregationalism," 62–77.

[12] The picture is even more complicated with the realization that other proximate authorities beside the leaders and members "participate" in congregational deliberation and decision-making. Christ's will is supposed to be understood with reference to the Bible as an inspired text, which is in turn interpreted by the pastor(s) in public preaching and teaching but also by lay congregants in both private and communal settings. Moreover, the Bible is not (and indeed cannot) be read in isolation from the

Introduction

Baptist congregationalism typically manifests certain procedural aspects derivative of these traits. The self-governance of a church appears in the form of regular gatherings of the membership—called "church meetings," "business meetings," "church conferences," or by similar titles—to deliberate and decide on matters of policy and practice. Responsibilities usually placed on the shoulders of the whole group include accepting and removing members, electing and dismissing officeholders, and approving budgets and bylaws. Lay leaders are appointed to committees, councils, or other such administrative organs that oversee aspects of church life. Churches exhibit a variety of processes for engaging discussion and resolving it with a determination. The latter is realized through some means of recognizing the will of the collective, such as a consensus affirmation or a majority vote.[13]

Defining Democracy

In the context of late-modern Western society, "democracy" is a term whose definition is more often assumed than clarified, but it does carry multiple meanings. When speaking of democracy, we may distinguish between two basic concepts: democracy as a political *structure* and democracy as, broadly speaking, a *culture* that manifests in various beliefs, inclinations, habits, and agendas.[14] The two expressions of democracy are interrelated in that the interpretation and implementation of one will affect the other.

The former concept, democracy as a structure, may be defined as "a political system in which all adults…determine public policy, generally

---

overlapping contexts that shape the community: namely, the experiences of the community and its individual members in their sociocultural setting and personal histories and the tradition(s) of biblical interpretation, theological reflection, and practices of worship, work, and witness. McClendon, in his perceptive "An Essay on Authority," argues for the interdependence of all such relative authorities through the metaphor of a "Ferris wheel of discernment" in which each mode of authority has a role in the deliberative conversation conducted under the final judgment of God. According to McClendon, the strength of congregationalism, when practiced well, lies in correlating these proximate authorities together in a dialogue marked by trust, openness, and attention to the Holy Spirit. See *Doctrine*, 2:454–88.

[13] Maring and Hudson, *Baptist Manual of Polity and Practice*, 71–77, 139–66.

[14] Ward, *Politics of Discipleship*, 40f.

through debating and voting."[15] As opposed to more elitist systems of government, democracy affirms that in principle all citizens may publicly express and give reasons for their opinions on common affairs. Because each person inevitably inhabits a distinct, limited perspective, different judgments on the proper course of action arise. The procedural structure of democracy allows such divergences to remain juxtaposed in a single polity and employs certain tools to manage conflictual diversity.[16] Democracy as a system is not value-neutral and already implies a bare minimum of democratic culture: namely, the fundamental equality of participants.[17] However, as critics have noted since ancient times, this bare egalitarianism can result in a "tyranny of the majority" in which the losers of a vote, though formally having the same per capita influence, are subject to unequal and finally oppressive outcomes. But as political theorist David Miller writes, pure majoritarianism can be checked both by constitutional protections as well as habits of respect and discussion.[18]

This dispositional dimension indicates how "democracy" can also name a culture—which may also be designated as a social way of life or an *ethos*—that informs procedure and shapes patterns of relationship between groups and individuals outside of formally "political" spaces and processes. Graham Ward defines democratic culture as the political values and practices that are idealized and lived out in societies governed according to democratic polity.[19] David Koyzis similarly distinguishes between democracy as a system and democracy as a "creed." The latter may manifest not only in governance but in the democratization of other spheres of human

---

[15] Jardine, *Making and Unmaking of Technological Society*, 35. See also Stout: structural democracy is "a form of government in which the adult members of the society being governed all have some share in electing rulers and are free to speak their minds in a wide-ranging discussion that rulers are bound to take seriously" (*Democracy and Tradition*, 4).

[16] Koyzis, *Political Visions and Illusions*, 127f.

[17] "[T]he moral and political virtue paramount in democracy is equality, understood as the maximal extension of the franchise and equality of opportunity" (Ward, *Politics of Discipleship*, 42).

[18] Miller, *Political Philosophy*, 48–53.

[19] Ward, *Politics of Discipleship*, 40.

Introduction

activity, such as economics, education, and religion.[20] Jeffrey Stout argues forcefully in *Democracy and Tradition* that, in the American context, democracy has always included a robust cultural formation. Specifically, democracy names an ethical *tradition* or unifying framework that instills solidarity in a pluralistic society. Democracy as a tradition "inculcates certain habits of reasoning, certain attitudes toward deference and authority in political discussion, and love for certain goods and virtues, as well as a disposition to respond to certain types of actions, events, or persons with admiration, pity, or horror."[21] The fundamental principle of this tradition, Stout contends, is that citizens see themselves as accountable to one another and thus give and receive ethical reasons for the judgments they make.[22]

A significant tributary of the democratic *ethos* in the contemporary Western world is the philosophy of political liberalism, and because of overlapping values and assumptions, the two distinctive visions are frequently conflated as identical.[23] But liberalism arose in the seventeenth and eighteenth centuries, before contemporary democracy, and there have been liberal societies that were not substantively democratic. Rejecting traditional social arrangements of hierarchy, class, and religion, liberals posited and worked for a "value-neutral" political system that elevates the autonomy of the individual as the chief political virtue.[24] Autonomy or sovereignty entails that each person may govern one's actions according to self-chosen norms. This respect for autonomy is qualified by the equal and inherent human rights of fellow citizens, which one's free choices must not violate.[25] Liberal theory holds that the state should possess constrained powers that primarily function to protect the rights of its self-sovereign constituents.[26] Over time, emerging national states expanded in resources and technological sophistication, and their economies transformed into

---

[20] Koyzis, *Political Visions and Illusions*, 128, 138–43. Although it must be noted that Koyzis offers a negative judgment of creedal democracy as a dogmatism that seeks to impose this mode of governance into social relationships where it may not be suitable.

[21] Stout, *Democracy and Tradition*, 3.

[22] Ibid., 6f.

[23] Koyzis, *Political Visions and Illusions*, 129.

[24] Ibid., 23, 43; Jardine, *Making and Unmaking of Technological Society*, 31.

[25] Koyzis, *Political Visions and Illusions*, 47–49.

[26] Ibid., 43f.

capitalist markets. Consequently, political liberalism has divided into two ideal types: classical liberals, who still limit the government's role as guardian of individual freedoms, and reform liberals, who give greater stress to equality of opportunity and who believe the government should intervene to support persons disadvantaged by economic and social conditions. In current Western societies, "conservatives" are generally classical liberals and those who identify as "liberals" or "progressives" are reform liberals.[27]

There can be no doubt that liberal societies have made vast improvements to the general welfare of their members. Those of us who live in such systems take for granted a wide range of freedoms that had been controversial or unthinkable until recent historical times: freedom to practice the religion of one's choice, freedom of opinion and expression, freedom from enslavement, and more.[28] Ideally, liberals aspire to treat persons fairly as unique beings with inherent worth instead of judging them as better or worse because they belong to a particular collective identity such as ethnicity, origin, class, or gender. In this regard, liberalism's orientation to human dignity coheres with the Christian understanding of persons made in the image of God, and it has been argued that liberal values are derivative of the West's Christian heritage.[29] Baptists are especially prone to spot resonances with their sectarian distinctives because from early in their history, they were advocates for religious toleration, the liberty of individual conscience, and finally the separation of church and state.

Yet liberalism has come under sharp and justified critique from Christian theologians and political theorists of various stripes. The liberal emphasis on sovereign individuals freely pursuing self-chosen ends has not just broken down antiquated constructions of power, but has resulted in a profound crisis of social alienation.[30] The goal of value-neutrality further catalyzes this fragmentation because political discourse becomes bereft of

---

[27] Jardine, *Making and Unmaking of Technological Society*, 33f., 37f.

[28] Ibid., 44.

[29] E.g., Bruce K. Ward, *Redeeming the Enlightenment: Christianity and the Liberal Virtues* (Grand Rapids: Eerdmans, 2010).

[30] Jardine, *Making and Unmaking of Technological Society*, 32, 91ff, 113. Extended sociological arguments detailing fragmentation in American society can be found in Robert N. Bellah, et al., *Habits of the Heart: Individualism and Commitment in American Life* (Berkeley: University of California Press, 1985); and Robert B. Putnam, *Bowling Alone: The Collapse and Revival of American Community* (New York: Simon & Schuster, 2000).

Introduction

not only a shared vision of the common good but, increasingly, even the most basic framework of agreements within which contestation can be productive.[31] Liberalism also possesses a tendency to equate politics with statecraft, with the consequence of expanding centralized power and smothering intermediate forms of community in which the democratic *ethos* most properly manifests and flourishes.[32]

Baptist ecclesiology certainly parallels democracy as structure or system, for in both instances a society establishes formal processes for discussing and deciding on matters of policy, often but not exclusively through the principle of one vote per member or citizen. Decisions may be the outcome of direct participation by the whole community, as in ballot initiatives or the approval of a congregational budget, or may be the responsibility of delegated representatives, whether presidents and legislators or pastors, elders, and lay committees. Indeed, both Baptist congregationalism and civil democratic forms instantiate in a variety of permutations as communities negotiate dynamics of authority and collective responsibility. Western liberal democracy bears resemblances but certainly not isomorphic equivalence with the pre-liberal, communal democracies of medieval Europe,[33] which made decisions through consensus-generating processes, and even the anti-liberal, constrained democratic spaces of the Islamic Republic of Iran, in which the populace may choose elected officials within the framework set by the Shi'a religious authorities.[34] Likewise, the moral habits that ideally characterize practices of deliberation and governance in Baptist churches overlap with those identified by theorists as the vitalizing conditions for a holistic democracy. In a democratic culture, constitutional processes are embedded in social norms of respect for the rights of fellow citizens and the conviction that political success should be achieved through the arts of persuasion rather than coercion. The norms that govern relationships among fellow believers are certainly more

[31] Coles, *Beyond Gated Politics*, 1, 8ff; Cavanaugh, "Killing for the Telephone Company," 254f.

[32] Cavanaugh, "Killing for the Telephone Company," 266; Black, "Communal Democracy and its History," 5; Moore, *Limits of Liberal Democracy*, 15f, 23f, 103f.

[33] See Black, "Communal Democracy and Its History," *passim*.

[34] For a history of how Iran's constitution was crafted amidst the complex and diverse opinions among the revolutionaries about the role of democratic practices in a society governed by Islamic law, see the relevant material in Axworthy, *Revolutionary Iran*, 122–86.

robust, given their shared baptismal commitment to walk together under the rule of Christ.

The differences between shared citizenship and shared discipleship does not dissolve the parallels between ecclesiology and civil democracy, but it contextualizes them within a theological register. Because Baptist churches are organized communities of human beings who make collective decisions about governance (which includes determining policy, allocating resources, and appointing officeholders), and are guided by moral principles of cooperative reasoning, I contend that they can rightly be labeled as "democratic." But the label is operative only if it is understood as analogical in character, so that the very real distinctions between Baptist and civil democracy is not elided. A Baptist church is not a democracy *simpliciter*, nor is its democratic functioning legitimated by the consent of the people alone. That very consent and embrace of the body politic as one's own is, in theological terms, a response to the divine grace that has called believers to repentance and into communion with God and one another. Moreover, the democratic character of congregations is a continuing expression of that grace as the Spirit endues believers with the panoply of gifts for interdependent enrichment and empowers them to represent the Lordship of Christ in their common life. Baptist "democracy" is not self-justifying or self-referential but serves the prayerful declaration that God's will be done on earth as in heaven. The Baptist Union of Great Britain conveyed this multivalency with its statement, "The Baptist Doctrine of the Church," in 1948. In this document, the British Baptists described the church meeting as outwardly democratic and also the place for submission to "the guidance of the Holy Spirit…that that we may know what is the mind of Christ."[35] To say that Baptists are democratic is to narrate the horizontal axis of discernment with and submission to one another, which is correlative to the vertical axis of discerning and submitting to the presence of the risen Lord.

Acceptance of the democratic label may be helpful in addressing two interrelated problems that plague the Baptist way of being church in the present moment. The first is the pervasive influence of political liberalism and the complicated ramifications that ensue. The consequences for Baptists, which will be spelled out in the following chapters, include: the incorporation of a pronounced spiritual individualism that threatens the

---

[35] Qtd. in Wright, *Free Church, Free State*, 123.

Introduction

communal character of churches as collectively discerning bodies, the sequestering of contestation to "private judgment" that undercuts the deliberative process, and the abandonment of participatory decision-making for the elective aristocracy of pastoral leadership.

The other problem is a perennial one for Baptists that may have been exacerbated by the influence of liberalism's exaltation of personal sovereignty or autonomy, but that is an intrinsic aspect of the ecclesial paradigm. Dissenting from established church traditions, Baptists also hold a long track record of contention and division among themselves. As Baptist historian Bill J. Leonard writes, participatory congregationalism "ensures dissent, disagreement, and the potential for schism at every turn."[36] The very first Baptist church became the very first Baptist church *split* as Thomas Helwys led ten members of John Smyth's community in Amsterdam to withdraw in protest over Smyth's overtures to the local Mennonites.[37] Early English and American Baptists coalesced into separate denominations that disagreed over the scope of Christ's redemption or the proper day for worship. During the First Great Awakening in mid-eighteenth-century America, the emerging "Separate" Baptists formed an independent movement apart from the disapproving "Regular" Baptists, but then they subsequently and gradually merged. Baptists across America united to support missionary work in the early nineteenth century until, in 1845, Baptists in the South separated and formed the Southern Baptist Convention (SBC) due to a dispute over slavery. African American Baptists also began to found their own churches and organizations in a process that accelerated after the Civil War. The original "fundamentalists" and other conservatives critical of perceived liberal inclinations left the Northern Baptist Convention in the 1920s and 1940s.

The most recent schism, and perhaps the largest, has been effected by self-identified "moderates" and "progressives" who removed themselves from the Southern Baptist Convention beginning in the late 1980s. Some two decades prior, more conservative Southern Baptists started raising vocal complaints against what they claimed was theological liberalism expressed by denominational leaders and seminary faculty. By the following decade, criticism expanded into active efforts to redirect the Convention. These efforts culminated in the election of a conservative candidate for

[36] Leonard, *Challenge of Being Baptist*, 40.
[37] Bebbington, *Baptists through the Centuries*, 38f.

president at the 1979 Convention. Resistance from theological moderates and progressives could not prevent conservatives from gradually gaining control over all denominational committees, agencies, and seminaries. By the mid-1990s, non-conservatives had abandoned efforts to influence the Convention and turned their attention to developing alternate institutions. Progressives formed the Alliance of Baptists in 1987 and moderates organized the Cooperative Baptist Fellowship (CBF) in 1991.

This large-scale survey of denominational conflict necessarily elides the innumerable, and largely undocumented, controversies that have affected individual congregations over four centuries of the Baptist tradition. Their participatory polity not only invites members to form habits of responsibility, attentiveness, creativity, and humility but also fosters vices of manipulation, bickering, partisanship, and abuse of power. In gathering together to discern what it means to be the church in a given time and place, any congregation will find itself to be a mixture of perspectives, visions, and convictions. Disagreement and conflict are unavoidable aspects of the decision-making process in a congregationalist church, which, if it remains true to this ecclesial vision, cannot short-circuit the conversation through appeals to the final authority of a minority elite.

To avoid the dangers of paralysis and division, Baptists must find a way to rethink their ecclesiology that anticipates and integrates the perpetual potential of conflict. Pious affirmations of Christ's Lordship by themselves are not enough to avert the turmoil generated by human finitude and fallenness. The question is whether Baptists can identify constructive approaches in which dissent and disagreement are fully embraced as necessary dimensions of discerning faithful discipleship in ever-changing seasons and contexts. Identifying with democracy opens avenues for engaging political theory and generating new insights. In the pages that follow, I wish to demonstrate that radical democracy in particular is an effective resource for envisioning this way of being the church.

Radical Democracy

The phrase "radical democracy" names a cluster of theories exhibiting shared origins in Western political thought and articulating common proposals for expanding conceptions of democracy beyond the reigning paradigm of political liberalism. In *The Politics of Radical Democracy*, Moya

Introduction

Lloyd and Adrian Little explain that radical democracy emerged in response to the crises of left-wing politics in the latter twentieth century: disaffection with Marxist orthodoxy, the emergence of new movements such as sexual-minority and environmental advocacy, and the demise of communism and spread of capitalism around the world.[38] Lloyd and Little separate this post-Marxist movement into two traditions—a critical theory version that aligns with the deliberative democracy paradigm and its emphasis on rational consensus, and a poststructuralist account that accepts disagreement as a continuing and necessary condition for democracy.[39] The extent to which the two strands can be segregated is debatable. Romand Coles, for example, fits in the latter camp, yet he interacts extensively with critical theorists including Jürgen Habermas, whose writings on communicative rationality have been central in shaping deliberative-democratic concepts.[40] Moreover, the different theories all align on one fundamental point; namely, a critique that liberal democracy is not democratic enough and that the way forward is to increase opportunities for direct participation in the political process rather than loading responsibility onto elected representatives and appointed bureaucrats.[41] Consequently, "radical democracy" is also a label applied to contextual, grassroots movements and actions of ordinary people challenging established modes of power.[42]

For my present aims, "radical democracy" will refer principally to a school of thought that prioritizes the roles of difference and dissent in political process. Owing to its roots in poststructuralism, radical democracy rejects efforts to establish a universal political grammar on a fixed foundation such as human rights or principles of rational discourse.[43] Such are problematic because every act of identification—be that identifying the

---

[38] Idem., "Introduction," in *Politics of Radical Democracy*, 1.

[39] Ibid., 2f.

[40] Gutmann and Thompson, *Why Deliberative Democracy?*, 9.

[41] Lloyd and Little, "Introduction," in *Politics of Radical Democracy*, 2f.

[42] Thus, in his introduction to the book co-authored with Romand Coles, Christian ethicist Stanley Hauerwas defines radical democracy more by deeds than by words; it is "the intermittent and dispersed traditions of witnessing, resisting, and seeking alternatives to the politics of death," a "lived pedagog[y] of hope," the "acts of tending to common goods and differences," and "the politics of small achievements" (*Christianity, Democracy, and the Radical Ordinary*, 3f).

[43] Tønder and Thomassen, *Radical Democracy*, 1.

THE CONTESTABLE CHURCH

limits of a community, the rules of discourse, the direction of history, etc.—necessary places itself over against a difference that cannot be encapsulated or subsumed according to the terms of identification. Identity requires the "Other" to take form and what lies beyond the boundaries remains ungraspable. According to Lars Tønder and Lasse Thomassen, radical democracy contains ontological imaginaries of both lack and abundance. The former refers to the incompleteness of a signification to name the reality of a thing and the latter emphasizes the endless possibilities for experimentation and transformation at the edges between identity and difference. Therefore, radical democrats propose that the heart of political life must be an *ethos* of "agonistic respect" in which discrepant visions of the common good listen to, and vigorously challenge, one another.[44] In other words, difference is never going away, so democracy must become the practice of tending to these inevitable conflicts.

The seminal work wherein the phrase "radical democracy" was coined is *Hegemony and Socialist Strategy* by Ernesto Laclau and Chantal Mouffe.[45] These theorists explicitly defined their work as a post-Marxist effort to challenge oppressive power structures through an expansion of agonistic, participatory politics. Political theory supports this work by acknowledging our incapacity to achieve complete objectivity and the concomitant abandonment of utopian desires for a harmonious social order.

The most influential American radical democrat has been Sheldon S. Wolin (1922–2015), whose key theoretical works are *Politics and Vision* (1960/2004)[46] and *Democracy Incorporated* (2008).[47] Wolin insistently

[44] Ibid., 2–7. In her wonderfully concise and lucid introduction to radical-democratic political theory, Chantal Mouffe (more on her below) explains the differentiation between antagonism, or conflict between enemies, and agonism, or conflict between adversaries. The distinction lies in how the opponent is ontologized not as sheer Other but as someone who, in good faith, contends for the hegemony of a specific interpretation of shared democratic principles. Positioning herself against both liberalism and other radical democrats, however, Mouffe insists that antagonism cannot be entirely eliminated from politics, but only sublimated beneath common democratic goals (see *Agonistics: Thinking the World Politically* [London: Verso Books, 2013]).

[45] Idem., *Hegemony and Socialist Strategy: Towards a Radical Democratic Politics* (London: Verso Books, 1985).

[46] Sheldon S. Wolin, *Politics and Vision: Continuity and Innovation in Western Political Thought*, expanded edition (Princeton: Princeton University Press, 2004).

[47] Idem., *Democracy Incorporated: Managed Democracy and the Specter of Inverted Totalitarianism* (Princeton: Princeton University Press, 2008).

Introduction

identifies radical democracy as an *ethos* rather than a form of government. The former continuously challenges the latter's attempts to limit the energies of democratic action within the stable and permanent parameters of a constitutional structure.[48] He designates this particular interpretation as "fugitive" democracy, meaning that democracy is really *democratization* as an ongoing process of innovation and contestation that can never be systematized and that cycles through periods of success and retreat.[49] Whereas bureaucratic forms of democracy practice the politics of *intending,* or the focusing and efficient utilization of power; fugitive, radical democracy practices the politics of *tending,* or attentiveness and active care for the myriad differences and commonalities that characterize communities.[50]

Another significant American theorist is William E. Connolly.[51] In theorizing about the shape of a multicultural democracy, Connolly identifies the pluralistic ethic as a "bicameral orientation" in which citizens of such a polity simultaneously contend for their convictions and generously attend to the perspective of their others who share the commons.[52] He notes how this orientation in grounded the distinction between individual or collective self and the other. Identity is formed relationally because its establishment and ongoing negotiation requires recognition of difference. Connolly calls for the positive affirmation of identity's contingency and an ethical stance of "nontheistic reverence" for the diversity of being.[53]

Another theorist, Romand Coles, is known for elaborating the concept of "receptive generosity."[54] As will be discussed in more detail in chapter 3, receptive generosity names a disposition of vulnerability in which a

[48] Wolin, *Politics and Vision,* 522.

[49] Wolin, "Fugitive Democracy," 42f.

[50] Wolin, *Presence of the Past,* 84–93.

[51] His significant works include *The Terms of Political Discourse,* 3rd ed. (Oxford: Blackwell, 1993); *Identity/Difference: Democratic Notions of Political Paradox,* expanded edition (Minneapolis: University of Minnesota Press, 2002); and *Pluralism* (Durham: Duke University Press, 2005).

[52] Connolly, *Pluralism,* 2–6.

[53] Connolly, *Identity/Difference,* xiv–xx, 64–68.

[54] His principal writings are *Self/Power/Other: Political Theory and Dialogical Ethics* (Ithaca: Cornell University Press, 1992); *Rethinking Generosity: Critical Theory and the Politics of Caritas* (Ithaca: Cornell University Press, 1997); *Beyond Gated Politics,* and *Visionary Pragmatism: Radical and Ecological Democracy in Neoliberal Times* (Durham: Duke University Press, 2016).

non-self-possessing subject both desires to benefit the other and has the humility to receive insight and critique beyond current perceptions of self and other. Coles's writing style is itself an expression of receptive generosity. By and large, his books consist of extended, close readings of philosophers, theorists, and democratic practitioners who represent a vast array of temporal and spatial locations. Coles expends great effort to read these others charitably, raise critical questions in response, and offer implications or reconsiderations of a person's thought that are not obvious and might even have been denied by the originator. Coles been especially concerned about the intertwinement of theory and practice and has written much about how one may inform the other. Seeking to live what he has written, Coles has also been an active participant in democratic organizing wherever he has lived.[55]

In summary, the general tenets of radical democracy could be stated as follows. This list is derived from William Connolly's outline of radical, or as he terms it, agonistic democracy, as presented in the preface to *Identity/Difference*:[56]

Radical democracy cares for the diversity of human existence by contending for the indispensability and necessity of conflict at the meeting point between personal or group identity and others in their differences.

Radical democracy departs from the "political minimalism" and individualism of liberal democracy. As opposed to limiting politics to discourse built on universalistic principles, agonism wishes to build political spaces in which multiple exertions and contestations of difference flourish.

Radical democracy also maintains a critical distance from the ideals of communitarian and deliberative democrats who set rational consensus as the principal goal of politics. Respect for the dignity of persons and their claims must include the proliferation of dialogical encounters that do not presume a certain terminus.

Radical democracy refuses to equate democracy or politics in general

---

[55] These political philosophers have been selected as representative due to their prominence, their scholarly engagement with one another, and their reception of, and/or incorporation into, Christian theological reflection. Other major American radical democrats include Bonnie Honig, author of *Political Theory and the Displacement of Politics* (Ithaca: Cornell University Press, 1993); and the Christian philosopher Cornel West, author of *Democracy Matters: Winning the Fight Against Imperialism* (New York: Penguin Books, 2004).

[56] Connolly, *Identity/Difference*, x–xi.

Introduction

with the operations and structures of a state entity. Radical democratic activity both exceeds governmental borders and percolates in small-scale, civil-society exercises of dialogue and argument. For some theorists, such as Wolin and Coles, democracy occurs primarily in the domain of the local, which is the most amenable frame for encountering difference and engaging in improvisation.

From Radical Democracy to the Contestable Church

Unsurprisingly, given their general tendency to identify with or originate in the political Left, radical democratic theorists are largely secular in orientation, if not explicitly writing as agnostics or atheists. The early works of Romand Coles, for example, presume a post-religious intellectual climate after the "death of God,"[57] but multiple fields of scholarly inquiry have entered the "religious turn," in which the arrival of "postmodern" critiques of Enlightenment rationalism, among other factors, has increased the visibility and intellectual viability of religion in arenas where it was once ignored or dismissed.[58] Thus Connolly, in *Why I Am Not a Secularist* (1999), criticizes a complacent and dogmatic secular liberalism that excludes the expression of religious viewpoints in the public square and offers proposals for constructive dialogue between the believing and the irreligious.[59]

The evolution of Coles's thought is instructive. By the time of Coles's third book, *Beyond Gated Politics*, his attitude toward traditional religion shifted dramatically in favor of critical appreciation. He develops insights for his radical-democratic project from Alasdair MacIntyre, a Catholic moral philosopher, and John Howard Yoder, a Mennonite theologian. He

---

[57] The phrase "death of God" recalls, firstly, philosopher Friedrich Nietzsche's declaration that belief in God and thus in objective morality has become intellectually untenable and, secondly, mid-twentieth-century theologians who accepted this conclusion and propounded a fully immanentist theology. See Solomon and Higgins, *What Nietzsche Really Said*, 84–102; McGrath, *Christian Theology*, 20f.

[58] See, e.g., Michael Hoelzl and Graham Ward, *The New Visibility of Religion: Studies in Religion and Cultural Hermeneutics* (New York: Continuum, 2008); John Panteleimon Manoussakis, *After God: Richard Kearney and the Religious Turn in Continental Philosophy*. Perspectives in Continental Philosophy 49 (New York: Fordham University Press, 2006).

[59] William E. Connolly, *Why I Am Not a Secularist* (Minneapolis: University of Minnesota Press, 1999).

raises critical questions in turn about the theoretical models of both thinkers although it will be shown that his pushback against Yoder is both mild and brief.[60] The last chapter of *Beyond Gated Politics* examines the politics of education via a case study of the clash between liberal "neutrality" and the convictions of "fundamentalist" Christian parents. Coles draws upon both Yoder as well as his concept of receptive generosity (of which more will be said later) to propose a method of localized solutions to such scenarios that respectfully accommodate radically disjunctive, sectarian visions of the good.

While teaching at Duke University, Coles took note of the Christian doctoral students from the department of religion who were being encouraged to register for his courses by the divinity school's famed theological ethicist Stanley Hauerwas. It was their participation that led Coles to explore the thought of Yoder, MacIntyre, Hauerwas, and other Christian thinkers. Concordantly, his involvement in the community organization Durham CAN (Congregations, Associations, and Neighborhoods)[61] while teaching at Duke was especially formative in helping him appraise the role of religious conviction in motivating communities' political involvement. Coles and Hauerwas began to dialogue, taught a course together, and co-wrote a book on the intersections of radical democracy and radical Christianity.[62]

---

[60] While Yoder may be a significant conversation partner for Coles, it would be unethical if I were to pass over in silence the sexual violence he committed against multiple women throughout his life. While some contend that Yoder the theologian may be retrieved with full and critical awareness, others have vowed to cease referencing his works to avoid what would be, in their judgment, complicity in his harms. I will continue to grapple with the ethics of retaining Yoder in the conversations of the theological academy, and I invite the reader to do the same. In the meantime, I have removed all direct citations of Yoder that were included in the dissertation from which the present work has been adapted. See Goossen, "'Defanging the Beast': Mennonite Responses to John Howard Yoder's Sexual Abuse," 7–80; Guth, "Doing Justice to the Complex Legacy of John Howard Yoder," 119–39; Porter, "Facing Harm: What to Do with the Theology of John Howard Yoder?"

[61] http://www.durhamcan.org/

[62] Stanley Hauerwas and Romand Coles, *Christianity, Democracy, and the Radical Ordinary: Conversations Between a Radical Democrat and a Christian* (Eugene: Cascade Books, 2008). The gradual shift in Coles's assessment of Christianity manifests a form

Introduction

Several Baptist theologians have begun to identify convergences between ecclesiology and the radical-democratic vision.[63] These previously noted congruencies between Baptist/Free Church ecclesiology and radical-democratic theory invite further dialogue. These publications have all identified similarities between the traditions. In terms of the transformative potential of the encounter, both Benjamin Boswell and Ryan Andrew Newson focus on the potential for the Free Church to offer a political-theology contribution to radical-democratic theory and practice, but the question that will animate this work reverses the dialectical arrow. Namely, how might a comparison of Baptist ecclesiology with the insights of radical democracy assist us in shaping churches that are intentionally hospitable to constructive conflict? In the following pages I will flesh out multiple points of similarity between Baptist ecclesial practice and theological writings, on the one hand, and radical-democratic theory on the other. The analogous emphases lay the groundwork that invites Baptists to consider receiving the gift of radical-democratic agonism as a fundamental component of discerning the mind of Christ in the power of the Spirit and through the voices of richly diverse believers gathered in the political bodies that are Baptist churches. Baptists who accept this affirmation of constructive conflict may justly, but only analogously, consider their ecclesiology to be radically democratic in character. This way of being the people of God in and through disagreement, with the aim of growing in faithfulness, I call the contestable church.

---

of radical democracy that escapes the criticism leveled by Bruce Ellis Benson in "Radical Democracy and Radical Christianity," 247–59. Identifying the philosophers Jacques Derrida, Alain Badiou, Michael Hardt, and Antonio Negri as representative figures, Benson charges radical democracy with a slight quantitative extension of liberal tolerance that still effaces differences and marginalizes religions under a secular universalism. But Coles echoes Benson's very concerns in his critique of liberal cosmopolitanism and the removal of religious contestation in the public sphere in *Beyond Gated Politics*, 43–78 and 239–63.

[63] See Boswell, "Liturgy and Revolution Part I: Georgian Baptists and the Nonviolent Struggle for Democracy," 48–71; idem., "Liturgy and Revolution Part II: Radical Christianity, Radical Democracy, and Revolution in Georgia," 15–31; Freeman, "Roger Williams, American Democracy, and the Baptists," 267–86; idem., *Contesting Catholicity*, 34–44; Schelin, "'In a Congregational Way,'" 22–36; Newson, *Radical Friendship, passim*.

Context and Conditions

This project will proceed through a close reading of and critical engagement with primary radical-democratic and Baptist theological texts, which are contextualized by secondary historical literature to provide the necessary empirical context regarding practices, ideas, convictions, and behaviors that shape the lived Baptist experience. Baptist theology possesses an endlessly self-interrogative quality, and its ecclesial form explicitly rejects centralized authorities who have the wherewithal and the legitimacy to make definitive pronouncements on matters of doctrine and practice. To identify any Baptist theological or ecclesiological statement as representative is a potentially misleading enterprise apart from careful qualification. Baptists are a diverse, global people of more than sixty million baptized believers whose communions have varying origins and histories and whose theologies differ dramatically. A familiar joke holds that where four Baptists are gathered there will be five opinions. So as not to be construed as representing some universal construct of "Baptistness," I will restrict my analysis to a particular lineal stream of communities and the theologians they have produced. This happens to be the ecclesial tradition in which I was raised and in which I continue to participate; namely, the denominations that have centered upon the southern region of the United States. These would be the aforementioned Southern Baptist Convention, the Cooperative Baptist Fellowship, and the Alliance of Baptists. For the sake of simplicity, I will refer to this family of Baptists as the *southern baptists*, using the small "s" to name their shared history and geographical center, and the small "b" to consider them together as a generic ecclesiological category while distinguishing the broader constituency from a single denomination that retains the name.[64] I will retain the capitalization of Southern Baptist for instances referring to this organization and to individuals who were or are self-consciously members thereof.

At the same time, southern baptists share a common inheritance with the majority of their national compatriots that lineally descends from the

---

[64] These bodies are also largely European American in ethnic makeup. The distinctive African American Baptist experience quite naturally exhibits theological and cultural divergences. These include a historical tendency to vest considerable authority in the person of the pastor within an overarching congregationalist polity. See Jenkins, "The African American Baptist Pastor and Church Government," 74-86; Madkins, "The Leadership Crisis in the Black Church," 102-12.

Introduction

Regular and Separate Baptists of the seventeenth through nineteenth centuries, who themselves were united by a common Calvinistic theology.[65] Southern baptists did not immediately dissolve all connections with their brethren upon the founding of the convention in 1845. Gradually, they began to establish separate institutions: the first SBC seminary was founded in 1859 and the first publishing house in 1891. Therefore, this thesis will consider as relevant sources both pre-SBC materials from the mainstream of the broader American Baptist heritage as well as Northern literature up to the end of the nineteenth century.

The difficulty of naming normative exemplars consequently poses a particular challenge for selecting a limited set of witnesses to Baptist thought. On the other hand, Baptist diversity and openness to critical reinterpretation allows many voices to come to the table. How, then, have I selected the figures who will be examined in the body of this work? Four criteria have guided the use of Baptist thinkers. First, each figure must stand within the southern baptist tradition. Second, this person must have achieved some level of public influence as a leader and writing theologian such that the figure's work holds or retains contemporary interest in the literature. Third, the thinker must have written on characteristic Baptist themes and express self-awareness of one's status as a Baptist theologian. Finally, the person's writings evidence substantial engagement with ideas that parallel radical-democratic thought.

The radical-democratic movement, meanwhile, is itself a heterogeneous set of theories that is aptly characterized by its own tensions, conflicts, and alternating proposals. An attempted comparison between southern baptists and radical democracy writ large would be too diffuse and unwieldy. Therefore, the political theorist Coles will be set as the conversation partner whose work will be reviewed and analyzed. The selection of Coles admittedly originates in contingent personal circumstances, but it is not idiosyncratic. His work exemplifies all four characteristics of radical democracy summarized earlier in this introduction. He has arguably engaged the Christian theological tradition more extensively than any other American radical democrat, and my argument builds upon the existing acknowledgment of shared concerns and proposals between Coles as a representative theorist and Baptist theologians. I will expand on the

---

[65] On the complexity of southern baptist appropriation of Calvinist doctrines, see Lemke, "History or Revisionist History?," 227–54.

tentative expressions of convergence by generating a focused and thorough dialogue between Baptist ecclesiology and radical democracy as envisioned by Coles.

The argument will proceed as follows. Chapter 1 will evaluate what southern baptists have intended by the self-description of congregational "democracy" and how they have instantiated democratic structures and cultures. The chapter begins by reviewing the origins and usages of democratic terminology as descriptive of southern baptist ecclesiology from the end of the Colonial era to the present day. Baptist writers deliver largely consistent explanations for the valence of "democracy" over time, with slight modifications in the direction of individualism and Americanization. The actual practice of Baptist ecclesiology, however, diverts sharply from the original vision of the Colonial era. As it stands, democratic language masks these transformations with a veil of continuity while insufficiently articulating the form of "democracy" that defines Baptists' participatory ecclesiology. Points of convergence will be drawn with radical democracy as well as unresolved tensions that may be addressed through the theoretical dialogue.

These subsequent chapters are ordered according to a sequence that serendipitously follows a logical ordering of theoretical questions, a chronological progression through Coles's corpus, and an equally diachronic movement through Baptist theologians. This logical development is one of increasing ontological complexity, beginning with an assessment of the political self, then examining the relationship between selves in their differences more closely, and finally to the patterning of community life as persons converse and decide on the political order.

The second chapter analyzes and compares the philosophical and theological anthropologies employed by Coles and the Baptists to justify the democratic *ethos* of vulnerable relationship with others. I begin by reviewing Coles's argument for the "artistic self" that he develops through an exegesis of Augustine, Michel Foucault, and Maurice Merleau-Ponty. Critical assessment of Coles is contrasted with the historic Reformed anthropology of fall and redemption accepted by most Baptists. This seemingly "negative" anthropology of natural inability is modified by a participatory anthropology in which believers are made participants in Christ's triple office of prophethood, priesthood, and kingship. I contend that E. Y. Mullins's influential doctrine of soul competency is an individualistic revision of this prior anthropology. Finally, I compare Mullins with Coles

Introduction

and suggest that the notion of interdependent artistic selves fills a lacuna in Mullins's thought and re-envisions interdependent soul competency as an anthropological basis for congregationalism.

Next, I turn to consider what form the expression of dissent should take in light of the above anthropological conclusions. The third chapter evaluates the modes in which persons express and convey their differences in relationship to one another. The chapter begins by noting the tension between two vectors in southern baptist life concerning dissent: the "more light" or mutability principle versus the ideal of preserving unity. I proceed to note that the practice of private interpretation or judgment is the most prominent mode for disseminating dissent among Baptists. While the right to reach personal hermeneutical and theological conclusions *does* have a long pedigree in the Baptist tradition, I point out how Baptist theologians have rightly criticized it as excessively individualistic. I then turn to Coles's book *Rethinking Generosity*, in which he elaborates *receptive generosity* as the programmatic practice of his version of radical democracy. I trace how Coles develops this concept through his readings of Immanuel Kant, Theodor Adorno, and Jürgen Habermas. I propose that twentieth-century Southern Baptist pastor-theologian Carlyle Marney offers a helpful point of contact with receptive generosity through his revisioning of Christian community as the crucible for the formation of persons. Marney is a bridge between Baptists and radical democracy, demonstrating that dissent and conflict are vital elements for spiritual maturation into the newness that Christ offers.

The vulnerable expression of the selves in committed dialogical encounter must be sustained by constructing supportive modes of authority. In chapter 4, I consider the practices through which the community channels both its received inheritance as well as innovative insight into processes of discernment and decision-making. Both Coles and Baptists are concerned with the interrelationship of leadership, or *episkope*, and the passing on/revision of longstanding markers of communal identity—the tradition or *traditio*. Coles helps southern baptists resolve a difficult paradox regarding the role of clergy as teachers and leaders in a body of mutually responsible believers while Baptists offer radical democrats the example of dynamic *traditio* that sustains rootedness in communal identity while encouraging new interpretations.

Finally, the conclusion will offer some tentative proposals as to how theory may become reality in the lived embodiment of the contestable church. I write as a theologian and for the Church, so I consider this project to be a failure if it does not support concrete proposals for ordering congregational life.

Although my primary aim is directed toward a theological reconsideration of how Baptists may institutionalize dissent and disagreement as necessary habits for the health of their common life, I will also suggest gifts of critical insight that Baptists may offer to radical democrats as an exercise of agonistic respect. My juxtaposition of Coles and Baptists reveals a recurrent theme that I recognize to be the chief difference that separates Baptist and radical-democratic conceptualizations of the political. Coles names a productive tension between two orientations in the democratic *ethos*. One is the teleological, by which he means the tendency toward making determinations, setting limits, and identifying the trajectories and goals of the political. The opposite orientation is the ateleological, or the disposition toward critique, novelty, the unexpected, or anything else that disturbs fixed reference frames. According to Coles, the ateleological and the teleological inform and interpenetrate each other, such that radical democracy demands a constant negotiation between the two in which neither is privileged. Agreeing with the radical democrats that there is no universal position from which to offer a critique, I will present two responses to Coles as a Baptist theologian. First, I will suggest that Coles himself is not able to maintain his balance, ultimately privileging the ateleological. Adjacent to this critique of internal incoherence, I will note that Baptists consistently frame the ateleological *within* the teleological, providing a referential stability to the dialogical process but while avoiding certain Colesian critiques of restrictively traditioned reasoning. In radical democracy proper, contestation has no end in sight, no utopia to be achieved. For the contestable church, conflict spurs Christians to be ever receptive and reforming, but in a prayerful expectation that dissent will be no more when God's peace quiets all our strivings.

CHAPTER 1

BAPTIST DEMOCRACY IN
THOUGHT AND PRACTICE

When we ask the question what "democracy" has meant to Baptists as a label for their ecclesiology, we can bifurcate the answer by separately analyzing the conceptual and practical dimensions of this claim. First, there is the matter of what Baptists have *said* about themselves when they speak of their churches as democratic. Second, there is the matter of what Baptists have *done* in their common life that instantiates democratic principles, both as an *ethos* and as a *structure* of formal deliberation and decision-making. Both the variety of democratic theories posed by political philosophers and the diversity of actual democratic polities represented by civil governments around the world remind us that the interface between concept and practice is itself a complex zone of contestation and reformulation.

While the *Baptist Faith and Message* of 1963 was the first Baptist confession of faith to apply the term "democracy" to church polity, it was but the latest instance in a century and a half of such identifications. To trace this history, I will review pamphlets, church manuals, systematic theologies, and other writings of influential and representative Baptist figures from the Early Republic to the present day. These texts demonstrate that, from the early nineteenth century, the notion that Baptists exemplify a form of democracy has been widely accepted. The descriptor serves as a shorthand designating a set of theological convictions that have been reiterated throughout the history of Baptists in America, but within this overall unity lies certain subtle shifts in understanding that imply the growing influence of liberal-democratic assumptions regarding personal liberty and popular sovereignty.

The historiography of Baptists has illuminated the concrete forms ecclesial democracy has taken and how these have also transformed over three centuries. How have congregations made decisions, resolved disputes, and sought counsel from one another? How have the beliefs held by Baptists expressed themselves in a democratic *ethos*, or how have they resisted democratization? The second half of this chapter will restate the conclusions of earlier Baptist historians regarding a noticeable shift in patterns of ecclesial life from the Colonial era to now. This transformation in practice lagged behind but inexorably followed changes in self-conception toward a heightened emphasis on autonomy for both individual believers and churches.

Pertaining to the comparative conversation with radical democracy, I will note general points of convergence and divergence between agonistic politics as summarized in the introduction and Baptist polity as it has been theorized and implemented. Moreover, this survey will demonstrate both discontinuity in the meaning of democracy for Baptists as well as perduring, unresolved questions about how it is to be lived out, especially in the case of managing dissent and conflict within the church. The failure to align consistently theory and action reveals the "democracy" of southern baptists to be an impoverished signifier in need of more rigorous articulation. It may be that the insights of radical democracy will be well placed to assist Baptists in clarifying what they mean by a democratic church and ultimately to enact it in a manner befitting their calling as disciples of Jesus Christ.

The Emergence of Democratic
Language among Baptists

While Baptists have organized as collectively governed communities from the very beginning of their existence, nearly two centuries would pass before a leading figure would label their polity as democratic. This lexical lacuna may be rooted in the negative judgment of classical political theory that democracy entails unrestricted mob rule.[1] The first explicit identification of Baptist ecclesiology with democracy occurs in a pamphlet published by John Leland in 1804. Leland was an influential Baptist minister and itinerant evangelist during the American Revolution and Early Republic who advocated prolifically for disestablishment and the liberty of conscience.[2] In his pamphlet called *The Government of Christ a Christocracy*, he raises the question whether the divine rule of Christ in the church may be compared either to monarchical or democratic government in the secular

---

[1] Koyzis, *Political Visions and Illusions*, 120f. Koyzis writes that democracy did not achieve a fully positive connotation in liberal societies until the twentieth century.
[2] Garrett, *Baptist Theology*, 162f.

realm.[3] Leland defines a democracy as the affirmation of equality between all men (*ethos*) and the exercise of self-government founded on a social agreement (structure).[4] He argues that church government resembles both monarchy and democracy yet stands apart as a unique polity. As in a monarchy, Christ is the unquestioned lawgiver and king who appoints subordinate officers (pastors). As in a democracy, the church is a corporate body of persons who exercise liberty (the most fundamental form being freedom from sin) and each member shares in the authority to govern (which has been delegated from God). This appears on earth as a congregational system in which each church governs itself under the Lord's dictates and so adopts a form which "greatly resembles[s] the genius of a republic."[5] Leland asks his readers to imagine the universal church as something of a hybrid system in which the many local church democracies are united within an "absolute empire."[6]

Because of its unique character, the system of government operant within the church is most properly labeled a "Christocracy."[7] This system is undermined whenever any authority is placed above a congregation and thus claiming to mediate between Christ and his subjects. Leland opposes all hierarchies but is especially critical of state-sponsored churches. Such do not belong to the roll of democracies that make up the Christocracy because they pollute Christ's government with an alien authority and become "creatures of state."[8] The pamphlet closes with the declaration that all establishments of Christianity are truly anti-Christocracies.[9]

Because of his prominence, and lacking any other candidate source, it is quite probable that Leland was the first public figure to equate Baptist

---

[3] Leland, "The Government of Christ a Christocracy," 273.

[4] Ibid., 274.

[5] Ibid., 275.

[6] Leland's ecclesial politics thus parallels the predominant view in contemporary political theory that the best form of government combines elements of monarchy, aristocracy, and democracy. This perspective, of course, guided the crafting of the United States Constitution and its division of federal authority into the executive, judicial, and legislative branches.

[7] Ibid., 275, 277.

[8] Ibid., 278.

[9] Ibid., 281.

polity with democracy.[10] However, because of the seemingly happy convergence between Baptist egalitarianism and republican values, it is certainly possible that other writers independently adopted the terminology. What is clear is that after the publication of Leland's pamphlet, Baptist ministers and theologians increasingly identified congregationalism as a type of democracy, perhaps even the most rarefied form. For example, in 1834 Jesse Mercer, minister and president of the Georgia Baptist Convention, wrote in the *Christian Index*, the convention's newspaper, that the model given in the New Testament for ecclesial organization is "pure democracy."[11]

Eleven years after Mercer's declaration, W. B. Johnson reiterated the concept of Christocracy for a new generation. Johnson was then serving as the first president of the newly formed Southern Baptist Convention when he wrote *The Gospel Developed through the Government and Order of the Churches of Jesus Christ* (1846).[12] Although he does not credit Leland, his discussion of the form of government in the churches closely resembles *The Government of Christ*. Johnson begins by remarking that congregational polity is sometimes called "democratical," indicating that the terminology must be fairly common by this point in time.[13] Johnson allows that the term is proper insofar as it is meant to describe the mode by which Christ's laws are administered. However, the church is dependent for its

---

[10] Leland is not the first, however, to describe congregationalism as a blend of aristocratic and populist government. The New England Puritans of the seventeenth century, who also practiced congregationalist polity, included a parallel statement in the *Cambridge Platform*, an ecclesiological confession adopted by synod in 1648. In chapter ten, the *Platform* states that church government is mixed, being a monarchy "in respect of *Christ*," resembling a democracy with regard to the power granted the whole body and including an aristocracy because of the institution of ruling elders in each church (emphasis original). See Walker, *Creeds and Platforms*, 217f. Especially because Leland was a Massachusetts native, it is conceivable to speculate that he was familiar with the *Platform*. However, I have not identified any references by Leland to that document. Given the separation in time of a century and a half, another hypothesis would be that Leland came across this depiction of congregations in general circulation absent a specific attribution. Finally, it is also possible that Leland conceived the monarchy-democracy binary independently.

[11] *The Christian Index*, 16 December 1834, p. 5. Qtd. in Wills, *Democratic Religion*, 33.

[12] In *Polity*, 161–248.

[13] Ibid., 172.

Baptist Democracy in Thought and Action

power on Jesus, the Head of the whole body, and because of this obedience monarchy is also an apt description of church government. Therefore, Johnson declares, "I know no single term that will better express the true character of this government than *Christocracy*—a government of which Christ is the Head, and in which his power is manifested in perfect accordance of the freedom of his people."[14] All the participants in a church fellowship are equal to one another in their "rights and privileges."[15] The relationship between churches is just the same, as the principle of Christocracy requires that no church should look to another to determine its pattern of communal life.[16]

Johnson acknowledges that the balance between the monarchical and the democratic is represented in the paradox of dutiful obedience to Christ and freedom to make responsible choices. He insists that the citizens of a Christocracy must determine their politics on the basis of Christ's laws and not their particular opinions.[17] However, Johnson further insists that this form of church government "does not treat the members of the churches as mere machines." Rather, as beings endowed with reason, the free exercise of their rational and moral power is necessary for the obligations of obedience. There exists a sublime consistency between the idea of equal rights and that of submission to Christ as king.[18]

This both-and conceptualization of local church governance is reiterated in a pamphlet published three years later by the Virginia pastor J. L. Reynolds. He summarizes congregational governance as the privilege of "self-government under Him [Christ]." Baptist polity is a demonstration of Christ's gracious confidence that his people, when given responsibility, will make their decisions on the basis of their fidelity to him.[19] For these antebellum southern baptists, spiritual democracy is made possible by the trust the divine monarch has placed in his subjects to remain faithful in their free decisions. While they do not explicitly address questions of dis-

---

[14] Ibid., 173–75.

[15] Ibid., 232. Although Johnson adds that distinctions between categories of persons must remain in the wider society, implying that equality within the church is no justification for a general revolution against conventions of deference.

[16] Ibid., 234.

[17] Ibid., 233.

[18] Ibid., 235.

[19] Reynolds, "Church Polity," 328.

sent and difference, Johnson and Reynolds's interpretation of congregational governance grants a theoretical space for voicing and addressing discrepant understandings of what is best for the church to be and do in a given context as it aims to fulfill its mandate.

These three Baptist leaders of the early-nineteenth century characterized their congregations as expressing a distinctive blend of two usually opposite poles of political organization: the exclusive prerogatives of a sovereign in monarchy and the collective aspirations of a population in democracy. Beginning with Leland, Baptists in America began to label their processes of collective decision-making "democratic." By this they meant that Jesus Christ, the Lord of the church, had devolved his authority upon the whole of each church instead of an elite segment. Each believer was fundamentally equal to the other, and so was each church. Johnson and Reynolds added that a church, while entirely submissive to Christ's Lordship, possessed the freedom to choose creative action within the limits imposed by divine commands. In their shared prioritization of God's authority to direct the church, all three figures distinguished ecclesial democracy from civil democracy in which, according to the theory of popular sovereignty, authority resides in the consent and will of the people without the supervenience of any external power.

Baptist Democracy in Mid-Nineteenth-Century Polity Manuals

Books and pamphlets on Baptist polity rolled off the printing presses at a prodigious rate toward the middle of the nineteenth century. The demand for writings that detailed the Baptist way of being church was generated by the expansion of America's largest denomination[20] both geographically into the frontier and demographically in terms of the number of adherents. Two of the most significant church manuals of this period were written by J. M. Pendleton, a founding figure in the Landmarkist movement,[21] and Edward Hiscox, whose work would become the most widely-used manual of the century, appearing in multiple editions into the twentieth century.[22]

[20] Corrigan and Hudson, *Religion in America*, 138.
[21] On the theology and significance of this movement, see below. On Pendleton, see Garrett, *Baptist Theology*, 225–27.
[22] On Hiscox, see Maring, "The Individualism of Francis Wayland," 137; Stewart, *Baptists and Local Autonomy*, 38.

Baptist Democracy in Thought and Action

The influence of both men helped to sustain the language of Baptist democracy into the post-Civil War period.

Hiscox adds a new dimension to Baptist writings on ecclesial democracy by addressing the issue of disagreement in decision-making. The government of the church is democratic because it falls upon the whole membership. Because this collective is formed by individuals whose opinions will not always coalesce, allowance is made for rule by majority.[23] However, Hiscox acknowledges that majorities are not infallible guides to Christ's will and their decisions may be judged inappropriate when they fall outside the "laws of Christ" revealed within the New Testament. He counsels majorities to "act cautiously" in pursuing decisions in the face of significant minorities that may yet have the right opinion on the issue. When a disaffected minority feels wronged, it has three options: withdraw to another church, form a new one, or request a council.[24] No means of redress exist beyond these.

Hiscox takes up the question of what Baptist democracy means for the relationships among churches or between churches and denominational bodies, but the answers he gives are contradictory. For Hiscox, the direct rule of Christ in self-governing churches marks them as "entirely independent" from the authority of other churches, denominational bodies, or governments.[25] Yet Baptists had long united their churches in regional associations, state conventions, and mission societies for the sake of fellowship, cooperation in ministry, and mutual accountability. Hiscox insists that an association holds no ecclesiastical authority over a church, meaning that it cannot dictate matters of doctrine and policy. However, he also argues that a church, when it is a member of an association, must "submit to be governed by its regulations."[26] Hiscox does not specify how this submission coheres with church independence or what conditions may justify overriding associational authority.

[23] Hiscox, *Baptist Church Directory*, 58. He prefers, but does not stipulate, unanimity in the admission and excommunication of members "and other important business" (79).

[24] Councils were ad hoc advisory bodies invited to assist the founding of a new church or the ordination of a pastor and to mediate internal church disputes. For Hiscox's discussion of councils, see pp. 128–31. See Shurden, *Associationalism among Baptists in America*, 11f.; Wills, *Democratic Religion*, 99f.

[25] Ibid., 56.

[26] Ibid., 132.

Hiscox revisited church polity and published his *The New Directory of Baptist Churches* after a gap of thirty-five years. In his updated manual, the notion of submission to the association disappears. Hiscox insists that church independence is not limited by the agreement to relate to other churches and the idea of interdependence between Baptist churches must be declared a fiction.[27] Hiscox distinguishes between membership, in which a church is absorbed by a larger body and surrenders some of its self-control, and fellowship, in which a church cooperates with the regional organization. Associations and churches are independent from one another, and an association can remove a church from fellowship if it deems the congregation to be errant in its beliefs or practices.[28] The metamorphosis of congregational self-governance into a stricter concept of congregational *autonomy* is likely indicative of some combination of Landmarkist influence (detailed below), the growing pervasiveness of liberal conceptualizations of liberty and self-determination, and theological responses to emerging scientific paradigms.[29]

In his *Church Manual* (1867), Pendleton lists three definitive features of congregationalism: governance by the whole membership, the authority of majoritarian decisions, and the non-transferable nature of a congregation's powers.[30] He contends that the proper response of the minority in a divided vote is submission, offering no provisos for error on the part of the majority. Because there is "no higher tribunal than a church," associations are only advisory bodies and Baptists must guard against any efforts to limit congregational independence.[31] Pendleton marshals several New Testament texts to defend the right of churches to self-governance. He finds the strongest argument to be the power of excommunicating and restoring members. Paul's deference to the church in Corinth in a disciplinary matter (2 Cor. 2:2-8) exemplifies the "majesty of democratic church sovereignty."[32] Surely, Pendleton notes, if Paul's churches exercised such a weighty responsibility, then they must have also governed themselves in every other matter.

---

[27] Hiscox, *New Directory for Baptist Churches*, 148.

[28] Ibid., 333–37.

[29] See Brackney, "Word Are Inadequate to Express Our Convictions," 15–37.

[30] Pendleton, *Church Manual*, 101f.

[31] Ibid., 173f.

[32] Ibid., 107.

The concept of "majority rule" encourages further comparison between the governance procedures of churches and of the nation. Though Baptists had previously been persecuted by the established churches during the Colonial era, they now felt comfortably placed in the mainstream as a prominent Christian denomination and significant influence upon society. As the American experiment in self-government continued to expand to include more of the populace as active participants, Baptists also increasingly prided themselves as the Christians who practiced democracy in church well before it became an operative principle of republican statecraft. Moreover, some saw fit to argue that Baptist churches were the model upon which the Founders drew inspiration. Such efforts signaled a greater willingness to closely align ecclesiology and secular republicanism than even that which was found in the "Christocratic" concept given by Leland and restated by Johnson.

A telling example is located in *The Baptist Denomination: Its History, Doctrines, and Ordinances* by Dudley Haynes. He cites an urban legend concerning Thomas Jefferson's alleged attendance of a Baptist church near his Monticello home about eight years prior to writing the Declaration of Independence.[33] According to the story, the pastor, Andrew Tribble, queried Jefferson for his thoughts on Baptist polity. Tribble remarked, "It is well known how democratic it is, and has been from the earliest times." Jefferson indicated that he was impressed by congregationalism in action. He found Baptist churches to be "the only pure form of democracy then existing," and he thought a civic equivalent would be "the best plan of government for the American colonies." Haynes triumphantly concludes this story with a rhetorical question, "Who can tell the influence this little church had thus upon the destiny of our country and the world[?]"

Whatever may have been Haynes's immediate source for this story, its original appearance in print seems to be an anonymous 1826 article for the *Christian Watchman*, a Baptist newspaper published in Boston.[34] There can be little question that the tale is fictional: Tribble was not elected pastor of the Baptist church in Albemarle County until 1777, the year after Jefferson wrote the Declaration. Jefferson left no mention of Tribble, nor

[33] Haynes, *Baptist Denomination*, 333f.

[34] The following is taken from "Andrew Tribble," Thomas Jefferson Encyclopedia, August 31, 2011, https://www.monticello.org/research-education/thomas-jefferson-encyclopedia/andrew-tribble/.

of the influence of Baptists, in any of his writings. Also, as befitting a widespread folk tale, several details in Haynes's account differ from the initial telling. The most significant addition is the inclusion of Tribble's boast, between his question to Jefferson and the latter's reply, that the Baptists have always been democratic and surpass the other churches with regard to their polity. This interpolation highlights the growing Baptist self-confidence of the nineteenth century: theirs was an ecclesiology that presaged the American Revolution, standing apart from the other denominations which had to adapt themselves to a less deferential political culture. The genius of the *novus ordo*, and indeed its superior, can be found in the democratic structure of the local churches scattered throughout the land. After all, for these Baptist writers the "pure democracy" that their movement models to the world is derived not from political doctrines of social contracts and equal rights but from a divinely ordained pattern of communal life. While independent of other churches or hierarchical organizations, each congregation operates as such because it is directly instructed by, and held accountable to, the authorizing God.[35] Yet that instruction is ascertained through the equal votes and voices of the membership.

Haynes adds that members of a church have rights to "private judgment" on matters not pertaining to fundamental articles of the faith.[36] His demarcation between legitimate church authority and personal conviction is likely derived from the writings of Frances Wayland, whom Haynes quotes in support of this statement.[37] While the delineation of a sphere of individual sovereignty is reminiscent of liberal political theory that is at the heart of the American experiment, Haynes spells out a key difference in that private judgment is not an unassailable good. He cautions his fellow Baptists to exercise this right with proper humility in the knowledge that they are still accountable to God for their beliefs and the consequences that may stem from holding them.

Hiscox and Pendleton add some texture to the portrait of Baptist democracy by forthrightly acknowledging the presence of ambiguity in a church's discernment of Christ's will. Disagreement will inevitably arise as

[35] Haynes, *Baptist Denomination*, 210.

[36] Ibid., 228f.

[37] Francis Wayland was the president of Baptist-founded Brown University in Rhode Island from 1827 to 1855 and a significant voice in denominational life. More will be said below concerning his role in shaping Baptist practice and self-understanding (see Garrett, *Baptist Theology*, 132–34).

34

a community reaches determinate conclusions, but due to majority-rules voting and congregational autonomy, the options of an aggrieved minority are limited. Haynes asserts the right of private judgment but, as with Hiscox in respect of majoritarianism, he urges humility in its practice. Meanwhile, his eager identification of Baptist polity and the American system demonstrates how comfortably settled Baptists now felt in society.

Early Twentieth-Century Systematic Theologians and Democracy

Around the turn of the century, two of the most prominent Baptist theologians in America employed democratic language in their broader theological treatises. Augustus Hopkins Strong, then President of Rochester Seminary in New York, treats ecclesiology in the third volume of his *Systematic Theology*. He echoes more than a century and a half of Baptist polity writings by declaring a church to be constituted by the laws of Christ, one of which being each member's right to have a say in church discipline and administration.[38] Although liberty of conscience for all and liberty of participation for believers are to be advocated, the defense of rights does not limit the nature of the church to that of a voluntary society. The principle of regenerate membership, symbolized in the notion of the Body of Christ, grounds the formation of the church in "the sovereign action of the Spirit."[39] Yet divine sovereignty is consonant with the principle of self-government, which has been instituted by Christ to train his disciples in the nature of Christian responsibility and liberty.[40]

The principle of regenerate church membership serves as a leveling agent for Baptist churches. If all partakers of the community life are genuine believers, then each owes a supreme allegiance to Christ with which others may not interfere.[41] Since each person communes personally with Christ, and each church receives instruction directly from him, individuals and congregations have equal standing with respect to one another.[42] This unmediated relationship with the divine also guarantees the exercise of private judgment in the interpretation of Scripture, which is not only a

[38] Strong, *Systematic Theology*, 3:890.
[39] Ibid., 893.
[40] Ibid., 898.
[41] Ibid., 897.
[42] Ibid., 898.

right but a duty as each person is responsible to attain knowledge and act in obedience to the Lord's commands.[43]

However, Strong avers that this leveling is not also an atomizing of the church into a mere agglomeration of individuals independently determining God's will for themselves. He explicitly critiques the Plymouth Brethren and Quakers for despising church organization and reducing ecclesial entities to "spiritual" bodies only[44]. Christ is an absolute monarch who guides believers and congregations alike, yet he chooses to speak most clearly through communal discussion:

> In ascertaining the will of Christ, however, and in applying his commands to providential exigencies, the Holy Spirit enlightens one member through the counsel of another, and as a result of combined deliberation, guides the whole body to the right conclusions. This work of the Spirit is the foundation of injunctions to unity.

Thus, the church, through the process of discerning and enacting Christ's commands, is an absolute democracy.[45] Strong devotes several pages to proving this statement, and defining its parameters, by New Testament passages. Through his exegesis he explains that democratic polity entails the responsibility of all members to maintain unity, preserve correct doctrines and practices, elect officers, and exercise discipline over one another.[46]

The emphasis on equal and unified participation is necessary to ameliorate the divisive potentialities of the democratic process. Members must always be aware that their companions also share the indwelling Holy Spirit from whom they seek guidance. Divine purpose is understood by comparing views and so requires the virtue of an open mind that may "welcome new light" and give up an opinion now found to be incorrect.[47] Strong explicitly rejects the notion that "majority rule" can be consonant with this absolute democracy. A large minority of dissent suggests that the "mind of the Spirit" is not yet known, for its signature is an inexorable movement toward consensus. Some intractable situations may call for division of a church, but such drastic steps should only come after waiting,

[43] Ibid., 900.
[44] Ibid., 895.
[45] Ibid., 903.
[46] Ibid., 904–908.
[47] Ibid., 904.

discussion, and prayer have failed to bring about the desired unity.[48]

Strong extends this principle of patient, collective listening for the Spirit in his conception of the relationship between self-governing Baptist churches. He insists on a balanced perspective that grants the absolute equality and responsibility of every congregation while arguing that it is improper for any church to ignore the work of other believers' gatherings.[49] Just as is the case with the discipline of individuals, each church should be willing to give and receive advice or admonition concerning its performance of Christian duties, and an association should withdraw fellowship from an erring church in the hope of eventual reform. Independence is juxtaposed with interdependence as each church acknowledges the presence of the Holy Spirit in her sister bodies. As Strong states explicitly: "[T]he law which applies to individuals applies to the churches, and the polity of the New Testament is congregational rather than independent." Although Strong had endorsed Hiscox's *The New Directory*, here he insists that a church's right to discern Christ's will apart from the counsel of other congregations must be considered only as a "last resort."[50]

Strong's contemporary E. Y. Mullins was perhaps the most influential Baptist theologian of the new century.[51] His most significant work was *The Axioms of Religion*, a modernist effort to restate Baptist theology on the basis of "primary and universal principles."[52] Mullins embodies a shift from the biblicist fideism of the nineteenth-century polity manuals toward theological rationalism, for church polity is determined not by the *laws* of Christ's lordship but the *principles* espoused by Christ's religion.[53] Mullins also redirects the locus of Baptist identity from the corporate fellowship to the individual soul. Influenced as he is by personalist philosophy,[54] at the outset of *Axioms* Mullins avers that the Kingdom of God manifests in personal, as opposed to propositional, religion. This religion consists in a call to individuals to respond to the offer of salvation. Such a response is antecedent to the formation of churches which serve as "social expression[s]"

[48] Ibid., 905.
[49] Ibid., 926.
[50] Ibid., 927f.
[51] See Garrett, *Baptist Theology*, 415–434.
[52] Mullins, *Axioms of Religion*, 26.
[53] Ibid., 27.
[54] See Garrett, *Baptist Theology*, 417.

of believers' personal experiences.[55] Whereas Strong roots his ecclesiology in the doctrine of the mystical Body of Christ, Mullins begins with the doctrine of individual salvation.

The heart of Mullins's conception of Baptist theology is the principle of "soul competency," which he describes as a spiritual capacity given by God and not a form of "human self-sufficiency."[56] This ability grants that each believer may receive and respond to God's will directly, thus bypassing coercive or mediating institutional arrangements that seek to manipulate and control religious expression. Consequently, a proper church polity operates democratically but also Christologically as the indwelling Savior directs the body through the Holy Spirit.[57]

Mullins devotes a chapter to the application of soul competency for his "ecclesiastical axiom." He explains that the equality envisioned by this doctrine is equal privilege and not equal capacities or qualification for offices of leadership.[58] This equal privilege is the direct relationship that Christ initiates with each individual.[59] The practice of democratic polity depends on this notion. Like his predecessors, Mullins sees Baptist ecclesiology as a paradoxical meeting point of absolute monarchy and absolute democracy. Mullins agrees with Leland by marking genuine adherence to Christ's Lordship as explicitly dependent upon the practice of congregationalism, but in a novel theological move he frames Christ's Lordship as always directed toward influencing the individual. Therefore, other Christian polities infringe on the exercise of that Lordship by enacting hierarchies.[60] Biblical congregationalism, however, stands apart not just from other church polities, but also every human form of government, by postulating an immediate relationship between the sovereign authority (Christ) and the citizenry (believers).[61] Mullins does warn that a potential shortcoming of this system is an "over-emphasis of individualism."[62]

Mullins elaborates on this point in the chapter, "Institutional and Anti-Institutional Christianity." He notes that some commentators,

---

[55] Mullins, *Axioms of Religion*, 28, 35f.
[56] Ibid., 53.
[57] Ibid., 54f.
[58] Ibid., 127.
[59] Ibid., 128.
[60] Ibid., 129.
[61] Ibid., 130.
[62] Ibid., 148.

Baptist Democracy in Thought and Action

grown disenchanted by denominational and doctrinal controversies, turn away from ecclesial relations in favor of the spiritual practice of self-sufficient individuals.[63] He contends that a less radical, but still dangerous, form of anti-institutional Christianity is the "open membership" position, which abandons the requirement of believers' baptism for new members who formerly belonged to paedobaptist churches. Mullins decries such efforts as a dissolution of the church as the social embodiment of the Kingdom of God and an ultimately subjective perspective that leaves individuals to act freely according to their wills.[64] This chapter underlines Mullins's conviction that soul competency is not an absolute liberty but a freedom that is fulfilled under the authority of God and the purposes of God for human flourishing. A church with no conditions of membership will lose its identity as *church*—that is, as a distinct social and political community formed under the Lordship of Christ.[65]

Mullins devotes much of *Axioms* to delineating how the principle of soul competency and its attendant axioms shape the manner in which Baptists relate to each other, the broader Christian tradition, and civilization as a whole. Baptists have chosen a cooperating structure over a representative one, in which participating churches reserve the right of free dissent or withdrawal from denominational bodies.[66] Mullins believes that unity is advanced and preserved by spiritual rather than bureaucratic or legislative means. Baptists have maintained, and hopefully will maintain, a remarkable consistency of faith and practice because the reigning Christ will guide the faithful toward harmony.[67] Mullins holds up Baptist polity as the necessary model to be adopted by the ecumenical movement in its search for visible Christian reunion. Voluntary unity, he claims, will be achieved when other Christian bodies abandon their elements which contradict the basic axioms he has outlined.[68]

Mullins contends repeatedly that soul competency should not be construed as an autonomous reasoning ability divorced from its origin in regeneration by the Spirit and its perpetuation through the indwelling of

---

[63] Ibid., 235.
[64] Ibid., 240.
[65] Ibid., 248.
[66] Ibid., 214f.
[67] Ibid., 219.
[68] Ibid., 232.

Christ[69]. He muddles the principle, however, by extrapolating its significance beyond the confessional limits of the church, criticizing various forms of human thought and organization that deny the "competency" of persons, generally understood. So, he claims that Christian theism is the only philosophy for a person who accepts soul competency because agnosticism denies the competency of the intellect.[70] Given his specification of soul competency as a spiritual gift concomitant with salvation, this statement is tautological. Mullins also says that political and social institutions must assume a moral competency of persons to better themselves "under God" for the welfare of society.

Mullins's most extensive syncretism is the assertion of soul competency as the principal catalyst for the progress of Western, especially American, civilization. Mullins holds an optimistic expectation for the emergence of an "ideal social order" and believes that the United States will lead the way because it is the location for "the free and full expression of soul competency."[71] America can be seen as a "Baptist empire" because of the principles in which its government is rooted.[72] Baptists provided the spiritual example for secular government to follow, producing a political system that recognizes citizens as competent to determine their own affairs.[73] Unlike Dudley Haynes, Mullins does not identify any specific and direct linkages between Baptist churches and the founders of the American political system. Rather, he sees that Baptists as furnishing a model that demonstrated democracy in action on a general basis. This model has been taken up and adapted for the civil sphere and now, through the global growth of democracy, entails the approach of "the Baptist age of the world."[74] The future of the world lies in the hands of democratic structures that respect the dignity and worth of human personality, and no better statement of principles can lead the progress of civilization than the axioms of religion.[75] Despite his definitional closure, Mullins's enthusiasm for the American project has led him to self-contradiction in that he can postulate soul competency as the fundamental ground of both Baptist and American

---

[69] Ibid., 40, 53, 55, 68.
[70] Ibid., 66.
[71] Ibid., 67f.
[72] Ibid., 255.
[73] Ibid., 270f.
[74] Ibid., 275.
[75] Ibid., 307.

democracy, which together constitute the hope of the world. More will be said concerning the consequences of Mullins's conflation in chapter 2.

One student of both Strong and Mullins, Walter Thomas Conner, influenced Southern Baptists through his professorship at Southwestern Baptist Theological Seminary.[76] In his theology handbook *Christian Doctrine* (1937), Conner reaffirms the traditional Baptist belief in the univocal New Testament witness concerning church government and the necessity of faithful adherence thereto. "To the extent that the church departs from a democratic organization and government, to that extent does it cease to be Christian in its principles and life."[77] What is notable about Conner's work is the exclusive manner in which he names Baptist ecclesiology as "democratic," passing over the theological descriptor "congregationalist" and only using "independent" as an adjective to elaborate what is meant by church democracy. His writing further demonstrates the strong sense of convergence Baptists felt between their polity and the liberal-democratic structure of American government. The nuanced analogical approach of someone like Johnson has been displaced by a firm belief in continuity.

Conner notes that the Christian traditions present four basic proposals for church polity, from the monarchical to the democratic.[78] When he argues for the final model, he combines the approaches of his teachers, first following Strong in pointing to scriptural proof and then following Mullins in identifying "fundamental principles." Unlike Mullins, Conner does not isolate a singular conceptual key such as soul competency that serves as foundation to subsequent axioms. Instead, he presents three separate ideas: Christ's complete Lordship, justification by faith, and the indwelling of the Holy Spirit in every believer.[79] The first principle refuses the recognition of any supervening clerical authority and the second erodes social distinctions in the light of universal sinfulness, but it is the final principle, the presence of the Holy Spirit, that Conner gives the most detailed explication. Because the purpose of the Spirit is to reveal and effect Christ's will in the world, every believer participates in the discernment of that will for the sake of the church's mission. This is a universal *charism* that is not limited to an "official class" of church leaders.

---

[76] See Garrett, *Baptist Theology*, 449–55.
[77] Conner, *Christian Doctrine*, 268.
[78] Ibid., 266.
[79] Ibid., 266–68.

American Baptists' systematic theologians of the early twentieth century continue to speak of their polity in the paradoxical framework of absolute monarchy and complete democracy as originally stated by Leland. They insist that the conjunction of Christ's Lordship and the equal standing of all believers justifies a deliberative process characterized by equal participation. This democracy is also pneumatologically oriented as they accentuate the guidance of the person of the Holy Spirit in the midst of the corporate fellowship. Both Strong and Mullins caution against overly individualistic accounts of the church even as they defend the right and responsibility of private judgment for each Christian. With Mullins, this shared concern to guard the integrity of the churches is threatened by his confusion of soul competency as a gift of grace with a general human competence that underlies democracy in the secular realm. This conflation of social and ecclesial aims carries the potential of distorting spiritual "democracy" by identifying it with a governmental system that is being articulated and defended in accordance with alternate concepts of human nature and purpose.

Postwar Concepts of Baptist Democracy

These aforementioned sources show that the 1963 revision of the *Baptist Faith and Message* drew upon the linguistic precedents set by the denomination's most prominent leaders and theologians. The article on the church was not a creative innovation in describing the local church as governed by "democratic processes under the Lordship of Christ." Leonard sees this language as conceptually implicit in congregationalism yet unmistakably the product of "the Americanization of Baptist polity."[80] As has been demonstrated, this importation of American political rhetoric into ecclesiology had been on-going by more than a century and a half upon adoption of the revised *BFM*. Although by this point such terminology had become comfortable and routine, Southern Baptist theologians could still see the need to clarify the meaning of such claims so as not to be misinterpreted as supporting the Enlightenment anthropocentrism at the heart of American political experiment. The chair of the revision committee, Herschell H. Hobbs, wrote a commentary on the new confession several years after its adoption. He remarks that local church "autonomy"

[80] Leonard, "In Search of the One, True Church," 165.

should not be construed as an absolute independence from the authoritative direction of Jesus Christ through the operation of the Holy Spirit. Baptists face two choices with regard to such terms: either they must be stripped of such anthropocentric connotations or, if such effort fails, other language in service of Baptist ecclesiological claims must be found.[81]

This outline of Baptist appropriation of democratic language will close with three recent voices. The first testimony comes from Stanley Grenz, a prolific writer whose writings have circulated widely across both Baptist and broader Evangelical circles throughout North America.[82] In his handbook on Baptist ecclesiology, Grenz identifies a unique perspective on the character of the church built upon Baptists' fundamental conviction of the "individual nature" of salvation.[83] This concept should not be confused with modern individualism because, following the New Testament, Baptists understand believers to be participants in covenant communities of interdependence.[84] Grenz presents a three-fold typology of church polity: hierarchical, representative, and congregational, with the last embodying the principle that each local church receives its authority to act directly from the risen Christ.[85] This congregationalism, however, can be further subdivided into "semi-presbyterianism," in which each independent congregation is directed by ruling elders, and "democratic congregationalism," in which final authority rests firmly on the entire membership.[86]

This power base generates two opposing threats to spiritual democracy based on the manner in which members participate, or fail to participate, in decision-making. On the one hand, active engagement by the congregation can devolve into factional "politicking" in which contrasting sides seek merely to overrule one another. On the other hand, apathy on the part of the majority can result in a *de facto* semi-presbyterian rule by the self-selected few. Grenz reflects that a proper democratic congregationalism entails the discernment of divine will by the whole body. He also warns that if this spiritual enterprise takes seriously this aim of discernment, then congregations should aim for widespread consensus instead of

---

[81] Hobbs, *Baptist Faith and Message*, 66.

[82] See Garrett, *Baptist Theology*, 690–96.

[83] *A Guide to Baptist Belief and Practice* (Valley Forge: Judson Press, 1985), 9.

[84] Ibid., 23.

[85] Ibid., 53f.

[86] Ibid., 56.

bare majority rule, which may be based merely on the personal preference of the greater number of members.[87]

In the latter decades of the twentieth century, the Southern Baptist Convention hemorrhaged members of a self-identified "moderate" theological persuasion as the conservatives (alternatively labeled the fundamentalists) gained control over the institutions of denominational life. The most prominent theological voice among the moderates has been historian Walter B. Shurden. His restatement of Baptist beliefs in *The Baptist Identity: Four Fragile Freedoms* has become something of a cornerstone for most moderates' theological identity. Like Mullins before him, Shurden arranges Baptist theology according to a set of axioms: Bible freedom, soul freedom, church freedom, and religious freedom.[88] Shurden defines church freedom as

> the historical Baptist affirmation that local churches are free, under the Lordship of Christ, to determine their membership and leadership, to order their worship and work, to ordain whom they perceive gifted for ministry, male or female, and to participate in the larger Body of Christ, of whose unity and mission the Baptists are proudly a part.[89]

Shurden posits that Baptists navigate a careful dialectic between the freedom of the individual and the responsibility each has to the community as a whole.[90] His own accent is toward the former: Shurden stresses the human capacity for choice and his description of church formation minimizes the work of God in calling persons to salvation. He also paints a realist portrait of Baptist polity in the wake of recent denominational conflicts, placing himself at a remove from the idealism and triumphalism of Strong and Mullins. While the *ideal* is for each church to act as a Christocracy, in practical terms Baptists must "*settle* for a democracy" as they hope to implement Christ's rule through congregational mechanisms.[91] Shurden also distinguishes himself from his predecessors by demurring that democratic congregationalism is necessarily biblical. Rather, Baptists

---

[87] Ibid., 57f.

[88] As one may notice from the names of the axioms, Shurden has set the concept of "freedom," which overlaps with Mullins's soul competency, as the distinctive and fundamental Baptist theological conviction.

[89] Shurden, *Baptist Identity*, 33.

[90] Ibid., 33f.

[91] Ibid., 37. Emphasis added.

have adopted this form of church governance because it provides the most freedom for the greatest number of persons. This utilitarian calculus is supported by the contention that equality of all allows more freedom for the guidance of the Holy Spirit. Finally, like Grenz, Shurden warns that congregational polity is threatened by the passivity of the majority.[92]

Malcolm Yarnell, III, Southern Baptist theologian at Southwestern Seminary, is similarly concerned that a longstanding tradition of democratic congregationalism is fragile and under attack.[93] He responds that this polity is the unambiguous teaching of the New Testament and he briefly reviews some key texts. Yarnell objects that recent efforts by Calvinist Southern Baptists to institute elder rule would establish "unbiblical lordship" over against "biblical leadership," contending that the shift derives not from exegetical study of Scripture but unsavory experiences in which pastors have suffered abuse from deacons or laity. In response to those who question the notion that a polity should be labeled democratic, Yarnell reiterates that salvation is a process in which each believer is called by God, indwelt by the Spirit, and made a participant in the shared priesthood of all. Thus, a genuine ecclesial democracy has a clear theological basis. He closes his article by retrieving the classic formula of the Baptist polity manuals that Christ is the absolute Lord who determines the laws of the church and who then calls his people to be faithful in executing them.[94]

These three voices demonstrate a desire in the late twentieth and early twenty-first century to preserve the Baptist witness of egalitarian congregationalism against two distinct but related threats. The first is the frequent disengagement by most members of a church from the decision-making process. This withdrawal from ecclesial politics undermines the notion of Spirit-guided corporate discernment. It is the likely factor behind the second threat, which is the advocacy among some Baptists of a form of "elder rule" in the churches. Grenz, Shurden and Yarnell each defend the fundamental equality of believers rooted in the Lordship of Jesus Christ and expressed in mutual processes of discernment. Their worries

[92] Ibid., 38.

[93] Yarnell favors Grenz's phrase throughout his article.

[94] Yarnell, "Democratic Congregationalism," SBC Today Print Resources, available at Internet Archive, accessed December 16, 2022, https://web.archive.org/web/20130116085132/http://whub21.webhostinghub.com/~sbctod5/wp-content/uploads/2011/04/democraticcongregationalism.pdf.

about the atrophy of such deliberation hint at the transformation of Baptist congregationalism that will be reviewed below.

Summary of Findings

From the original comparison of Baptist polity with secular forms of government by Leland, to the most contemporary ecclesiological writings, the idea of "Baptist democracy" has been envisioned according to the same constitutive elements. First, all are agreed that such democracy does not mean sovereignty properly belongs to the gathered body as an "autonomous" church. Rather, *the Lordship of Jesus Christ is the paramount authority*. Baptists differ from episcopal or presbyterian traditions by concluding that this rule is delegated or discerned through the whole body of believers and not any select individuals or groups. A frequent motif in the nineteenth-century polity manuals, restated by Yarnell, is the contention that Christ determines the law of his people and the churches administer that law.

Second, this diffusion of the kingly rule through the whole entails the *fundamental equality of believers*. Each person has been freed from the power of sin and possesses the indwelling Holy Spirit as a guide, therefore each is entitled to share in governance. Moreover, each church is in some way responsible to hear the discernment of other congregations although there is disagreement about the relative value of ecclesial self-governance versus interdependence. The idea of democracy makes the discernment of religious truth as a political and corporate act, but Baptist writers also introduce the idea of private judgment, generating a certain tension between individual and corporate deliberation. In the work of Mullins, the individual is given spiritual and logical priority over the church, and this is carried forward in Shurden's ordering of his four freedoms.

Finally, from the beginning of Baptist "democracy" some writers explicitly address the natural *affinity with the values and practices of the American constitutional system*. While all of these writers celebrate their homeland's form of government, we find an emphasis in Leland and Haynes on the uniqueness and superiority of church government over against secular. That this sentiment was widely shared at the time may be intimated by the fact that Mercer was given a medal by his colleagues that was inscribed with the words, "Government is in the Church."[95] By the time of Mullins,

---

[95] Wills, *Democratic Religion*, 29.

46

the distinctions are blurred, however, such that the Baptist churches and the American state, albeit formally separate, are conjoined partners in a shared task of transforming the world.[96]

What points of convergence exist between these marks of ecclesial democracy and the agonistic *ethos* of contemporary political theorists? With regard to the issue of conflictual difference, some figures openly wrestle with the question of managing dissent during the decision-making process. Johnson and Reynolds's integration of divine sovereignty and creaturely freedom implies the emergence of productive tensions in that multiple, creative visions of enacting Christian faithfulness may be voiced in congregational deliberations. Whether competing viewpoints recognize one another as both seeking the good, or that the other has compromised integrity to the gospel, what is to be done when difference persists? Pendleton defends simple majoritarianism, whereas Hiscox and Strong agree that the outcome of a vote does not end dialogue. Hiscox suggests three courses of action for the aggrieved minority, but two out of three entail schism rather than the opposing parties striving together in their differences. It is Strong whose understanding most closely compares with radical democracy. Insisting that the Holy Spirit leads a church *through* contestation, he advises disciplined patience as disciples give and receive reasons for their perspectives, pray, and wait for clarity.

The surveyed theologians also express an ambivalent evaluation of individualism. It is undeniable that Baptists have articulated a high view of the human person as capable of relationship with God in Christ through the Holy Spirit, who is consequently empowered to speak from one's own experience. Precisely because of this theological orientation, the conviction of personal liberty of conscience does not reduce entirely to an expressivist individualism, for the purpose of democratic congregationalism is formation in Christ as all discern together what is proper to the Christian life. Even Mullins, the most individualistic of these writers, cautions against pure subjectivism. This tension between respect for selves as agents and recognition of their essential relativity occupies both Baptist and radical democratic anthropology and will be considered in more detail in the

---

[96] See Canipe, *Baptist Democracy: Separating God from Caesar in the Land of the Free* (Macon: Mercer University Press, 2011). Canipe argues that the first quarter of the twentieth century is a period in which Baptist leaders most strongly perceive an overlap between Baptist principles and American democracy.

next chapter.

That fundamental, theological orientation of congregations names an irreducible differentiation between ecclesial and radical democracy. The extent to which Baptists are willing to proliferate dialogical encounters, at least as they occur within the interior political terrain of the church, is limited by the governing *telos* of the gospel. While these writers accept that there will be different interpretations, they believe that the democracy of Baptist churches ultimately steers in one direction. Should churches wander in times of patient dialogue, it is to more clearly see the path toward a fuller realization of God's Kingdom here and now.

These ecclesiological writings offer the impression largely of consistency in the Baptist understanding of church politics. This apparent continuity is tempered by the emergent individualization and Americanization of some writings, yet one could conclude from this survey that, in large measure, what was then is also now. What is written and what is performed in the churches may be quite contradictory, however. Even as the language remains fairly constant over time, how do the practices of Baptist "democracy" shift and evolve? Do they exhibit transformations that detail what is implied in these ecclesiological texts? If so, then perhaps there is no consistent pattern of Baptist democracy that may be readily identified.

The Practice of Baptist Democracy in the First Two Centuries

This section begins with a survey of what can be known about Baptist ecclesial governance in the early American period preceding Leland's explication of Christocracy, specifically the eighteenth and early nineteenth centuries. How Baptists lived their ecclesial convictions will be summarized in three themes: purity, equality, and interdependence.[97]

Baptist *purity* meant that churches were gatherings of believers "regenerated" by the Holy Spirit to live a holy life, which was enacted through separation from the carnality of the world. Throughout the Colonial era, Baptists in North America constituted a tiny, marginalized sect. In New England and the southern colonies, they were restricted by the church es-

---

[97] This necessarily general overview is not intended to obscure the diverse array of Baptist beliefs and practices that can be found in any historical survey, e.g., Weaver, *In Search of the New Testament Church.*

tablishments, but even in the freer middle colonies their growth was limited.[98] The combination of external legal restrictions and an internal self-conception as rightly ordered gospel churches heightened Baptists' self-conception as a distinct society from the one around them. Indications of their "high" political ecclesiology may be found in the writings of Benjamin Griffith, who was commissioned to pen treatises on behalf of the Philadelphia Baptist Association, the earliest interchurch Baptist body in America. In his booklet on Baptist polity, Griffith repeatedly characterizes a congregation as a political body endowed with the authority of Christ to govern and judge its members. The "spiritual body" of the visible church is ruled by Jesus as the "political head."[99] Those who consent to church membership adopt the laws of Christ as binding and submit to his government through the body as a whole. Griffith presents an egalitarian interpretation of Matthew 16:19, stating that all church participants share together in self-governance by the power of Christ.[100] This egalitarianism is far from anarchic, though, for mutual submission entails the possibility of receiving judgment for sinful behavior, and Griffith describes excommunication in judicial terms.[101]

Griffith's pamphlet exemplifies how early American Baptists portrayed their churches as covenantal bodies formed by solemn mutual consent and sustained by a diligent adherence to divine commands. This adherence was maintained by practices of mutual exhortation and examination. Baptists took great care to regulate their churches as regenerated fellowships of genuine believers. The Great Awakening of the second quarter of the eighteenth century exacerbated this tendency as the emergent "new light" or "Separate" Baptists insisted that converts prove themselves by testifying to an unambiguous "conversion experience."[102] Because of their influence, into the mid-nineteenth century Baptist churches of the South generally required membership candidates to give their testimony before the gathered congregation. It was the responsibility

[98] Hinson, "The Baptist Experience in the United States," 221.
[99] Griffith, "A Short Treatise Concerning a True and Orderly Gospel Church," 96.
[100] Ibid., 96, 99.
[101] Ibid., 106f.
[102] Hinson, "The Baptist Experience in the United States," 221.

of the current members to determine whether an individual had truly experienced saving grace or not.[103]

Baptists also regulated their societies through the corollary practice of discipline and excommunication. Members brought each other before the whole body to face accusations of moral or doctrinal impropriety. The responsibility to ensure a church's moral purity was entrusted to all persons, male or female and Black or White. Discipline was regarded with such seriousness that it made up the majority of discussion in church meetings.[104] Because Baptist churches understood themselves to be entrusted by Christ as a distinctive witness against the sinfulness of unregenerate society, they embraced a sweeping and intrusive authority to regulate even the households of their constituents. The most frequent charges brought against men in the Colonial era included adultery, abuse of family and slaves, and abandonment of family.[105] Such authority could only be granted by the consent of the members who viewed participation in their church fellowship as a matter of highest importance. However forceful and persistent a congregation could be in its discipline, its power remained noncoercive. Nevertheless, early Baptists who advocated for the general liberty of conscience also maintained that a church should vigorously police the standards of behavior to which its members had assented.[106]

In comparison to a wider culture that reinforced longstanding distinctions of class, race, and gender, early Baptists were a relatively *egalitarian* religious movement. While Baptists recognized individual men as specially called by God and ordained them into the responsibility of pastoring or eldering their communities, significant authority was reserved to the corporate body of a church. As noted above, an individual was received into membership, investigated, tried, acquitted or convicted, and excommunicated by the whole congregation. It was thus necessary that there be set times to gather not primarily as a worshiping body but a deliberating body. From their English forebears, the American Baptists inherited the practice of these church meetings, which were typically called "conference meetings" or even "days of discipline" (with the latter phrasing based upon

---

[103] Allen, "Spiritual Discernment, the Community, and Baptists," 114.
[104] Ibid., 19; Najar, *Evangelizing the South*, 68.
[105] Mathews, *Religion in the Old South*, 249.
[106] Bebbington, *Baptists through the Centuries*, 182.

the predominant item on the agenda).[107] However, other points of discussion included candidates for membership or ministry, finances, and even doctrinal and ethical questions. Conference meetings were typically held once a month, most often on Saturdays but sometimes after worship on Sunday or on another day of the week. Baptists took their self-governance so seriously that the male members of the church—and sometimes the female members as well—were required to attend conferences unless adequate excuse had been submitted in advance. Minutes of the meetings and decisions were recorded in "churchbooks."[108] Early Baptists highly prized their non-hierarchical ecclesiology in which each church was free to discern its own policies and principles under divine guidance. Moreover, the Separate Baptists who emerged from the Great Awakening were additionally, and quite severely, opposed to the privileging of educated clergy or upper-class laity within congregations.[109]

Historians have claimed that when Baptists came together to form churches, welcome converts, and judge adherents, they frequently granted rights to women and African Americans that sharply contrasted with conventional social hierarchies. Some recent evaluations have pushed back against overstated arguments that compared early Baptists more favorably to prevailing ethical standards than is warranted.[110] Jessica Madison steers a middle course in her analysis of church discipline records from South Carolina for the late eighteenth and early nineteenth centuries. She proposes that, with respect to gender, Baptists generally adhered to a shared "moral economy" that defined proper behavior according to a person's social station. Madison distinguishes between oppression and subjection, contending that women were generally willing recipients of the former. Their restrictions formed a subset of a larger spectrum of mutual subjection and reciprocal obligation expected of all believers, including White males.[111] Baptists distinguished themselves most clearly from prevailing social customs by the extent to which they censured men for actions that were considered acceptable or even praiseworthy in the honor-bound Southern culture, such as gambling, violence, and adultery.[112]

---

[107] Wills, *Democratic Religion*, 18.
[108] Najar, *Evangelizing the South*, 68.
[109] Hudson, *Baptists in Transition*, 71.
[110] See Spangler, "Democratic Religion Revisited," 30–50.
[111] Madison, *In Subjection*, vii–ix.
[112] Ibid., 58–90.

With an awareness of these complexities, examples of Baptists seeking a form of spiritual equality in a hierarchical society may be noted. Church covenants of the era listed the charter members of the body, and on the roll of names could be found Black men as well as women of both races.[113] Baptists debated the extent to which women could participate in church government. One church queried the Philadelphia Baptist Association in 1746 on the propriety of female ecclesiastical suffrage. The attending messengers concluded that, while women cannot "lead" in church, they do have the right to vote,[114] but some Separate Baptist churches gave women greater responsibility, appointing them to serve officially as "deaconesses" or "elderesses" in ministry to their sex.[115] During the third quarter of the eighteenth century, they also briefly experimented with the public preaching and testimony of female "exhorters," much to the chagrin of the more formal and "orderly" Regular Baptists.[116] More typically, women participated in the disciplinary process of the churches, serving as accusers, investigators, and jurors. Ecclesial disciplinary proceedings served as a check on domestic patriarchalism, such that husbands were held to account for spousal abuse. However, such a process could be used to reinforce conventional gender norms. Husbands sometimes charged their wives with disobedience before the church.[117]

Black participation in the Baptist movement was minimal during the Colonial era. One estimate has African American participation in evangelical (largely Baptist and Methodist) churches at around five per cent by 1800.[118] Yet those who did choose to align themselves with the Baptists entered a social realm of unparalleled opportunity. In contrast to civil judicial procedure, slaves could testify concerning Whites' behavior in church meetings.[119] Slave marriages were recognized in churches even though they were not acknowledged in law.[120] Disciplinary oversight of the household included checks on the treatment of slaves by their masters. For example, one Virginia church debated the question, "Is it Lawful to

---

[113] Najar, *Evangelizing the South*, 54.

[114] Durso, "Baptist Women in America, 1638–1800," 207f.

[115] Ibid., 205.

[116] Lumpkin, *Baptist Foundations in the South*, 69.

[117] Heyrman, *Southern Cross*, 249; Najar, *Evangelizing the South*, 81.

[118] Heyrman, *Southern Cross*, 46.

[119] Wills, *Democratic Religion*, 24.

[120] James, "In the world but not but not of the world,'" 88.

punnish our Servants by burning them &c in any case whatever?"[121] Another church forbade its members from separating married slaves through sale.[122] Monica Najar remarks that the Colonial Baptists took seriously their convictions about an egalitarian spiritual society, such that the primary dividing line was not between one race or another but between the church and the world.[123] The tension between the conventions of the broader culture and the commitment to the gospel was keenly felt by Baptists. Churches and associational bodies passed various abolitionist resolutions, fomenting heated discussion about the morality of slavery.[124]

Alongside their congregationalist practice, Baptists also in principle acknowledged the existence of a universal, yet invisible, church that encompassed and connected all the scattered gatherings of believers. Baptists in seventeenth-century England had to band their churches together in "associations" for mutual support, and in the following century Baptists in America gradually came to embrace associations as well. Baptists thus practiced an *interdependent* congregationalism in which churches were to discern the will of Christ together.

Shurden's study of associations in Colonial and Early Republic America establishes their origins in two practices of the early 1700s.[125] One was the calling of "church councils," which were temporary bodies consisting of representatives of several churches requested by one experiencing internal conflict. It would be the duty of the council to mediate the dispute in the hope of encouraging, but not dictating, a resolution. Another practice was the structuring of churches into distinct, geographically dispersed congregations or "arms" that convened occasional joint meetings. Over time, the arms often became independent churches, yet the fellowship gatherings continued. One such grouping of churches became the Philadelphia Baptist Association in 1707.

In the minutes of the original meeting, it is stated that the body would meet yearly "to consult about such things as were wanting in the churches, and to set them in order."[126] From the beginning, associations were seen

[121] Qtd. in Najar, *Evangelizing the South*, 140.
[122] Lumpkin, "The Role of Women in Eighteenth Century Virginia Baptist Life," 160.
[123] Najar, *Evangelizing the South*, 142f.
[124] See Najar, "'Meddling with Emancipation,'" *passim.*
[125] Shurden, *Associationalism Among Baptists in America*, 11–13.
[126] Qtd. in Keep, *What is a Baptist Association?*, 27f.

not just as places of convivial fellowship but as forums for mutual deliberation and accountability. Theologically, the association was viewed as something of a church meeting writ large. Just as individual believers freely assembled to determine God's will for their churches, so did the churches for their common efforts. The character of this process is defined in the official documents commissioned by the Philadelphia Association and written by Griffith. In his *A Short Treatise Concerning a True and Orderly Gospel Church* (1743), he writes that the associational delegates, by consent of the churches:

> ...may declare and determine the mind of the Holy Spirit revealed in Scripture...and may decree the observation of things that are true and necessary...And the churches will do well to receive, own, and observe such determinations, on the evidence and authority of the mind of the Holy Ghost in them.[127]

One may note the tension between "decreeing" observance and calling churches to ratify associational decisions through their own judgment. Griffith disclaims any power of the association to dictate to churches and reiterates this point in his *Essay on the Power and Duty of an Association* six years later. An association is not a "superior judicature" above the churches, but a body of mutual counsel supported by churches that agree on matters of doctrine and practice.[128] To use the frequent language of early Baptist polity, they must share essential convictions concerning the laws for Christ's society. For Griffith that shared understanding does grant the association dispensation to discipline aberrant defections from the consensus that unites the congregations, even to the point of censuring individuals or factions in any participating church.[129] As Shurden notes, associations sometimes viewed themselves as guardians of individuals over and against churches that had practiced harsh or inappropriate discipline.[130]

Just as churches would excommunicate unrepentant or egregiously sinful members, so to would associations disfellowship Baptist assemblies that strayed from the prized purity affirmed by all. Such an action could do nothing in itself to change the leadership or constitution of the self-

---

[127] In *Polity*, 112.

[128] Griffith, "An Essay on the Power and Duty of an Association," qtd. in Keep, *What is a Baptist Association?*, 71.

[129] Ibid., 74.

[130] Shurden, *Associationalism among Baptists in America*, 149.

governing churches, yet, as Shurden indicates, the benefits of associations were so well regarded that a recommendation would often be "little less than an ecclesiastical law."[131] As a small, often impoverished minority in Colonial America, Baptists had a great stake in remaining united as much as deemed feasible.

The association was also a forum for democratic deliberation on matters not easily settled by appeal to Scripture or confessional norms. Congregations often found that their internal debates required the aid of other voices in reaching a settled decision. Thus, the annual meeting became a venue for receiving and discussing "queries" brought by messengers. Attention has already been given to the 1746 query to the Philadelphia Association on women's role in church government. Other matters of discussion at early association meetings include the morality of slavery,[132] the reception into membership of an adult immersed by an Anglican minister,[133] or the validity of discipline in response to apparent economic exploitation.[134] Sometimes an association would refuse to give advice on a particular issue out of allegiance to the Baptist concept of the responsible church. On the other hand, associations would also disfellowship churches for refusing to follow their conclusions.[135]

In summary, Colonial Baptists were communally oriented, relatively egalitarian, and determined to maintain high standards of moral and doctrinal purity. The individual could share his (and sometimes *her*) judgment as part of corporate deliberations but was also expected to submit to the decision of the whole as the will of God. This pattern was copied on a larger scale with the understanding that churches in association were responsible for deliberating together and for acknowledging the judgment of the extra-congregational body. This was a simultaneously populist and rigorist movement. It began to attract significant interest as the colonies marched toward revolution, resulting in fundamental consequences for the future of Baptist life.

---

[131] Ibid., 135f. See Wills, *Democratic Religion*, 101. This was particularly the case in Shubal Stearns's Sandy Creek Association; see Sparks, *The Roots of Appalachian Christianity*, 87–94.

[132] Query of Rolling Fork Church, Kentucky, to its association in 1789 (Najar, *Evangelizing the South*, 153).

[133] Keep, *What is a Baptist Association?*, 29.

[134] Namely, "Shall we hold members in fellowship who sell corn at $1.00 per bushel?" Qtd. in Shurden, *Associationalism among Baptists in America*, 65.

[135] Ibid., 123, 131.

Shifting Norms After the
American Revolution

The Revolutionary era heralded a significant transformation of the American Baptist experience. At the start of this period the Baptists were a small, struggling sect that chafed against the strictures of ecclesial establishment that prevailed in most of the colonies. By the turn of the century, they had become the largest denomination in a republic that guaranteed religious liberty for all.[136] This remarkable elevation of Baptists' place in society would have a profound reorienting effect on their perceptions of themselves and the world around them.

Baptist historians commonly remark that this small Christian movement suddenly found itself happily compatible with the spirit of the age. "To a people fiercely devoted to liberty and highly individualistic in temperament," writes Winthrop Hudson, "Baptists had a built-in appeal."[137] This previously marginalized sect now offered a model of free association, popular participation in government, and equality of rights for persons across the traditional boundaries of social status. The influx of converts increased dramatically.

Meanwhile, Baptists saw an opportunity for one of their key principles to be recognized and enforced by the governing powers. Many Baptist groups not only embraced the revolutionary cause but also petitioned for freedom of religion as one of its necessary components. In 1775, Virginia Baptists stood apart from other religious bodies by proposing before that colony's convention both independence from Great Britain as well as complete religious liberty.[138] Following the war, Baptists were an important voting bloc that allied with such prominent figures as James Madison and Thomas Jefferson to secure the separation of church and state in the Bill of Rights of the United States Constitution.[139]

Now that their newly independent country acknowledged religious liberty and increasingly allowed for the participation of the common man in politics, Baptists began to see the political and the spiritual orders as

---

[136] A guarantee, it must be remembered, that did not eliminate entitlements granted for particular denominations by the various states. Such state establishments would gradually phase out during the early decades of the nineteenth century.

[137] Hudson, *Baptists in Transition*, 79.

[138] Lumpkin, *Baptist Foundations in the South*, 114.

[139] Ibid., 119.

Baptist Democracy in Thought and Action

two mutually supportive realms of human belonging. It was now conceivable, perhaps even inevitable, to be "both good Baptists and good republicans."[140] The increase in social visibility and in conversions pressured Baptists to conform more closely to general cultural conventions and partially to rein in their experimental, egalitarian practices. Although more Black Christians were joining Baptist churches, they encountered a diminished space of freedom compared to their forebears. The majority of churches that had allowed them to vote withdrew this recognition around the start of the nineteenth century. Congregations also regularly sought masters' permission before welcoming slave members. African Americans were disciplined less but excommunicated at a higher rate.[141] Women also found their ecclesial suffrage abolished even as they became the majority of adherents at the end of the Colonial era.[142] In this respect, Baptists fell in step with a rising social trend of defining "proper," limited roles for women.[143] Restricted to their domestic domain, women had less recourse to appeal to their churches with disciplinary charges. By the 1830s, evangelical denominations were imagining the home as another "church" in which the male head held sway. Congregations slackened their oversight of family life out of a concern with alienating their voting membership of White males.[144]

By the beginning of the Early Republic Baptists were far more numerous and somewhat less countercultural in their practices than they had been in their sectarian era. In most respects, however, their ecclesial practices remained consistent with their longstanding vision of a spiritual fellowship vigorously guarding its own purity. Discipline was exercised widely and thoroughly in the antebellum era, especially in the South. Gregory Wills tallies an excommunication rate of 2 percent of adherents yearly during this period.[145] Women and slaves were still able to present charges, even if they did so only rarely,[146] and Black and White people

---

[140] Najar, *Evangelizing the South*, 130.

[141] Heyrman, *Southern Cross*, 69.

[142] Durso, "Baptist Women in America," 208.

[143] Lumpkin, "The Role of Women in Eighteenth-Century Virginia Baptist Life," 159f.

[144] Heyrman, *Southern Cross*, 158f.

[145] Wills, *Democratic Religion*, 22.

[146] Ibid., 38.

were typically investigated by the same procedure.[147] The Palestine Baptist Church in Mississippi, for example, made an official statement in 1834 that it would apply the discipline guidelines of Matthew 18 equally to Black and White or male and female.[148]

The churches responded variably to the question of dissent concerning their rules and decisions. A general preference for consensus and reconciliation remained intact even as communities navigated thorny disagreements or revolts. Wills's study of Georgia churches finds that most required unanimous votes for the admission or reconciliation of members but only a bare majority for excommunication.[149] The rationale for these procedures was the preservation of church unity. Most members subordinated their consciences to the authority of the church, and those who challenged it were usually and summarily excluded. On occasion, however, a church could listen and learn from a member in the dock. Wills describes an incident in 1817 at Powelton Baptist Church as recounted by its prominent pastor, Jesse Mercer. One member had allowed social dancing at his house as a part of his daughter's wedding celebration. After he admitted his guilt, he proceeded to push back against the church by railing against sins in the fellowship left untouched by discipline. Mercer was overcome by emotion during the trial and urged the congregation to see it as an opportunity for renewed attention to the work of the Holy Spirit.[150]

Individualist and Populist
Revisions of Ecclesiology

The political context of the Revolution, followed by the developments of Jeffersonian and Jacksonian democracy, began to impinge on Baptist polity. The consequences entailed a sharpening of individualistic tendencies and a loosening of interchurch structures of action and accountability. Transformation of Baptists' self-understanding and, subsequently, their practice, was inaugurated through the writings and the activism of influential leaders in the denomination during the period of the Early Republic. These figures largely understood themselves as faithful guardians of their

[147] James, "'In the world but not of the world,'" 84.

[148] Ibid., 96.

[149] Wills, *Democratic Religion*, 30. See Sparks, *Roots of Appalachian Christianity*, 149, on the alleged requirement of consensus among early Separate Baptists.

[150] Wills, *Democratic Religion*, 26f.

Baptist Democracy in Thought and Action

inherited tradition and stewards of the New Testament teachings, but they were also innovators who introduced subtle shifts in the theology of their movement.

The earliest prominent innovator was Isaac Backus, a former Congregationalist and a minister in Massachusetts who advocated persistently for religious liberty. In this effort he drew upon not only longstanding Baptist principle but also the writings of John Locke concerning tolerance and the purposes of government. As a result, his argument for freedom of conscience revised a familiar talking point. In a tract written to the Massachusetts public in 1780, Backus stated that "religion is ever a matter between God and individuals."[151] His wording echoes the famous declaration of Helwys in *A Short Declaration of the Mystery of Iniquity* that "men's religion to God is between God and themselves."[152] A casual comparison of the two statements suggests a faithful reproduction of a classic Baptist teaching. However, the switch from plural to singular is significant. Baptists traditionally defended liberty of conscience so they would have the ability to form communities that would together discern and implement the "laws of Christ." It was in these church gatherings that the primary interaction with God was realized. By instead defining religion as primarily a discourse between God and persons independent of their corporate associations—as *individuals*—Backus rhetorically displaces the central role of the congregation as Baptists had historically understood it.[153]

Leland also adopted this redefinition of religion as centered upon the interaction between God and individuals.[154] Both he and Backus saw the act of salvation as an event occurring separate from, and logically preceding, a person's participation in a local church body.[155] Leland separated baptism as the act of incorporating a believer into Christ from a church's decision to welcome a baptized believer into its particular fellowship.[156] Both men were also very suspicious of denominational bodies as potential

[151] Qtd. in Maston, *Isaac Backus*, 78.

[152] Helwys, *Mystery of Iniquity*, 53.

[153] For a close, contextual reading of Helwys's statement as rooted in theological concerns for the kingship of Christ over the true church, see Freeman, *Contesting Catholicity*, 67–71.

[154] Leland, "The Rights of Conscience Inalienable," 181.

[155] Gaustad, "The Backus-Leland Tradition," 110.

[156] Leland, "Letter to Thomas Bingham, esq., July 1833," 643.

THE CONTESTABLE CHURCH

threats to the responsible self-government of the churches these elect individuals would join. After three years' hesitation, Backus finally led his church into the Warren Association once he was convinced that it would never hear grievances from either the excommunicated or from current members. For his part, Leland helped facilitate the union of Regular and Separate Baptists in Virginia, only to later denounce national mission societies as centralized structures of control.[157]

The individualistic and localist tendencies expressed by Backus and Leland were taken up and radicalized by Francis Wayland, another New England Baptist who served as president of Brown University and editor of *American Baptist Magazine*. Wayland's works were very influential on the development of Baptists during the nineteenth century. One book in particular, *Notes on the Principles and Practices of Baptist Churches*, is the first notable publication written for the purpose of explicating the distinctive attributes of the Baptist tradition. Although Wayland styles himself as a simple expositor of the inherited, common wisdom of his denomination, he is adapting that tradition to cohere with the broader political milieu.[158]

Wayland's ecclesiology is built upon an atomistic anthropology that celebrates the innate possibilities for the spiritual development of the average person. Early in his *Notes* he contends that Scripture has been designed by God so that each person reading it—that is, by oneself—may understand and apply its teachings.[159] The Bible is not primarily read and discussed within the believing community, but in the personal experience of each person who studies the text under the "absolute right of private judgment." This natural right does not entail a natural ability, however, for the Holy Spirit, who is available to all believers, is required to correctly understand the written word.[160]

The right to private judgment implies that individuals will reach divergent conclusions on biblical interpretation and Christian doctrine. For earlier Baptists, as well as many of Wayland's contemporary peers, separation from Christians espousing incorrect teaching is a necessity for main-

---

[157] Gaustad, "The Backus-Leland Tradition," 123–26.

[158] Freeman, et al., remark that this work "tells more about Wayland and the democratization of American religion than about the earlier generations of Baptists he meant to describe" (*Baptist Roots*, 220).

[159] Wayland, *Notes on the Principles and Practices of Baptist Churches*, 15.

[160] Ibid., 132.

60

taining a pure and faithful church; however, Wayland writes, in *The Limitations of Human Responsibility*, that schism is, instead of a deplorable consequence of human fallibility and sin, a "natural and healthy result of freedom of opinion" as each person reaches their own determinations. Wayland still insists on the propriety of church discipline although he doesn't say much about how this coheres with his exaltation of personal choice. He justifies the compatibility of established Baptist practice and his individualism by insisting that discipline is a matter of submitting to Christ and not, strictly speaking, to the other members of one's congregation.[161] But if the will of Christ is discerned only by individuals in private judgment, what justification is there for attending to the disciplinary judgment of the church?

We have seen that Baptists transposed their congregational governance into a comparable pattern of associational life. Likewise, Wayland reinscribes the individualism of private judgment as the independence of local church action. He insists that a Baptist church is characterized by "absolute independence."[162] Like Backus before him, he denies any opportunity for persons to appeal to their association in a disciplinary issue. He also insists that when Baptists delegates gather in associational meetings they have no authority to serve as representatives of their churches and to make decisions on their behalf.[163] This insistence undercuts the older deference to associations that saw them as special occasions for discerning the mind of Christ together.

Early in his career, Wayland argued that Baptists should develop a unified organizational structure through the national level.[164] At this time, the Triennial Convention, which was formed in 1814, would meet with delegates from local or regional Baptist bodies to determine the course of international mission work. Proposals were being made to unite the convention with other Baptist organizations, such as the Baptist General Tract Society,[165] to form a single national body that would oversee education, publications, and missions. As Wayland's perspective turned more

---

[161] Wayland, *Limitations of Human Responsibility*, 124f.

[162] Ibid., 177.

[163] Ibid., 178–81.

[164] Maring, "Individualism of Francis Wayland," 156.

[165] Later renamed the American Baptist Publication Society.

individualistic he became an opponent of this proposal. He eventually distinguished sharply between the duties of a church and those of an individual: the church enjoins a member's dedication to the sharing of the gospel, but it is up to each person to decide whether and how to give to, or participate in, foreign and domestic mission endeavors.[166] Wayland was an influential figure in the 1826 meeting of the Triennial Convention, when the body voted to remain a society dedicated solely to foreign missions and whose membership was based on individual or corporate financial contributions. Baptists rejected an alternative plan to become a more closely connected communion of interdependent churches.[167]

Wayland's hyper-autonomous viewpoint was carried forward to future generations of Baptists through the dissemination of materials by the American Baptist Publication Society.[168] In 1833, the New Hampshire Baptist Convention adopted a confession of faith that defined the church exclusively in terms of the local congregation, with no reference to the universal body. One member of the drafting committee, John Newton Brown, unilaterally revised the confession twenty years later and published it in his church manual.[169] His version was also included in the manuals written by Pendleton and Hiscox and became the basis for the *Baptist Faith and Message* adopted by the Southern Baptist Convention in 1925.

The heightened individualism of these Baptist leaders modulated the emphasis on the church as a pure and unified outpost of righteousness in a sinful world. Christ's will was discerned not primarily in the gathered community as it prayed, deliberated, and acted, but in the mind of each believer as they prayed and studied Scripture in private. While their emphasis on each person's right and responsibility to deal with God expanded the ecclesial container for dissent to be expressed, their de-emphasis of the community ironically sidelined such processes by attenuating the political character of Baptist churches as collective decision-making bodies.

Such revision to Baptist polity as proposed and argued by leadership figures may not have taken hold were it not for transformations occurring from the "bottom up." To be sure, much of what persons like Wayland claimed about Baptist ecclesiology did not suddenly emerge in structural

---

[166] Wayland, *Notes on the Principles and Practices of Baptist Churches*, 189f.
[167] Maring and Hudson, *Baptist Manual of Polity and Practice*, 209f.
[168] Hudson, "By Way of Perspective," 27.
[169] Garrett, *Baptist Theology*, 129.

Baptist Democracy in Thought and Action

revisions. Hudson points out that the practices of churches and associations remained fairly traditional for much of the nineteenth century[170] while Wills's study of Georgia churches demonstrates a strong commitment to discipline, Calvinist orthodoxy, and the priority of communitarian congregationalism over personal liberty. The sectarian, communal ideal of the older Baptist churches was increasingly challenged by the rise of the revivalist evangelical movement. In the swirl of religious ecstasy stirred by the Second Great Awakening, mass crowds flocked to hear populist, lay preachers operating outside the bounds of congregational structures.[171] The "camp meeting" became the locus of the conversion experience as persons responded immediately to the emotional appeal of the folk religious figure. Through these meetings the concept of salvation in Christ was divorced from contextual formation in the teachings and disciplines of a believing community. Baptist churches felt compelled to quickly approve and admit new members who testified to the religious devotion they now felt as a consequence of the revivals. This displacement of the months-long examination of candidates for membership was inevitably corrosive of the traditional Baptist perspective that a church must zealously guard the boundaries of its fellowship and carefully preserve its doctrinal commitment from creeping error.[172]

The evangelical movement encouraged indifference to questions of church order and specific doctrinal traditions. Moreover, revivalism spawned a number of new religious sects, such as the Disciples of Christ and the Mormons, who competed fiercely for converts on the western frontier and who sparred constantly over theological interpretation. Out of this period of intense debate, the second third of the nineteenth century witnessed the rise of the Baptist "Landmarkist" movement, which spread largely through the American South. The name comes from the title of a pamphlet written by J. M. Pendleton in 1854, *An Old Landmark Reset*. Like Wayland before them, Pendleton and his cohorts, John Robinson Graves and Amos Cooper Dayton, characterized their work as defending or restoring traditional Baptist practice, but, in a novel development, they argued for the existence of an unbroken succession of true gospel churches

---

[170] Hudson, "By Way of Perspective,"27; Hudson, *Baptists in Transition*, 130.

[171] Hatch, *Democratization of American Christianity*, 133–38.

[172] On the transformation of the conversion experience, see Allen, "Spiritual Discernment, the Community, and Baptists," 118f.

all the way back to Jesus Christ. Their "high church" view of the Baptists entailed a rejection of pulpit affiliation and baptismal recognition to ministers and believers from churches of differing polity and practice. Although Wayland was an influence on Pendleton and Graves, they clearly rejected his *laissez-faire* attitude toward theological differences. What they did draw from him, however, was a suspicion of the missionary societies and conventions.[173] They instead believed that churches alone are responsible for fulfilling the "Great Commission" and should do so by funding missionaries directly.[174] This biblicist logic also rejected the delegation of authority by churches to representatives attending meetings of larger bodies. For the Landmarkists, anything that did not appear to them expressly supported in Scripture could not be theologically justified.

The combined force of theoretical and practical transformations effected a sea change in Baptist ecclesial identity. Both the "Backus-Leland" tradition and the Landmarkist theologians resisted the empowerment of organizational bodies beyond the local church, shifting Baptists toward a sharper insistence on the "autonomy of the local church." The Landmarkists preserved, but also made stricter, the older Baptist ideal of the pure and separated church while Baptists influenced by Backus, Leland, and Wayland interpreted their faith according to a more anthropocentric individualism, with the result that Baptist democracy began to appear more congruent with liberal-democratic notions of personal sovereignty. The revival movements drove individualistic new Christians into the churches who were themselves enculturated according to this paradigm, and who insisted on membership based on their personal testimony rather than the judgment of the church as to their spiritual state.

While Wayland depicts dissent as having a positive valence, he breezily accepts the division of churches as the proper outcome. Difference in Wayland's vision does not lead to a contestable church, but to a sort of amicable divorce as Christians who come into conflict simply agree to part ways. This suggestion of schism over a difference is neither traditionally Baptist nor radically democratic, but instead coheres with the political minimalism of the liberal tradition in its attempts to reduce conflict by containing most differences within private spheres of interest.

[173] Garrett, *Baptist Theology*, 216.
[174] Robert G. Torbet, "Landmarkism," 180.

The Demise of Discipline and Current Efforts
at Ecclesial Renewal

The radical localism of Wayland, Hiscox and the Landmarkists seized upon native suspicions of coercive church establishments and took root in American Baptist life. The formerly robust vision of associations was weathered down, and the more recent denominational structures were largely limited to serving as fiscal establishments for evangelistic work, but on the whole the practice of church discipline remained intact. One reason may be the enthusiasm with which many ordinary adherents embraced the judgment of a bench of peers. Through the relative egalitarianism that Baptists retained, women, Black people and poor alike found a measure of dignity that would not be granted in culture at large. Moreover, leading Baptist opinion-makers did not contend against discipline as they had against extra-congregational authorities. Even the most ardent proponents of individual interpretation of religious truth, such as Wayland, still recognized the right and duty of each church to hold its membership to account on matters of doctrine and ethics. The moral and confessional democracy that Baptists had long practiced held firm for a longer time than the interdependent democracy of associational and denominational life.

Yet by the second half of the nineteenth century, Baptists realized that the seams of church discipline were beginning to fray. In Hiscox's revised manual, *The New Directory*, he notes a trend of relaxing disciplinary strictures.[175] One of the first arenas in which churches ceded their authority was likely the doctrinal debate between Calvinism and Arminianism. The vast majority of Baptists had subscribed to Calvinistic theology and thus was in the mainstream of early American religious thought. They maintained this doctrinal stance even as other populist religious movements mounted a sustained rhetorical attack.[176] For the early Baptists, as Wills notes, orthodoxy was taken seriously as the bulwark of morality, and even a self-proclaimed Calvinist who rejected one of the major tenets could be excluded from church fellowship.[177] By the middle of the century, allowances were made for Arminianism as a personal opinion so long as it

[175] Hiscox, *New Directory*, 168.
[176] Hatch, *Democratization of American Christianity*, 170–79.
[177] Wills, *Democratic Religion*, 85, 89.

was not voiced publicly or given any sanction by the church.[178] This confidence in the self-evident necessity of doctrinal purity eroded even further, such that in 1874 J. S. Lawton, co-owner of the *Christian Index*, the Georgia Baptist newspaper, could write in favor of toleration for, and unity with, non-Calvinist Baptists. Lawton did not defend this stance with traditional biblicist arguments, but rather with one echoing value neutrality: "[N]one of us are infallible."[179]

This period also witnessed increasing reluctance to police social pursuits that were not obvious violations of scriptural commandments. Second Baptist Church in Atlanta, Georgia, engaged in an extensive debate on the question of "worldly amusements" during winter 1870–1871. The congregation finally decided that it would investigate such matters on a case-by-case basis. Consequently, Second Baptist never again held a disciplinary hearing on social activities.[180] One longstanding source of conflict had been the official opposition to dancing. While before congregations had stood solidly against this amusement, a surge of young members generated unease about cutting off a new generation of adherents that was resistant to the old taboo.[181]

Weaver and Wills both note that discipline was less likely to be effective as a greater share of churches became urban, larger and wealthier.[182] However, the influence of urbanization should not be overestimated. Especially in the South, Baptists remained a rural movement. A 1916 survey found that 92.4 percent of the membership of the Southern Baptist Convention resided "outside the principal cities."[183] Although the toleration and anonymity characteristic of urban life was surely a contributing factor, the erosion of discipline came by means of a current swollen by several tributaries: increasing doctrinal ambivalence, evangelical revivalism, weariness over the hard work of discipline, and the pervasiveness of liberal-democratic assumptions about the rights of the individual. By the end of the 1920s, church discipline had all but disappeared.[184] The case of a small, rural church in Texas illustrates the change of approach that nearly all

---

[178] Ibid., 103, 106.

[179] Qtd. in ibid., 107.

[180] Weaver, "Second Baptist Church, Atlanta," 86f.

[181] Wills, *Democratic Religion*, 124–26.

[182] Ibid., 129; Weaver, "Second Baptist Church, Atlanta," 86.

[183] Harrell, "Evolution of Plain-Folk Religion in the South, 1835–1920," 34.

[184] Wills, *Democratic Religion*, 116.

Baptists experienced. Cego Baptist Church stopped excluding errant members after 1925. Decades later, one elderly church member said to her interviewer that the congregation worried it would forgo the possibility of correcting members in the wrong if they were excluded from fellowship.[185]

Because the concept of Baptist churches as self-regulating moral societies was disappearing, a new organizing principle was called upon to fill the vacuum. Around the turn of the nineteenth century, Baptists began drawing consciously from the management models of American businesses.[186] The Southern Baptist Convention organized management boards for missions and education in emulation of the governing structures of large corporations.[187] The sweeping vision of the church as a community covenanting together in obedience to the gospel was narrowed down to institutional and instrumental articulations. With many of the old doctrinal, ethical and social concerns now placed outside the purview of ecclesial deliberation, the churches were recast as enterprises that existed to deliver one product: converted souls.[188] Toward that end, Baptists retooled seminary education and literature dissemination to encourage "best practices" toward this seemingly quantifiable goal. The most popular church manuals of the interwar period, such as *The Efficient Church* and *Building Better Churches*, were written by Gaines Dobbins, who held the position of Professor of Church Efficiency at Southern Baptist Theological Seminary.[189] The new practices included detailed and exact record-keeping as churches were encouraged to keep track of such figures as attendance, bringing personal Bibles to church, faith-commitment decisions, financial contributions, and so on.[190]

The practice of church government among Baptists in the United States has by and large continued in the amalgamation of individualistic piety and corporate organization that came to dominance around the turn of the twentieth century. Certain key features that characterized congregational deliberation in the Colonial and Early Republican era are all but non-existent. The approval of membership candidates is typically a brief

[185] Jonas, "Keeping the Faith in the Open Country," 107.

[186] Allen, "Spiritual Discernment, the Community, and Baptists," 121.

[187] Hinson, "Oh Baptists, How Your Corporation Has Grown!," 20.

[188] Hudson, *Baptists in Transition*, 131.

[189] Hinson, "Oh Baptists, How Your Corporation Has Grown!" 27; Hinson, "Baptist Experience in the United States," 227.

[190] Hinson, "Baptist Experience in the United States," 227.

formality[191] and the work of discipline is so foreign that its absence is "not even noticed."[192] Meanwhile, the regular church meeting is most often called a "business meeting," a label that Hudson and Norman H. Maring note is symptomatic of the reductive account of its purposes that now prevails as questions of doctrinal, moral or social import are rarely discussed.[193] Although controversies between factions of Baptists have sometimes generated discussion,[194] associations generally do not serve as extra-congregational venues of spiritual democracy because, for the American Baptist Churches USA, they have largely been displaced by denominational regions,[195] and, for Southern Baptists, they are rarely more than annual fellowship meetings.[196]

By the middle of the twentieth century, Baptist historians and theologians began to sound the alarm about the hollowed-out nature of ecclesial community.[197] Among southern baptists, two notable responses have arisen to arrest the slide toward an ecclesial version of political liberalism. The first has been made by conservatives in the Southern Baptist Convention who insist on the recovery of regenerate church membership—principally through robust church discipline, providing extensive historical analysis and suggestions for reinstating the practice.[198] A key leader in this effort, both as a scholar and practitioner, has been Mark Dever, who pastors Capitol Hill Baptist Church in Washington, DC. Dever founded the parachurch ministry organization 9Marks, which enumerates and advocates for a set of practices deemed necessary for healthy churches—church discipline being among them. Materials produced by the organization provide both biblical justification for church discipline and practical guidance

---

[191] Hammett, "From Church Competence to Soul Competence," 162.

[192] Mohler, "Discipline: The Missing Mark," 43.

[193] Maring and Hudson, *Baptist Manual of Polity and Practice*, 71f.

[194] See Carter, "Dealing with Doctrinal Conflict in Associational History," *passim*.

[195] This despite attempts to revive associationalism. See Maring and Hudson, *Baptist Manual of Polity and Practice*, 224–30.

[196] Stewart, *Baptists and Local Autonomy*, 48.

[197] Hudson played a key role through his publications, particularly *Baptist Concepts of the Church* and *Baptists in Transition*.

[198] E.g., Mohler, "Discipline: The Missing Mark," 43–58; White, "The Why, How, and When of Church Discipline," 199–226; Hammett, *Biblical Foundations for Baptist Churches*, 109–26.

68

on implementation.[199]

Moderate and progressive figures affiliated with the Cooperative Baptist Fellowship and the Alliance of Baptists have also contend for a revived communitarianism although their emphasis has been on communal reading of Scripture, the celebration of the sacraments, and a stronger sense of rootedness in the broader Christian heritage, with minimal attention to the practice of discipline per se. The seminal document of the communitarian or "catholic" Baptists is the *Baptist Manifesto*, originally published in 1997.[200] These Baptists emphasize the egalitarian aspect of Baptist ecclesial democracy and stress the responsibility to attend to divergent perspectives in the process of determining faithful Christian living in the present. This process is exemplified by the edited anthology *Sources of Light*, in which various Baptist theological voices offer a written conversation on engaging in contextual, church-centered theology.[201]

Briefly comparing the overall state of southern baptist ecclesiology between the Colonial era and now, the following admittedly general statements can be made. Southern baptists have shifted from an emphasis on purity and separation to greater laxity in upholding doctrinal and ethical standards. The egalitarian impulse has remained and, due to societal transformations in the twentieth century, has been more fully recovered and even extended as older norms of gender and racial hierarchy have been rejected; however, this egalitarianism has become more individualized, so that its aim is less at equal participation in and responsibility for the church but in the assertion of equal rights to determine the truth for oneself. The Landmarkist movement has faded and Baptists have accepted a greater degree of interdependence in their denominational structures, but associational life lacks the character of deliberation and discernment it once expressed. In recent experience, Baptists have taken the route of separation rather than contestation in shared spaces.

---

[199] E.g., Leeman, *Church Discipline: How the Church Protects the Name of Jesus* (Wheaton: Crossway Books, 2012).

[200] Produced as an appendix in Freeman, "Can Baptist Theology be Revisioned?," 303–10. Originally published as "Re-Envisioning Baptist Identity," 8–10. More will be said about the Bapto-Catholic movement in chapter 4.

[201] Chilton and Harmon, eds., *Sources of Light: Resources for Baptist Churches Practicing Theology*. Perspectives on Baptist Identities (Macon: Mercer University Press, 2020).

Comparing the history of southern baptist ecclesial practice with radical democracy allows for the following conclusions. First, southern baptists have a mixed record regarding the value of difference and the role of conflict in their churches and associations. Early Baptists were simultaneously rigorist and deliberative, imposing strict discipline on matters they saw as decided by Scripture but, through the use of queries, engaging in fertile discussion regarding the application of biblical teaching in situations that were more ambiguous and open to debate. Over time, southern baptist zeal for discipline waned, but so too did their willingness to engage in extended theological conversation regarding relevant issues. Baptists are much more accepting now of theological and ethical diversity but far less apt to hold vulnerable discussions in which the variety of opinions is examined, tested, and shifted through argument and persuasion. Engagement with radical-democratic theory may potentially support Baptists in finding the right balance between a settled identity that too readily assumes the divine will, on the one hand, and an uncritical tolerance that prevents dissent from serving as a community-shaping challenge.

What the history of Baptist ecclesial practice shows is a fundamental agreement with radical democracy on the necessity for local, participatory politics in which persons formed disciplined habits according to an *ethos* of receptivity and mutual care. Recent efforts to renew Baptist ecclesiology from both conservatives and moderates stress precisely this point over against atomistic conceptions of personal faith and spirituality. For radical democrats, democracy is learned and sustained in the *doing*, and for Baptists Christ has commended the living out of the gospel to the care of gathered communities who seek to understand and enact their mission in witness to the world. Attention will need to be paid to patterns of community life that encourage active participation while avoiding the dangers of either apathy and individualism on one side or strict boundary lines and schism on the other side.

Conclusion

In this chapter I have set out to clarify what southern baptists have intended when they speak of themselves as "democratic." A simple, and understated, answer would be that they are not entirely sure. As Hudson has observed, the practice of church governance has seen much improvisation but no certain direction.[202] In all likelihood this is the case because the church is now generally understood as a secondary organizational elaboration upon an individual's primary religious experience. The rising individualism from the Revolutionary era onward has reshaped Baptist ecclesiology in a decisive manner. Wills remarks that the Baptists of 1850 identified their "democracy" as the authority of a congregation collectively bearing the responsibility of Jesus Christ's rule. The Baptists of 1950 (and of today, for that matter) have more often seen their "democracy" as the freedom of the individual who makes private judgments in religious matters and who brings their direct experience of Christ to the church.[203] The monumental differences are masked somewhat by a continuity of terminology and basic structures. Baptists have persisted with a bare skeletal outline: the fundamental equality of all believers, the authority of the congregation as a whole, and the freedom of each congregation from coercion by external agencies. Yet the flesh placed on this skeleton has rotted away and been replaced by a new body that is easily recognized as molded from the constituent elements of America's liberal-democratic *ethos*.

Baptists in America seized upon the language of democracy because they saw it as a fitting, if still only analogous, representation of their distinctive manner of discerning the will of Christ as corporate fellowships of believers. Over time, Baptists came to understand their democratic vision in more individualistic terms as respecting the rights of people to know God and God's will for themselves. There exists a fundamental tension at the heart of the claim to be democratic. As a result, it is apparent that Baptists have yet to clarify what it means to be a spiritual democracy. Any restatement of their ecclesiology within such linguistic parameters must, in order to be intellectually viable, expound upon their core convictions and take account of their shifting political patterns. A theological conversation with radical democracy may provide the impetus for redefining the idea of Baptist democracy for the present day.

[202] Hudson, "By Way of Perspective," 28.
[203] Wills, *Democratic Religion*, 139.

CHAPTER 2

SOUL COMPETENCY AND
THE ARTISTIC SELF

The practice of democracy expresses an implicit claim or set of claims concerning the human person. Authoritarian regimes, when not simply resorting to violent coercion, have traditionally justified themselves by postulating a fundamental distinction between the elite who rule and the commoners who serve and obey. This difference has been attributed to heredity, class socialization, education, or some combination of these factors. Even in reformist movements of the early modern period, "democracy" was considered a dangerous and radical notion. Liberty must be tempered by order, lest radical elements wreak havoc on social stability. Thus, the Founding Fathers of the American Revolution generally believed that the republic should be organized as the benevolent rule of the more prosperous and refined on behalf of the masses.[1] Much of subsequent American political history can be quite accurately summarized as a protracted battle over extending the franchise.

The democratization experienced in the United States and elsewhere has entailed the progressive abandonment of longstanding historical precedent. Barriers to participation forged of ethnicity, gender, and economic status have formally lifted although prejudices and structural inequalities have persisted. Mature democracies take it as axiomatic that all citizens are intrinsically capable of involving themselves in the political process, with limitations only imposed under exceptional circumstances (i.e., disfranchisement for criminal conviction). What understanding of the human person allows or requires the modern belief in an emancipated populace? The early modern period declared the existence of natural "rights" but as a naked assertion this postulate stands inadequate. Why should all persons be considered the bearers of equal rights?

This secular question finds a parallel in ecclesiological discussion. The Baptists who emerged in England during the seventeenth century followed their Separatist forebears in practicing a congregationalist polity. Explicitly

---

[1] See Wilentz, *Rise of American Democracy*, 3–39.

opposing the hierarchies and synods of the Anglican or Presbyterian polities, Baptists have, with much consistency, insisted upon the full responsibility of a congregation as a whole for governing and maintaining itself. In doing so, Baptists have also rejected a longstanding tradition that considers the proper functioning of churches to be dependent upon a distinction between clergy and laity, the former of whom exercise their office through the principle of apostolic succession. The first chapter of this work documented the Baptist sense of being "democratic," but now the question must be asked, "Why is this so?"

This chapter will explore the anthropological justifications given for democratic practice within radical democracy and Baptist theology. What is the nature of persons such that they can, or perhaps must, enter into vulnerable relationships with different others? The search for an answer will begin by analyzing the anthropology developed by Coles in *Self/Power/Other* (*SPO*). Coles seeks a concept of the self that may support his dialogical ethic. His review of three philosophers and his conclusions about the "artistic self" will be presented and discussed. Then this chapter will explore Baptist statements on anthropology. First, the differences between Coles and the traditional Reformed theology of original sin and redemption will be presented. Then a more "positive" anthropology of participation in Christ's triple office will be articulated. Finally, the anthropology of "soul competency" expressed by Mullins, perhaps the most influential southern baptist of the twentieth century, will be juxtaposed with Coles's notion of the artistic self. Despite the primary metaphysical differences between Coles's vision and Baptist theological anthropology, the vision of interdependent artistic selves provides a helpful enhancement of soul competency for Baptist ecclesiology that resolves the dilemma of individual and community.

The Anthropology of *Self/Power/Other*

Before examining the contents of *SPO*, it will be helpful to provide a working definition of the first word in this work's ternary title. Coles does not himself explicate the term and likely expects the reader's basic familiarity with philosophical discussion on the subject. Significant ink has been spilled because the concept is one that, on the face of it, is readily understood as an immediate experience pertaining to each person—yet effort is needed to clarify just what is being communicated by the term "self."[2] Space cannot be afforded to this extensive topic apart from briefly noting some relatively recent definitions. Charles Taylor, in his book *Sources of the Self*, defines the self as a being complex enough to possess an identity, the latter term representing the recognition of existing as a particular thing oriented in reference to its surrounding environment and other beings.[3] Richard Sorabji also sees the self in the human being as claimant of a particular identity, but differs from Taylor in seeing this identity shaped intrinsically through accepting ownership over one's "psychological states and actions."[4] John Smith defines the self as a developing autobiography centered upon a pervading awareness and intention of who a person is striving to be.[5]

These descriptions of the self typify modern Western philosophy's rejection of two polar positions: Rene Descartes's idea of a substantial and permanent self that lies, unchanging, beneath the evolving life history of a person, and David Hume's reduction of the self to a mere agglomeration of perceptions that lacks a coherent unity.[6] The common supposition in newer perspectives on the self is the denial that the self is a unitary "something" exhibiting substantial permanency. Rather, the self is a dynamic *process* as an individual observes their life story unfolding in time, ordered by a meaningful sequence of events, and shaped by experiences that can be analyzed "internally" as one's emotional states and thoughts or "externally" as initiating and receiving action in the world. The definitions given above differ as to the degree by which externality is responsible for shaping the self. It is this conversation that Coles builds upon as he searches out his anthropological justification for the radical-democratic project.

Self/Power/Other, Coles's first book, is an extended reflection on the nature of self in its relationship with the other as presented in the writings of three theorists—St. Augustine of Hippo, the French philosopher and literary critic Michel Foucault, and the French phenomenologist Maurice Merleau-Ponty. He exegetes their works in this order so that his reading of Foucault may critique Augustine and then his reading of Merleau-

---

[2] Smith, "Freedom as Self-Determination," 84.
[3] Taylor, *Sources of the Self*, 32–36.
[4] Sorabji, *Self*, 21.
[5] Smith, "Freedom as Self-Determination," 86f.
[6] Ibid., 84.

Ponty may both critique and extend elements in Foucault's thought.[7] Coles presents the hopeful aim of determining "the *highest* possibilities of our lives with others" in a setting explicitly modern and consequently post-theological.[8] His intent is to justify a democratic ethic of reciprocal dialogue and he sees the answer in an ontology of inter-generative selfhood. This anthropology contends that human flourishing depends upon, and occurs through, the thick interaction of permeable selves.[9]

In his introduction, Coles rejects any form of substantialist essentialism, whether pertaining to an individual or a social group, which would render its existence and identity to be self-defined and self-sufficient. To conceptualize an alternative account, he draws upon the science of ecology to provide an introductory metaphor. Naturalists have found that the edges between ecosystems, formally known as "ecotones," tend to manifest a greater diversity and density of living organisms than the interiors. This natural analogy suggests to Coles that the quality of humanness is best expressed at the tensional edges of identities, yet the history of human politics is littered with the desire to eliminate edges, whether through hegemonies of violence or those of value that seek to "obliterate the other's otherness."[10] The imaginary of the edgeless self is maintained even in modern liberal theory, according to Coles. On the one hand, the prominent theorist of political liberalism, John Rawls, envisions atomistic, rational selves in his hypothetical "original position," who reason from first principles. Communitarian theorist Michael Sandel, on the other, critiques the idealization of a self constituted solely by detached reflection, but Coles argues that Sandel constructs the self only through its *agreements* with the other. Contradicting both thinkers, Coles believes that the self forges both its very being and its freedom to act through dialogical encounter with the others in their very differences. As an *ethos*, the encounter includes the pursuit of a common good that is given definitional texture by the cultivation of diverse perspectives.[11]

---

[7] In this and the following chapters, my discussion will analyze Coles's presentation of these thinkers and will not determine the validity of his exegesis.

[8] Coles, *Self/Power/Other*, vii–viii. Emphasis original.

[9] Ibid., ix.

[10] Ibid., 1f.

[11] Ibid., 3–6. For these theorists' original arguments, see John Rawls, *A Theory of Justice* (Cambridge, Massachusetts: Belknap Press, 1971); Michael Sandel, *Liberalism and the Limits of Justice* (Cambridge: Cambridge University Press, 1982).

In *The Confessions* and *The City of God*, Coles discovers St. Augustine's views concerning the formation of the human person. He sees the central question behind *Confessions* expressed in Book X, Chapter 17: "What then am I, my God? What is my nature?"[12] Augustine finds his answer in the act of constituting a "confessing self," Coles writes. This understanding of the self evokes a conscious rejection of the "pagan" world that stands in tension with the ascendant and now politically empowered Church. The unbelieving elite of old Rome fashioned malformed selves through the vice of pride, which includes not just a moral lapse of judgment but an ontological falsehood by deeming individuals to be self-generative. Having rejected the notion of dependence, the proud pagan thus abdicates responsibility to others and God and substitutes this with the freedom of self-rule.[13] This conceit in which nothing is owed to the external world results in acts of violence to appropriate the other as an object that exists in service to the self.[14] The old Roman world thus generated unreflective selves that became enslaved by their lusts for personal satisfaction, having refused to investigate the complexities of their internal depths.[15]

For Augustine, the Christian gospel opposes such self-assertion as an exercise of fruitless vanity. Augustine postulates as an alternative the "confessing self," which turns inward to discover the deepest truths about its nature.[16] The self that would be a citizen of the City of God must continually expose itself to interpretive review if it is to uncover its true nature.[17] For Augustine, the self is revealed as an interior multiplicity riven by competing desires—a remarkably modern understanding of the self, echoing the definitions shared above. Even the exercise of the will is not singular. Confession of these diverse (and, it must be said, generally sinful) desires to God intends the goal of restoring unity out of the many strands of personality.[18] This is accomplished by drawing attention away from the fleet-

---

[12] Coles, *Self/Power/Other*, 14. This quotation is from St. Augustine, *Confessions*, 194.

[13] Coles, *Self/Power/Other*, 17f.

[14] Ibid., 19f.

[15] Ibid., 26.

[16] Ibid., 14.

[17] Ibid., 28–30.

[18] Ibid., 32f.

ing desires that come and go in the experiential, present moment and toward a narrated personal history gleaned from memory. In *Confessions* the self is equated with the scope of memory.[19] The self-revelatory account disproves the prideful ontology of the pagan world and reveals instead the imperfections and dependencies of its existence.[20] Moreover, only unyielding self-examination under God may collect and bring under control the competing strands of personality, thus heralding true freedom.[21]

Coles employs the metaphor of "depth" to summarize how Augustine views the being that is partially uncovered through confession but which remains, in this life, beyond full disclosure. Beneath the exterior lie the hidden cravings and motivations that truly define the self. Those who do not confess remain "flat" by denying the ambiguous or even unknowable aspects of their existence.[22] Augustine presents the spiritual exploration of the multiplicitous self as a polemical point against conceited Roman anthropology, but Coles finds another totalizing conceit in the confessional process. So long as the Christian story is contestable as truth, Augustine's appreciation for the diversity of being is itself a hegemonic exertion. The differences contained inside the self must be subjugated to the solitary voice of Faith. The differences that exist beyond the Christian vision must also be judged contrary to the will of God and rooted in willful disobedience.[23] The result is imperialism reborn.[24] The world's rainbow of colors must merge into the white purity of God's holy light or else be deemed as belonging to the dark nothingness of sin.

The concept of depth indicates, in Augustine, a multifaceted being persisting through intertwined strands of desire and memory. These must be purged through confession in order for the remembering self to achieve freedom and genuine self-realization. The notion of the inner turmoil named by depth, however, is rejected by Michael Foucault in his works. According to his social analysis, "depth" names an imposition upon the self by subjugative powers. He critiques modernity as the advancement of the "normalizing gaze" by dominant social structures in order to exclude

---

[19] Ibid., 34–37, citing again X.17. See Smith's definition of the self, given above.
[20] Coles, *Self/Power/Other*, 37f.
[21] Ibid., 46f.
[22] Ibid., 44–48.
[23] Ibid., 47, 51.
[24] Ibid., 51f.

what is considered abnormal from the allowed spectrum of diversity.[25] The practice of disciplinary power extends beyond the visible separations to judge interior motivations and attachments.[26] Depth is defined by the regulatory system as the true meaning of the self that must be uncovered by the expertise of analysts trained to reveal hidden truths; i.e., therapists and priests. Coles summarizes this critique by Foucault: "We discover within, the being we have been fabricated to be; and we perpetuate and intensify this form of being when we exalt it as truth."[27] The image of the self that appears is a false profundity, imposing interpretations that serve the privileges of external interests.

Foucault traces the trajectory of modernistic ontology back to the collapse of the classical concept of the universe structured according to the "Great Chain of Being" descending from the divine realm into the world of manifestation.[28] In this stable and given order, human beings recognize differences arising within and testifying to a seamless fabric of existence where everything has its place. With the coming of the Enlightenment the classical framework gives way to an opaquer existence in which humanity lacks transcendentally defined relationships with the world. Conscious of finitude, human beings make themselves the wellspring of stabilizing truth, resulting in the pressure to eradicate the instability of difference.[29] The dimension of "sameness" is now the trajectory imposed upon society rather than the ground upon which it is founded.

Rejecting the common reading of Foucault as merely nihilistic, Coles believes that his thought offers a counter-ontology of dynamic dialogue in place of modernity's bent toward oppressive unity.[30] The unified depth fashioned by the disciplinary gaze is dismissed in order to uncover the heterogeneity of being. Foucault rejects any imposition of "truths" upon the self that would distort its character to fit prior conceptualizations. Thus, the constraints of metaphysics, both classical and modern, are rejected in favor of "the artistic fashioning of ourselves in dialogical engagement with

[25] Ibid., 56f.

[26] Ibid., 59.

[27] Ibid., 62.

[28] See Arthur O. Lovejoy, *The Great Chain of Being: A Study of the History of an Idea* (Cambridge: Harvard University Press, 1936).

[29] The preceding summarizes and reorders the presentation of Foucault as presented by Coles in *Self/Power/Other*, 66–72.

[30] Ibid., 75f.

the differences within ourselves and between ourselves and others."[31] The world beyond the observer is always other at least in part. The recognition of such demands an attitude of openness toward specificity beyond and outside of predetermined categorization. This epistemic stance, Coles argues, is not a counsel of despair but the fecund ground for the creative freedom of self and society.[32] With no divinely given ground, Foucault declares, "we have to create ourselves as a work of art."[33]

Coles identifies the notion of self as art form to be Foucault's *ethos* or his non-prescriptive depiction of a positive way of life.[34] The self is created by the questions raised at the boundaries where one's being meets different others. The exercise of this creative freedom impels an ethical vision of society as the space shaped by the goal of enhancing differential expression.[35] However, Coles remarks that Foucault's ontology includes a disturbing shadow that imperils his ideal, for Foucault believes that all expressive acts are marked by an innate violence toward difference. How can any sort of ethical belonging to others operate in the midst of inextricable discord?[36] This dilemma prods Coles to seek an ethics rooted less in aesthetic judgment, leading him to turn to Merleau-Ponty.

The metaphor of "depth" regains a positive function in the phenomenology of Merleau-Ponty although, in distinction to Augustine, this depth is located in the exchange *between* self and other rather than *within* a single person's inner life. Coles writes that Merleau-Ponty sets out in *Phenomenology of Perception* to craft a "philosophy of being" by engaging theories of human knowledge.[37] Faulting both rationalism and empiricism for failing to acknowledge the presence of indeterminacy in the world, Merleau-Ponty argues that perceptive experience necessarily arises from the differentiation between an object and a background. Any "thing" is only noticed as such by virtue of emerging out of indeterminacy. The perception that discriminates figure and ground is not itself determinate of objective reality but rather determined by one's history of experience and

---

[31] Ibid., 77.

[32] Ibid., 80.

[33] Ibid., 81, citing Foucault, "On the Genealogy of Ethics," 237.

[34] Coles, *Self/Power/Other*, 85.

[35] Ibid., 92f.

[36] Ibid., 96f.

[37] Ibid., 104.

expectation.[38]

Self and world are thus inextricably related, for the latter is revealed through perception while the former remains situated within particular fields of influence such as cultural and political context.[39] It is in the act of perception that "depth" emerges as the rational delineation between object and background.[40] To the percipient, this structuring both presents as well as hides the many qualities of existence, for perception cannot contain the fullness of a world that exists as, in Merleau-Ponty's words, "wild Being."[41] Depth ensures both the distinction between things as well as the inescapable otherness of things in themselves beyond the act of perception.[42]

The self is discerned simultaneously with the different others. "At the instant that I become aware of another perceiving being," Coles writes, "so too, for the first time, I become aware of myself."[43] Personhood is constituted through the intersubjective, even intercorporeal, relationships of tension and recognition. This dialogical encounter grants the distinctiveness of the world as well as the setting and limits of one's own vision.[44] Just as Augustine was concerned that pagans had flattened the self into the predetermined patterns of pagan pride, so Merleau-Ponty finds danger in modernity's "flattening of being" that would shape different individualities into normalized and purportedly objective patterns.[45] This drive toward universality is problematic because the self is defined not in relation to the dynamic indeterminacy of wild Being but rather to a fixed and seemingly eternal perception of how things are or ought to be.

In contradistinction to the objectifying gaze, Merleau-Ponty envisions the self forging its own meaning within the turbulent interconnections of existence. Coles discovers in this assertion, much as in Foucault, the notion that the self is both artist and art form. Merleau-Ponty proposes the individual production of "styles" of being in which the truth of oneself

---

[38] Ibid., 105f.
[39] Ibid., 106.
[40] Ibid., 114.
[41] Ibid., 118f. Citing Merleau-Ponty, *Visible and the Invisible*, 170.
[42] Coles, *Self/Power/Other*, 126.
[43] Ibid., 132.
[44] Ibid., 134f.
[45] Ibid., 135–37.

is not unveiled but unfolded in dynamic creativity.[46] This dynamism remains perpetual, for the production of self as expression of relationship with the world is fragmentary. Beyond these concretions lies "a tremendous plenitude of otherness" that demands ongoing dialogue with the world.[47] The self comes into determination as far as it is realized through and because of the encounter with the other.[48]

This anthropology of the emergent self provides, in Coles's estimation, the ground upon which to fashion a radically interrelational politics. The vitality and freedom of the artistic self depends upon the enlightened self-interest of attending to the formation of fellow artists of humanity.[49] For the artistic enterprise to work, social structures and institutions must embody this interest and reject dehumanizing practices. Merleau-Ponty thus rejected capitalism and favored Marxist theory for some time before criticizing its own negation of difference and coming to affirm the value of parliamentary democracy as a vehicle for creative contestation.[50] Its promise would find fulfillment not in particular bureaucratic procedures but in the willingness of the chosen leaders to cultivate the artistic *ethos*.[51]

Conclusions

Coles retraces his journey through these three thinkers in his concluding chapter. He commends Augustine for opposing the conceited ontology of Roman paganism, yet remains troubled by the theological hegemony that edges toward "monological being."[52] The multiplicity contained within the confessing self is characterized by irrevocable conflict instead of dialogue.[53] Coles wants to know if there may be an ontology that turns away from Augustine's triumphalism without simply falling into the nihilism that gives up on the search for truth beyond the mere assertion of the self.[54] He

[46] Ibid., 144–46.
[47] Ibid., 149.
[48] Ibid., 151.
[49] Ibid., 152.
[50] Ibid., 153–59.
[51] Ibid., 168.
[52] Ibid., 170–72.
[53] Ibid., 173.
[54] Ibid., 179.

finds that Foucault replaces the humility characteristic of Christian obedience with a secular analogue expressed in appreciation for differences, within and without, generating artistic self-construction.[55] Recognizing greater similarity between Foucault and Merleau-Ponty than they themselves or other philosophers might acknowledge, Coles senses a rich theory of the artistic *ethos* as he conjoins their work. Nevertheless, Coles favors the more optimistic ontology of Merleau-Ponty, who rejects reducing discourse about things to the imposition of violence upon them.[56] While both agree that otherness remains perpetually beyond our categorizations and concepts, Merleau-Ponty sees a world of possibilities that evoke creativity, rather than transgressions that instill fear.[57] It is this openness to the endless arising of the world that Coles wishes to define the self and, subsequently, the grounding ethics for radical, democratic politics.

SPO sets the pattern for Coles's theoretical writing in all future works. He extensively plumbs the works of other thinkers, providing analysis and teasing out novel readings as yet unexplored. Along the way, he offers his critiques or his elaborations of his dialogue partners as they relate to his quest for a justified politics of ethical contestation. Committed as he is to this interactionist *ethos*, Coles leaves his own conclusions comparatively underdeveloped. The following discussion is an effort to interpret the interpreter so as to elucidate his anthropological conclusions regarding the artistic self.

First, at least during this stage of his career, Coles inhabits a perspective that assumes the intellectual nonviability of God. There is no question of rescuing the Christian narrative from the buffeting storms of the Enlightenment. The gospel shuffles away "in its dusk," and those who seek to live ethically in the modern world must do so absent any normative directive from the Divine.[58] If God is contestable, at the least, or outright indefensible, at the worst, then the Christian vision is not simply incorrect but just as much imperialistic as the Roman story that Augustine rejected.[59] Human nature must be understood in terms other than blind adherence to a belief system that has taken so many violent turns in the quest

[55] Ibid., 180.
[56] Ibid., 187.
[57] Ibid., 188, 190.
[58] Ibid., viii. See 9.
[59] Ibid., 51f.

Soul Competency and the Artistic Self

for a unitary politics.

Second, and speaking more broadly, Coles sides with Foucault and Merleau-Ponty by engaging in an explicitly post-metaphysical search for acceptable forms of life together. Beyond the Christian notion of God, there are no other contenders for some form of unconditioned Ultimate that guarantees a clear delineation between proper and improper expressions of human nature. Rather, as Merleau-Ponty argues, perception enables each person to recognize a hidden otherness that flickers in and out of observation but remains perpetually beyond complete interrogation. It is impossible, then, to discern a permanent structure that is given and in which each soul must play its part, as in the "Great Chain of Being" concept of the medieval philosophers. There is only the perpetual production and passing of forms that engender multiple, evolving responses from the self formed through recognition of their appearance.

Third, perhaps because of this rejection of metaphysics, Coles employs pragmatic reasoning as the masonry to construct his anthropology. It is true that Augustine's confessing self is rejected because Coles finds his theological presumption intellectually untenable, but this rejection is also conditioned upon the fruit borne by the monological pressure to conformity that Augustine exerted not simply in writing but in action as a bishop of the state Church. Augustine cuts short the possibilities for edge-enhancing practice in order to conquer and silence those who reject his vision. Coles does not so much argue the error of Augustine's turn to compulsion as he points to its incompatibility with his own project. Similarly, Coles lifts up Merleau-Ponty's ontology of depth between figure and background not because it is necessarily "true" as opposed to "false." While Coles certainly finds the phenomenology of depth to be logically coherent and demonstrably relevant to human experience, he does not attempt to argue its formal validity. In the end, it is accepted because it is useful for his project of constructive contestation.[60]

Affirming the deconstruction of any metaphysical or theocentric essence to the human being, and disclaiming any pretension at objective discourse, Coles adopts for his anthropology the common account of the self as art form that is shared by Foucault and Merleau-Ponty. Both philosophers dismiss the notion that the self is discovered through an exclusively or predominately internal process. There is no hidden depth waiting to be

---

[60] More will be said on Coles's pragmatic methodology in the next chapter.

plumbed through prayer and penance, contra Augustine. Nor, as Foucault is so concerned, is the self to be defined in conformity to the predeterminations of disciplinary authorities. In the dialectic between the reflexively individualistic gaze and the conformist collective vision, Coles rests his hope on the creative, on-going formation (and re-formation) of the distinctive self precisely through its interaction with a world of differences.

The ethical and political claims on behalf of participatory democracy flow from this insight on the self as contingently situated within the expansive background of life in its fullness. Any person's self-development as artistic being *requires* the presence of diverse others. On the one hand, Foucault notes that the coexistence of separate forms of human be-ing open one to possibilities as yet unknown and untried.[61] The play of interaction enables a person to imagine new ways of practicing their "art." And as previously noted, Merleau-Ponty defends democratic pluralism as the practical means for ensuring that each artistic self is allowed to explore its own development. If the "nature" of human beings is their capacity to create themselves, then the most fit social expression of this capacity will be found in a participatory democratic culture that both protects and fosters the mutual respect, encounter, and challenge of humans one to another in their concurrent personal experiments.

Finally, it should be noted that Coles's belief in artistic, interdependent selves remains a sustained premise of his later works has he continues to engage other prominent thinkers. In his second book, *Rethinking Generosity*, Coles reads Adorno as claiming the self only exists through its generous relationships with the other.[62] He sees in Habermas's theory of communication the understanding that personal identity is defined by the process of relating to others.[63] In *Christianity, Democracy, and the Radical Ordinary*, Coles writes approvingly of Anglican theologian Rowan Williams because the latter articulates Christian identity being granted by Christ as believers encounter him through their experience of the wider world.[64] Each of these instances are used as exemplars of the dialogical selfhood Coles places at the heart of his project.

---

[61] Ibid., 88.
[62] Coles, *Rethinking Generosity*, 99.
[63] Ibid., 157.
[64] Hauerwas and Coles, *Christianity, Democracy, and the Radical Ordinary*, 181.

Historic Baptist Anthropology:
Fall and Redemption

At the outset, a comparison between the radical-democratic anthropology of Coles and the theological anthropology of mainstream Baptist theology may appear hopelessly fruitless. Coles explicitly develops a post-Christian, post-metaphysical conception of the human person, whereas Baptists remain firmly rooted in a theological orientation. Whereas Augustine's hegemonic confessionalism serves as foil to Coles's artistry of the self, Baptists are inheritors of a tradition that prizes the bishop's doctrines of sin and redemption. This section will begin by reviewing how Baptists in America have typically defined the human person and how this has informed their congregational ecclesiology.

The early English Baptists and their American cousins all emerged within a tradition of Christian theology that may be broadly termed "Reformed." The early leaders of this movement operated out of central Europe and most typically in the German states and Switzerland. The most prominent theologian, whose work would be seminal for all later Reformed thought, was the French lawyer John Calvin. Calvin drew upon Augustine to teach the doctrine of total depravity. According to this belief, the sin of Adam and Eve in the Garden of Eden brought about the fall of humanity from a state of innocence and righteousness. All subsequent individuals are born in a "state of sin," that is, possessing an inclination away from love of and service to God. Moreover, no one is capable of repenting of this orientation and redirecting the will back toward its original created aim. According to Calvin, God predestines and unilaterally rescues only the "elect" from perdition. The Dutch Reformed theologian Jacobus Arminius blunted the force of total depravity by introducing the idea of prevenient grace. Arminius agrees that no person retains an *intrinsic* capability of willing the good that is God. However, God universally extends to all a partial restoration of free will so that the offer of salvation may either be chosen or rejected.

Whether adopting Arminianism, and thus being known as "General" Baptists, or Calvinism, receiving the label "Particular," these new communities professed a shared teaching that the primal Fall resulted in an inherited disposition toward evil choices.[65] Helwys, leader of the faction in Smyth's church that eventually returned to England, writes that the sin of Adam has been imputed to subsequent generations, with the result that individuals retain "no disposition or will unto anie good."[66] The *Second London Confession* of Particular Baptists (1677) reiterates the Calvinist perspective on total depravity. It specifies in Article IX that conversion results in an imperfect ability to choose the good, and Article XIII states that sinful desires are progressively weakened in the process of sanctification.[67]

The first significant Baptist confession on American soil, the *Philadelphia Confession* authorized by the Philadelphia Association in 1742, reproduced the text of the Second London Confession with a few added articles.[68] It would remain the most influential confession among the majority, Calvinistic Baptists until the *New Hampshire Confession* of 1833 became widely disseminated. This confession also recounts the Reformed system of fall, regeneration, and progressive sanctification.[69] No person possesses a will free enough to choose obedience to God until the empowering grace of the Holy Spirit allows the opportunity to respond.[70] The *New Hampshire Confession* was adapted and augmented to become the *Baptist Faith and Message*, which has retained this map of sin and redemption to the present day.

---

[65] The major exception may be John Smyth and his followers at the very beginning. In *A Short Confession of Faith in XX Articles* (1610), Smyth writes that no one is born with original sin. Rather, each person retains a free ability to discriminate between good and evil. Nevertheless, Smyth accepts that genuine righteousness derives exclusively from God's act of regeneration. See Lumpkin, *Baptist Confessions of Faith*, 100f. In *Propositions and Conclusions concerning True Christian Religion* (1612), Smyth writes in Article 14 that free will is a "natural faculty" of the human person, therefore teaching a different concept from Arminius" prevenient grace. Article 21 states that, instead of receiving the inherited consequences of Adam's sin at birth, every person recapitulates the stages of innocence, fall, and potential restoration in their own life (*Propositions and Conclusions*, 126, 127).

[66] *A Declaration of Faith of English People Remaining at Amsterdam*, Articles 2 and 4, in Lumpkin, *Baptist Confessions of Faith*, 117f.

[67] Ibid., 264, 268.

[68] Ibid., 348f.

[69] Ibid., 362–64.

[70] Ibid., 370–73.

While Arminians and Calvinists differed on the extent to which depravity resulted in the abolition of the human will toward the proper spiritual and moral ends, the consensus stated in Baptist confessions is clear. Human beings possess a distorted nature that is incapable, by itself, of attaining genuine right living according to the will of God. Regeneration brings freedom from the guilt of sin, whether conceived as personal or inherited from Adam, and grants the ability, not perfected in this life, of choosing the good.

At the turn of the twentieth century, A. H. Strong organized the beliefs expressed in American Baptist confessions into a systematic theology. Strong elaborated a conception of humanity's original state according to the "image of God" concept in Genesis 1. For Strong, the image included both a "natural likeness to God," or personality, and a moral likeness.[71] Personality incorporates the powers of self-consciousness and self-determination while the moral likeness is defined by a will directed toward God as one's end, resulting in the appropriate actions.[72] Strong holds that the original sin of Adam and Eve spawned grave consequences, resulting in the turning of the will from its appropriate end and the loss of any ability to redirect this course.[73] Human beings in the state of sin are incapable of performing a genuine good that is innocent of self-gratification.[74] What goodness remains in unbelievers must be sustained by an "immanent divine power" that is none other than Christ dwelling, to a certain degree, within all human lives.[75] Therefore, the regeneration of a human being results not just in a reorientation of the will but an intensifying of the grace of the already-present Lord. "All men are naturally one with Christ, the immanent God," Strong writes, "and this natural union prepares the way for that spiritual union in which Christ joins himself to our faith."[76] Nevertheless, the power of sin remains within believers—although no longer exclusively controlling the will—and thus necessitates cooperation with the Holy Spirit to be effectively and progressively combatted over time.[77]

Stanley Grenz offers an opposing view to Strong in his systematic

[71] Strong, *Systematic Theology*, 2:514.
[72] Ibid., 515–18.
[73] Ibid., 591f.
[74] Ibid., 570.
[75] Ibid., 550–52.
[76] Strong, *Systematic Theology*, 3:798.
[77] Ibid., 3:869f.

theology while retaining a shared commitment to the general outline of communion with God, fall, and restoration initiated by divine grace. Drawing upon advances in scholarship that illuminate the ancient Near Eastern context for Genesis, Grenz identifies the "image of God" concept as expressive of the purpose or function as opposed to the substance of the human being.[78] Humans cultivate and bear the image relationally as recipients of divine love and as agents who may represent the divine will to one another and enact it in dominion over the world. The image is only fully realized through participation in community with God and other persons.[79] The consequence of the Fall, therefore, is not a permanent devolution of human beings in essence or structure. Rather, original sin initiated a disordered valuing of the self over God, passed along not so much as the inheritance of a depraved constitution but as the malformed education in alienation and self-centeredness which are inevitably modelled for developing young minds.[80]

Grenz accepts the idea of depravity, however, in the sense that each human being is so conditioned by the pervasiveness of sin as to be incapable of willingly correcting this disordered orientation.[81] However, he rejects the notion that the unregenerate must also be intrinsically incapable of performing genuinely good actions.[82] Salvation entails the empowering presence of the Holy Spirit to convict persons of sin and grant them the capability of accepting the gospel summons.[83] Contrary to Strong's Calvinist perspective, Grenz believes that the presence of the Spirit enables the human will to choose, rather than determining the outcome.[84] The regenerated discover freedom, defined not as autonomous choosing but as "the ability to live in accordance with our destiny" as believers are invested with the potential for serving in ordered community once again.[85]

These two representative theologians differ on the manner and extent of the original fall from grace as well as the process of salvation that restores individuals to their created purpose. Strong identifies the "image of

[78] Grenz, *Theology for the Community of God*, 174f.
[79] Ibid., 177–80.
[80] Ibid., 188, 192, 205.
[81] Ibid., 209.
[82] Ibid., 185.
[83] Ibid., 412, 414.
[84] Ibid., 415.
[85] Ibid., 437f.

God" and its disruption in substantialist terms: each person instantiates the image in discrete qualities that are impaired because of an inherited nature. God elects to save part of the human race, restoring the original character of these qualities and allowing believers to truly live morally upright lives. Grenz sees the "image of God" as a label for certain modes of human interaction that are damaged owing to a reorientation of the will away from genuine fellowship. This framework of human behavior is primarily socialized to each new generation rather than directly passed in some quasi-genetic fashion. Persons are capable in themselves of knowing and doing the good to a partial extent but remain so definitively conditioned by sin that divine intervention is required to be truly liberated back to their created end. Salvation is a restoration of relationship with God that allows for truer and better communion with one another.

Their voices exemplify a general consensus held by most Baptists concerning the nature of human beings. First, all persons attain a disordered condition of being bent toward sin. This condition, whether seen as immediately heritable or embraced by each person owing to insurmountable environmental influence, has unfailingly passed down through the centuries. At the moment of conversion, however, the Holy Spirit effects regeneration, or a transformation of a person's nature such that the new believer exhibits a desire to serve God and a graced ability to resist sin. At the outset, one is *justified*, or granted an acquittal in God's judgment of sin. The Christian self is not instantly made perfect and so must engage in a process of progressive transformation as the old actions and intentions are abandoned for a life in keeping with the will of God. Traditional Baptist soteriology embraces a sober realism about the still-fragmented character of the Christian self. In this respect, it remains thoroughly Augustinian.

Because sin is not fully eradicated from the human person, the question arises as to who may even be capable of leading Christian communities in discerning and enacting the will of God. Rejecting the clericalist answer predominant in Christian history, Baptists have entrusted accountability for sin not in the hands of a select hierarchy but in the membership as a whole. The frequent refrain in the confessions that members "watch over one another" indicates that a central purpose of the church is to nurture growth in Christian understanding and deed. Such advancement is made possible by the disciplined care Christians exercise over one another through ecclesial fellowship. For Baptists, all have equally fallen and been redeemed, and therefore all have a share in this work of shaping new spiritual selves. As will now be shown, this democratic accountability is made possible by more than a simple, clean sweep of the slate. Rather, the new life in Christ grants a new capacity for each person to serve the other by serving as a vehicle for Christ's activity in the world.

The traditional emphasis on the inability of human beings on their own to discern and act upon the good may suggest that any comparison between radical democracy and Baptist theology would be an uncomfortable admixture. Coles provides an unreservedly "positive" assessment of the human person that accepts no imposed restrictions on moral or rational action. He firmly rejects the validity of any metaphysical narrative for orienting the democratic process toward predetermined values or beliefs. Baptists, on the other hand, have historically maintained the existence of limitations to the human will, on the one hand, and a definitive *telos* for human ethical aspirations, on the other. This distinction is ameliorated by the awareness that these limitations are overcome in the life of the Christian beginning with the regenerative encounter. While the doctrine of original sin raises questions as to how Baptists understand and participate in the political processes of a world considered fallen, it does not directly bear on the nature of participation in the politics of the *ecclesia*. Regeneration is the doorway to a new form of human be-ing—or what Baptists might name a "new creation" in the words of the Apostle Paul (2 Corinthians 5:17). For life after the salvific encounter with Christ, Baptists have indeed postulated a more "positive" anthropology that will now be explored, one in which human beings are authorized to manifest the purposes of God in the created world.

The Participatory Anthropology of the Triple Office

Genealogically rooted in the Reformed tradition, Baptists are heirs to an elucidation of Christ's redemptive work known as the "triple office" or *munus triplex*, a concept of some prominence in Calvin's theology. Calvin writes that the title of "Christ" refers to three different roles in the politico-religious life of ancient Israel: prophethood, priesthood, and kingship. Each of these roles constitutes an element of Jesus's redemptive work as teacher of truth, simultaneous officiant and sacrifice for atonement, and supreme governor of the redeemed.[86] The doctrine of Christ's *munus triplex* was adopted by English Separatists of the late sixteenth century as justification for the right of independent churches to assemble and determine their polity and practice. One such congregation, with its membership divided between its original London base and its emigrant majority in Amsterdam, drew up *A True Confession* in 1596. Article 10 announces Christ as the rightful mediator between God and humans and the eternal prophet, priest, and king of the Church. Article 12 declares that the triple office cannot be transferred, in whole or in part, to any other persons.[87] This declaration annuls the prerogatives of a priestly or royal elite to define ecclesiastical statutes. The subsequent articles describe how this office is nevertheless manifested through the participatory framework of believers' personal and direct union with Christ. Article 13 contends that Christ prophesies to the Church through the agency of his chosen ministers.[88] The derivative prophethood of preachers bears no marks of hierarchy because true ministers are ratified as such by the churches that recognize and ordain them (articles 21–23).[89] The right of sharing in Christ's priesthood is given to the Christian community as a whole, so that each may present pleasing "spirituall sacrifices" (article 14).[90] Finally, Christ exercises his kingly prerogative over each person directly (article 15). Because he dwells within all believers, he governs their inward selves, or their "hearts," by means of the Holy Spirit.[91] *A True Confession* also claims that Christ governs through the mediation of the formal ministry (article 17), yet the affirmation and supervision of clergy by the church at large places a check on the accumulation of power by the official leadership. Each person is responsible for discerning the will of Christ through the witness of the Spirit, both as it is perceived internally and through the counsel of other believers. Therefore, the triple office of Christ is realized as his people share in an interdependent common life.

---

[86] John Calvin, *Institutes of the Christian Religion*, 2.15, Christian Classics Ethereal Library, accessed December 16, 2022, https://ccel.org/ccel/calvin/institutes/institutes.

[87] Lumpkin, *Baptist Confessions of Faith*, 85.

[88] Ibid.

[89] Ibid., 89.

[90] Ibid., 85f.

[91] Ibid., 86.

THE CONTESTABLE CHURCH

Another Separatist congregation fled to Amsterdam under the leadership of Smyth in 1608. By the following year, Smyth arrived at the conviction of believers' baptism, rebaptizing himself as well as his congregation. Smyth drew up his *Short Confession of Faith* in 1610, wherein he specified Christ to be "the only King, Priest, and Prophet of the church."[92] The word *only* is another signal for the rejection of privileges pertaining to a distinct class within the Christian Church. The language would be echoed the following year in the confession of faith penned by a faction of Smyth's church overseen by Helwys.[93]

Sometime after Smyth's death in 1612, his remaining followers issued a confession titled *Propositions and Conclusions Concerning True Christian Religion*. Notably, article 30 explicitly claims the extension of Christ's mediatorial office to all Christian believers. By virtue of their relationship to Christ, "the faithful through Him are thus made spiritual Kings, Priests, and Prophets."[94] The Smyth faction came to a distinctive, experimental conclusion as to what this union meant in congregational practice. Article 61 declares that the "new creature," or the regenerated believer, does not require the exterior, physically manifested elements of religion such as the Bible or the ordinances to be rightly guided in the will of God. Rather, as the next article states, such "outward things" are only necessarily employed for the sake of others (presumably the unregenerate participants in community events).[95] Such was their faith in the unmediated experience of God made available to all members as an abiding spiritual communion. A service was understood to begin when the Bible and all other books were set aside, thus allowing "spiritual" worship under God's inspiration. This habit of conducting services remained with Baptists for much of the century.[96]

Subsequent Baptist confessions during the seventeenth century would regularly specify Christ's triple office as an article of belief.[97] None explic-

---

[92] Ibid., 100.
[93] Ibid., 119.
[94] Ibid., 128f.
[95] Ibid., 135f.
[96] Ellis, *Gathering*, 46f.
[97] These include *The First London Confession* (1644), *The Faith and Practice of Thirty Congregations* (1651), *The True Gospel-Faith* (1654), *The Midland Association*

itly state that Christians are made to be participants in that office. However, they do continue to assert that each believer is spiritually united with Christ and consequently derives a capacity to engage in mutual oversight. *The First London Confession* avers that the benefits of Christ's priesthood and prophethood include his governing the faithful through his presence within their hearts.[98] The Church is the community wherein believers are both joined to Christ and to one another for the sake of following the established commands of the Lord.[99] *The Somerset Confession* remarks that Christ rules through the indwelling Spirit, granting every repentant and baptized person "fit capacity" to exercise faith through the gifts of the same Spirit.[100]

As demonstrated in the first chapter, Baptist writers in America would frequently justify their polity in legalist rather than anthropological terms. Polity and discipline manuals speak of Christ granting each church the "power of the keys" for administering his pronounced commandments. Jesus is the supreme lawgiver who, according to the metaphor linking American republicanism and Baptist ecclesiology, established a constitution for the churches in the form of Scripture. The manuals do continue to identify the *munus triplex* as a point of reference for congregational polity although the accent would be on Christ's governing authority as king or—in the preferred language of the eighteenth and nineteenth-century manuals—as "head" of the Church, his Body.[101] Nevertheless, the triple office would still on occasion be referenced as an anthropological principle. This can be seen in the polity manual published by Reynolds in 1849. In his opening chapter, Reynolds stresses that the kingship of Christ is an authority not simply exercised *over* believers, but *through* them by virtue of their spiritual participation in him: "By the mysterious incarnation, he

---

Confession (1655), *The Somerset Confession* (1656), and *The Orthodox Creed*. Cited respectively in Lumpkin. *Baptist Confessions of Faith*, 166, 178f, 193, 199, 207f, 310. These confessions represent both General and Particular Baptist churches.

[98] Ibid., 162f (article xix).

[99] Ibid., 165 (article xxxiii).

[100] Ibid., 208 (article xviii), 211 (article xxvi).

[101] See Griffith, "A Short Treatise Concerning a True and Orderly Gospel Church;" "A Summary of Church Discipline;" Jones, "A Treatise of Church Discipline;" and W. B. Johnson, "The Gospel Developed Through the Government and Order of the Churches of Jesus Christ;" respectively, in Dever, ed., *Polity*, 96, 119, 127, 142, 175, 232.

formed the connecting link between the subjects of his kingdom and himself, allying his divine nature to theirs, and making them partakers of his own. Every real member of Christ's kingdom bears the likeness of its great king."[102] A gathered congregation, called together by grace and guaranteed the presence of Christ in its midst, is not only entrusted with self-government but made competent through regeneration to effectively realize Christ's intended aims.[103]

Two influential Baptist figures of the first half of the nineteenth century also refer, however briefly, to the transformation of the believer as a participant in Christ's mediatorial office by virtue of relationship with him. Wayland is perhaps the first prominent Baptist to utilize the phrase "priesthood of believers." He defines this as the right of each Christian to approach God through the mediation of Christ as High Priest.[104] This priesthood is properly derivative of Christ exercising his own priestly role. Leland, in a brief essay published in 1836, describes the individual believer as one who is adopted by God, treated alongside Jesus Christ as a "Son of God," and (employing the language of Revelation 1:6 and 5:10) made to be "a king and priest to God and the Lamb."[105]

Later systematic theologians of the turn of the century advance the motif of the triple office. The Northern Baptist theologian Alvah Hovey, in his *Manual of Systematic Theology and Christian Ethics* (1877), identifies Christ as the unique priest and king appointed by God in fulfilment of the description found in Psalm 110.[106] This is the implicit ground for declaring all believers to be "kings and priests unto God" whose standing within the church is not defined by external markers of social or civil status. Each possesses the simultaneous duty and privilege of disciplining one another, acting as authorities in the context of collective ecclesial action.[107]

The belief that the regenerated Christian participates in the triple office is restated in the work of Strong. It was noted above how Strong includes "union with Christ" as an element of the conversion experience. Strong further declares that the convert is so closely joined to Christ that

---

[102] Reynolds, "Church Polity," 300.
[103] Ibid., 329, 345.
[104] Wayland, *Notes on the Principles and Practices of Baptist Churches*, 131.
[105] Leland, "Advertisement – Great Reward Offered," 682.
[106] Hovey, *Manual of Systematic Theology and Christian Ethics*, 176.
[107] Ibid., 302f.

Soul Competency and the Artistic Self

one has the "legal standing" to participate in Christ's traditional, mediatorial offices of prophet, priest, and king.[108] Christians are made prophets in the sense that each has the responsibility and right to proclaim the teaching of Christ. This task is not delegated exclusively to ordained ministers. Rather, all possess the potential to receive from Christ the understanding necessary to interpret the meaning of the Scriptures.[109] Christians are priests for one another through the exercise of prayer and they are kings in the exercise of authority over the created order for the glory of God.[110]

From the beginning, Baptists have used the triple office as a rationale for their congregationalism. Just as all equally have fallen under condemnation through sin, so all who are saved are equally restored to intimate fellowship with God. Christ's mediatorial roles are implied or explicitly stated as being exercised through the body of Christians as a whole. Spiritual union with him grants a derivative status to each believer as one who manifests the ongoing work of prophethood, priesthood, and kingship in concert with others.[111] The "democratic" nature of Baptist ecclesiology is therefore supported in a twofold manner. First, the lingering presence of sin in the lives of believers requires mutual accountability and submission in discernment. As surely as all fell under the weight of total depravity, so too do all the redeemed find their restoration in the likeness of God to be an incomplete and ongoing process. Second, each Christian is equally empowered for this journey of sanctification by participating in the work of Christ. This participatory anthropology grants each Christian a new identity as a responsible agent for God's mission in the world and the capability to pursue this work in concert with the Church as a whole, which is the very Body of the Prophet, Priest, and King.

At the turn of the twentieth century, one prominent Southern Baptist theologian sought to integrate essential Reformed soteriology and participatory sanctification in one intrinsic and uniquely Baptist insight about the human person in relation to God. Mullins's notion of what he termed

---

[108] Strong, *Systematic Theology*, 3:805.

[109] Ibid., 2:712.

[110] Ibid., 2:775f.

[111] Baptists have typically denied any fundamental distinction between clergy and laity concerning their aptitude for embodying these qualities within the framework of congregational participation. The difference between the two categories of Christian believer is explained in terms of function rather than capacity. Baptist perspectives on ordained and pastoral ministry will be further detailed in chapter four.

"soul competency" would become a default anthropological statement of Baptist convictions for much of the next century. Because of his distinctive approach and tremendous influence, his doctrine of soul competency will now be considered as a justification for spiritual democracy.

The Anthropology of Edgar Young Mullins

E. Y. Mullins was an outsized figure in turn-of-the-century Baptist life, serving as president of Southern Baptist Theological Seminary as well as the Southern Baptist Convention and the Baptist World Alliance (BWA). His primary theological project was the restatement of Baptist doctrines and principles for a new era. Such was the motivation for his magnum opus, *The Axioms of Religion*, in 1908. It is in this work that Mullins defines the concept of soul competency.[112]

He introduces the concept as a resolution to the central question of his third chapter, "The Historical Significance of the Baptists." Mullins reviews several teachings presented as distinctive to the Baptist tradition—religious liberty, the separation of church and state, individualism, justification by faith, biblicism, and regenerated church-membership—and declares them all to be extrapolations of one antecedent principle.[113] He names the principal axiom from which they all derive as "[t]he competency of the soul in religion."[114] Upon introducing this novel phrase, Mullins immediately clarifies that such competency is exercised "under God" and does not constitute an autonomous human capability. Competency does not overturn the traditional Baptist beliefs concerning God's grace in regeneration or the authority of Scripture.[115] It does not stand as an innate

---

[112] For a fuller biography of Mullins and his impact, see Garrett, *Baptist Theology*, 415f.

[113] In this respect, Mullins's work is unequivocally representative of the modernist philosophical concept of *foundationalism*, which Christian philosopher Nancey Murphy defines as "the theory of knowledge, based on the metaphor of knowledge as a building, that requires all beliefs to be justified by tracing them to a special category of beliefs that cannot be called into question. See Murphy, *Beyond Liberalism and Fundamentalism*, 2. See pages 11–35 for Murphy's discussion of the role foundationalism has played in constructing contemporary conservative and liberal theologies, and pp. 85–109 for philosophical critiques of foundationalism.

[114] Mullins, *Axioms of Religion*, 44–53.

[115] Ibid., 53.

Soul Competency and the Artistic Self

capacity that remains intact in all persons despite the pervading consequences of the Fall.

Mullins is quick to say how soul competency should not be misconstrued, but what is its positive character as theological anthropology? He contends that soul competency displaces coercive human mediation in religious matters, as exemplified by hierarchical ecclesiology and infant baptism, with the practice of religion as "a personal matter between the soul and God."[116] Soul competency justifies the aforementioned teachings of the Baptists as well as the practice of democratic church governance. Thus, polity is based upon the ontology of Christ dwelling within believers and therefrom exercising authority.[117] The personal encounter of humanity and divinity derives from the biblical concept of the image of God, understood as an attribute of the relatedness between the two such that God may reveal himself intelligibly.[118] Mullins summarizes his account of soul competency in the following chapter: it is "the soul's capacity, right, and privilege to approach God directly and transact with him in religion."[119]

Synthesizing these statements, soul competency is the assertion of the unmediated access to God available to each Christian. Mullins does not accept, however, an independent and self-referential capability that is free from either prior or external conditioning. He does not intend to claim soul competency as a natural human characteristic preceding the transformation wrought by God in the conversion experience. This is made clear by Mullins's statement earlier in *Axioms* that the freedom of the Christian believer from religious coercion is justified by God's grace. Regeneration involves the appearance of God within the human person (for Mullins, the "soul"), inculcating "a state of moral power."[120] Mullins further writes that soul competency is established by the initiative of God to approach human beings in Christ.[121] Moreover, the experience of direct encounter with God does not render moot the Christian's obligation to interpret Scripture in order to determine the divine will. Rather, personal reading of the Bible is a key instantiation of this direct relationship with God. Because Mullins

[116] Ibid., 54.
[117] Ibid., 54f.
[118] Ibid., 58.
[119] Ibid., 63.
[120] Ibid., 40.
[121] Ibid., 68.

trusts that the Bible is inspired text, he rejects any independence of Christian experience apart from responsible hermeneutics. Soul competency, though, is a refusal to grant elite status to a particular class of individuals within the church to delineate the parameters by which one may say God authentically speaks through Scripture.

By seeing this clearly, continuity may be discerned between Mullins's notion of soul competency and the participatory anthropology of the triple office. Both teachings assert a human capacity that is derivative of spiritual fellowship between the believer and Christ. The ability to act responsibly in religious matters, says Mullins, is one that occurs through and under the power of God. So also does one's potential for teaching, interceding, and mutual oversight in the church come through the manifestation of the roles that remain primarily Christ's and are only properly exercised through his supervision. Mullins does not explicitly name the triple office in *The Axioms of Religion*, but the tenor of his argument indicates a partial restatement of its anthropological implications in new terms. This does not equate the triple office with soul competency. The triple office may be characterized by two aspects: the *interior* dimension of personal encounter with God and the *exterior* dimension of shared duties to fulfill God's mission in the world. The doctrine of the triple office prioritizes the latter within the framework of the Christian community while soul competency emphasizes one's privilege by means of the direct divine-human encounter. Moreover, as will now be shown, soul competency has been critiqued as a doctrine that weakens the theological and communal orientation held by Baptists and exhibited by the participatory anthropology of the triple office.

The Critique of Soul Competency
and a Reassessment

Mullins's restatement of the defining Baptist spirit was celebrated widely upon the publication of *The Axioms of Religion*. It quickly received endorsements as a clear apologetic for Baptist beliefs and sold well in the United States and abroad.[122] From the beginning, however, some figures expressed concern about the utility of soul competency as an organizing principle.

---

[122] See Weaver, "The Baptist Ecclesiology of E. Y. Mullins," 18; Hinson, "E. Y. Mullins as Interpreter of the Baptist Tradition," 116f.

One contemporaneous critic believed that Mullins failed to emphasize sufficiently the Baptist appreciation for the authority of Scripture.[123] James Leo Garrett Jr. cites European Baptists who expressed reservations about the doctrine's apparent hyper-individualism and anthropocentrism.[124] A particularly scathing denunciation was penned by Northern Baptist theologian Winthrop S. Hudson at midcentury. He also faulted soul competency for excessive individualism and for being a product of the cultural environment of Mullins's day rather than biblical interpretation. According to Hudson, Mullins eliminated the need for the church by "mak[ing] every man's hat his own church."[125]

Despite these criticisms, Mullins's doctrine of soul competency was seen as an interpretive key to southern baptist beliefs during the twentieth century. In the wake of the conflict between moderates and conservatives in the SBC, however, members of both sides have reassessed his legacy. On the right, Mullins has been labeled a doctrinal minimalist. One of his successors as president of Southern Baptist Theological Seminary, Al Mohler, interprets Mullins as a modernist who prioritized personal experience over biblical revelation.[126] On the left, communitarian or "postliberal" moderate Baptists have sustained the critique of individualism. The *Baptist Manifesto* contrasts soul competency with "shared discipleship" and rejects the former for inscribing faith as a private transaction between God and individuals "who inherently enjoy unmediated...experience with God."[127] Contemporary defenders of Mullins have written rebuttals to these criticisms.[128]

This is not an exhaustive list of challenges to Mullins's soul competency doctrine,[129] but these citations indicate that soul competency is no longer an unproblematic, generally accepted tenet among southern bap-

---

[123] Hinson, "E. Y. Mullins as Interpreter of the Baptist Tradition," 116f.

[124] Garrett, *Baptist Theology*, 427. See McClendon Jr., *Ethics*, 29, 31, for an American example of the same.

[125] Hudson, "Shifting Patterns of Church Order in the Twentieth Century," 215f.

[126] Mohler, "Baptist Theology at the Crossroads," 4–22.

[127] Freeman, "Can Baptist Theology be Revisioned?," 304.

[128] E.g., Dunn, "Church, State, and Soul Competency," 61–73; Dilday, "The Significance of E. Y. Mullins' *The Axioms of Religion*," 83–93.

[129] For a fuller bibliography, see Garrett, *Baptist Theology*, 427–34.

tists. Some critiques address the cogency of soul competency as the distinctive and unifying principle of Baptist theology. This chapter will also not evaluate the doctrine's standing in this regard, but only as an expression of theological anthropology, irrespective of its validity as the Baptist epitome. The more modest goal at present is to retrieve soul competency as a heuristic for Baptist notions concerning the responsible Christian self. This will be accomplished by correcting a common misreading of soul competency. Then the critique of undue individualism will be acknowledged. Finally, Coles's vision of the artistic self will be engaged as a means for revising soul competency as an interdependent self-realization under God's grace. Such an expression of soul competency can be argued as continuous with a trajectory in Mullins's writings.

This reassessment begins by clearing away a misinterpretation of Mullins's concept, one that fails to acknowledge Mullins's stated limitations of soul competency as referenced above. Both defenders and detractors have understood soul competency as a statement of universal human privilege regardless of their standing with respect to salvation. Timothy George, who writes appreciably of Mullins, defines soul competency as the right and responsibility of all persons, not just Christians, to approach God directly.[130] On the other hand, Malcolm Yarnell rejects soul competency precisely *because* he understands it as access to God prior to regeneration.[131] It should be apparent from the review of soul competency provided above that Mullins does not define soul competency as a natural or general human capacity. Despite his innovative language, his soteriology is firmly rooted in the Reformed tradition's convictions concerning the priority of divine grace. Mullins uses the concept to emphasize a synergy between God and individuals in their spiritual development, yet he regards God as the exclusive initiator of this process. In his systematic theology text, *The Christian Religion in its Doctrinal Expression*, Mullins explicitly states his discomfort with the supposition that humans have a "natural ability" in religious matters, defined in terms of willpower. Rather, preceding divine grace initiates a person's free response to God.[132] No person can acknowledge sin, repent, and express faith without the operation of the

---

[130] George, "The Priesthood of All Believers and the Quest for Theological Integrity," 284.

[131] Yarnell, "Changing Baptist Concepts of Royal Priesthood," 245.

[132] Mullins, *Christian Religion in its Doctrinal Expression*, 294f.

Holy Spirit.[133] Mullins's doctrine aligns with Reformed soteriology just as much as it does with participatory anthropology.

This misreading of Mullins likely originates in his incautious correlation of Baptist principles with those that define the American political system. *The Axioms of Religion* is published more than a century after Baptists first began to equate the politics of church and state even while supporting their official separation. Lee Canipe calls this a perspective of "complementary convergence," which he contends was especially prevalent among leading Baptist figures in the early part of the twentieth century.[134] This was a period in which political figures frequently appealed to a divine destiny for the United States, inspiring Baptists to believe that democracy and the gospel would spread in tandem around the world.[135] Canipe faults Mullins as one such leader who threaded ecclesiology and secular politics into an apparently seamless garment.[136]

This characterization of Mullins is undoubtedly accurate. One of his later chapters is titled "The Contribution of Baptists to American Civilization." In the first paragraph he declares that "we may regard American civilization as a Baptist empire, for at the basis of this government lies a great group of Baptist ideals."[137] Because Mullins believes that America is influenced by Baptist practice, he sets about discovering analogues between soul competency, his six axioms, and the principles of American democracy.[138] He does not see the virtues of church and state as identical, but as mutually supportive means for fulfilling the petition in the Lord's Prayer that God's Kingdom would arise on earth.[139] The future ascendance of democracy, Mullins believes, is also the coming "Baptist age of the world."[140]

It cannot be denied that certain of Mullins's statements merge political and religious competency into one human faculty. He identifies the American principle of popular sovereignty as the "political side" of soul

---

[133] Ibid., 366–75f.
[134] Canipe, *Baptist Democracy*, 3, 10.
[135] Ibid., 11f.
[136] Ibid., 92, 109–25.
[137] Mullins, *Axioms of Religion*, 255.
[138] Ibid., 270–74.
[139] Ibid., 274.
[140] Ibid., 275.

THE CONTESTABLE CHURCH

competency.[141] Moreover, he names soul competency as the religious principle that animates multiple endeavors of modern civilization, listing art, science, and philosophy specifically.[142] Although he still asserts that these human activities are performed "under God,"[143] or most properly achieved when animated and directed by God, Mullins clearly accepts that they may function outside the borders of the Church. He does not argue any detailed theological justification for this novel expression of prevenient grace. As Canipe has pointed out, Mullins's theology is a product of an age when Baptists and America were viewed as two instantiations of one progressive, advancing ideal.[144] Nevertheless, in spite of this conflation of church and society, Mullins still distinguishes between competency under God, in general, and the particular form of soul competency that he believes animates Baptist life.

The other major charge against Mullins from contemporary theologians is his pronounced individualism. Ironically, this is a criticism Mullins himself makes of other Christians in his own day. Early in *Axioms*, he warns against a tendency toward anti-institutional Christianity that would collapse the faith in a "ring of dancing atoms, each moving aimlessly around its own center."[145] When he enumerates his list of the "spiritual laws" of the Kingdom of God, his fifth law declares the interdependence of believers.[146] He explicitly rejects individualism as the definitive Baptist principle because human beings are necessarily social creatures.[147] He believes that Baptists often over-emphasize individualism in their polity.[148] In a separate volume on Baptist faith and practice, Mullins asserts the practice of discipline as the means by which churches protect themselves "against the disorderly individual."[149]

So why, despite these overt statements, does Mullins merit the charge of individualism? Freeman suggests that Mullins borrows from a contemporary, the philosopher and psychologist William James, the notion of

[141] Ibid., 271.
[142] Ibid., 65f.
[143] Ibid., 218.
[144] Canipe, *Baptist Democracy*, 155.
[145] Mullins, *Axioms of Religion*, 19.
[146] Ibid., 40.
[147] Ibid., 51.
[148] Ibid., 148.
[149] Mullins, *Baptist Beliefs*, 65.

communal religion as a derivation of the individual's primary experience.[150] The competent soul can interpret the Bible and its own conversion experience without mediation from others. Because Mullins has defined this capacity as an exclusively "one-on-one relationship," he offers no substantive justification for ecclesiology. He embraces a disembodied anthropology in which the soul holds priority over the body and social action by the church is rendered inappropriate.[151]

The perspective of corporate religion as secondary is explicitly stated in *Axioms*. "Religious privilege and religious duty," he writes, "subsist between men and God in the first instance in their capacity as individuals and only secondarily in their social relations."[152] Mullins describes the conversion experience exclusively in terms of God coming directly to the individual in the exercise of grace. Christianity's essence consists of "spiritual truth" conveyed and verified immediately to the soul by the Holy Spirit.[153]

What Mullins lacks is any accounting for how the individual may recognize regeneration for what it is, or even to express the mental assent to the gospel message that Baptists understand as essential to genuine faith; surely there is a form of "interference" in personal religion from the very beginning in that each new Christian has at some point received this message through human mediation. No one can interpret an apparent conversion without employing the conceptual categories that have been imparted by others, even if those categories may be modified by one's direct, personal experience. Mullins argues that the Kingdom of God "comes in the first instance to the individual,"[154] but it cannot do so in any strict sense of privacy.

Turning to Mullins's justifications for Christian community in *Axioms*, it can be seen that he views the Church in thoroughly utilitarian terms. It arises subsequent to conversion as individuals relate to one another via their similar religious experiences and common beliefs.[155] Mullins believes that Christ is supreme over the churches while simultaneously re-

---

[150] Freeman, "E. Y. Mullins and the Siren Songs of Modernity," 34.

[151] Ibid., 35f.

[152] Mullins, *Axioms of Religion*, 93.

[153] Ibid., 96f.

[154] Ibid., 39.

[155] Ibid., 35f.

marking that a given congregation is an assemblage of autonomous individuals who come together because of "common interest."[156] This is an extraordinarily voluntarist account of the Church as an aftereffect of regeneration. Mullins certainly does not see the Church as irrelevant; rather, a given church fosters "important relations" between individuals who are "organized for a great end and mission."[157] He also expresses his disdain for contemporary efforts to "spiritualize" the Church, such that it is not visibly distinguished from the world, or to dissolve it in a subjectivity that "leaves each man free to do as he wills."[158] For Mullins, each person has the competence and responsibility to regulate one's "inner life" according to Scripture. Without a clear conception of the community's authority to interject in such regulation, soul competency runs the risk of falling into the very spiritualization and subjectivity that Mullins rejects.

It is clear that, in Mullins's theology, Christian identity is formed largely through the direct encounter between the individual and God. This encounter is defined and proceeds in part through the study of Scripture, which each believer has the right to privately interpret. Mullins insists that God's grace generates the capacity of each person to sustain and grow in this divine-human relationship—a capacity which he names soul competency. The context of *Axioms* indicates that his concern is to provide a clear apologetic for Baptist congregationalism over against other forms of ecclesial organization. Mullins stresses soul competency as a justification for the democratic polity of the Baptists. Other structures of governance effectively establish a spiritual elite who may determine the contours of spiritual experience and biblical interpretation for the body as a whole. In place of this schema, Mullins posits that every person holds responsible agency to discern the voice of God through the presence of the Spirit.[159] In this respect, his terminological novelty should not be allowed to mask Mullins's continuity with earlier Baptist theology. He is restating the conviction that Christ's Lordship is exercised through the whole Church and by each Christian's participation in the mediatorial offices through spiritual union with him. Soul competency is the mode through which believers are all empowered to embody the triple office.

[156] Ibid., 129.
[157] Ibid., 55.
[158] Ibid., 235, 240.
[159] Ibid., 262.

What Mullins lacks is a sufficient rationale for the necessity of the Church with regard to the individual believer's development as a competent soul. Although he disclaims hyper-individualism and asserts a social dimension to his doctrine, his ecclesiology is considerably weakened by defining genuine religion primarily and predominately in terms of the direct encounter with God. He provides no reflection on the indisputable fact that any person's spiritual experience must be interpreted in relation to intelligible categories communicated by those who already share in the common life of the Church. For Mullins, competency is granted exclusively by God in a relationship that seems to transcend the burdens of social context. As it stands, soul competency is at best inadequate and at worse naïve concerning the actual manner in which persons come to identify themselves as participants in the Christian faith. Consequently, the most influential anthropology for modern southern baptists, and the one given the most attention, is also one that weakens the conception of the Church as a site of spiritual democracy. This is because the church makes no effective contribution to the formation of Christian selfhood.

Artistry and Mutual Competency

By attending to the notion of the artistic self that Coles draws out of Foucault and Merleau-Ponty, the possibility of re-envisioning the doctrine of soul competency arises. The juxtaposition with Coles reveals in Mullins an undeveloped trajectory toward spiritual interdependence that can find a fuller expression in the very inter-expressivity of dialogical selfhood.

It was shown above how Mullins has been criticized for defining away the necessity of the church through soul competency. In place of the communion of believers sustained and elevated by the Holy Spirit he values Christian faith primarily in terms of a private correspondence between the individual and God. Christian experience centers upon the discernment of God acting inwardly for the regeneration and continued renewal of the believer. Mullins's doctrine of soul competency mirrors Augustine's description of the anthropological division between the inner and outer person, in which one's humanity is made more perfect through attentiveness to the interior dimension where the light of God may shine for the sake of better self-understanding.[160] While both Mullins and Augustine declare

---

[160] See Taylor, *Sources of the Self,* 129–34, 141.

that one's true nature is realized through this private fellowship of soul and God, neither accept that the spiritual encounter would ever result in a "revelation" that counters the established sources of theological conviction. Mullins insists that the establishment of doctrine depends both on this immediate encounter with Christ and on Scripture properly respected and interpreted.[161] He reiterates throughout his corpus that each Christian has the prerogative to make their own interpretive judgments, yes, but that these are judgments specifically about how to understand and apply the Bible.

Nevertheless, Mullins also explicitly rejects atomistic individualism and contends for the interdependence of Christian selves. His objection in *Axioms* is regrettably more rhetorical than substantial, leaving the reader uninformed as to why or how Mullins would construe the requirement of interpersonal relationships for the sake of a better-developed Christian life. One may begin to see a resolution of this problem, and the beginning point of congruence with Coles's vision of the artistic self, in another Augustinian aspect of Mullins's theology. In keeping with southern baptist theology in general, Mullins accepts a salvation-historical narrative of humanity's fall from original fellowship with God, the communication of a disposition toward sin from one generation to the next, and the gracious initiative of God in delivering salvation. For this traditional Western soteriology, the reception of grace at conversion does not eliminate the possibility of sin as a choice of the will going forward. The Christian life, therefore, is characterized by the process of sanctification, or realizing the power of the newly freed human faculties toward their proper end in God. These faculties include the cognitive aspects of the person such as reason and knowledge, which have been perverted in the post-Eden world. Mullins writes in *Freedom and Authority in Religion* that a believer's consciousness "never grasps all of the religious Object [that is, God] because of sin."[162]

A Baptist congregation's practice of "democracy" is based, therefore, not only on the equality of personal access to God but also the equality of "fallenness" or the limitation of one's moral, spiritual, and intellective faculties through sin. In other terms, God exhibits a "depth" that extends

---

[161] Mullins, *Christian Religion in its Doctrinal Expression*, 164.
[162] Mullins, *Freedom and Authority in Religion*, 298.

beyond the understanding of even the most earnest and devout of believers. The discernment of the divine will emerging from God as Depth requires the gathering together of selves, each separately but never entirely illuminated by the Spirit of God. In this manner of construing the Baptist perspective on church governance, one recognizes the parallel with Merleau-Ponty's notion of the depths of "wild Being."

What is not paralleled between the thought of Mullins and Merleau-Ponty, or Mullins and Foucault, is the notion that the self is constructed through encounters with others in their differences. Mullins retains a conventionally substantialist understanding of the self as expressed in the body-soul duality prevalent in the history of Christian theology.[163] While body and soul are both necessary for the existence of a complete human being,[164] Mullins situates human consciousness and personality in the soul, which is a permanent entity that perdures even as its moral and spiritual attributes are transformed through regeneration.[165] This "static" concept of the self implies, like Kant's subjective sovereign, an entity that takes nothing from others, sharing of itself but not transformed by encounter.

However, alongside Mullins's dualistic schema he discusses the notion of the developing and composite human *self*, the concept of which he identifies as one of the "fundamental facts of psychology."[166] He decomposes the whole self into three components: the physical body, the social self affected by involvement with others, and the spiritual self that is aimed toward the highest ends of human flourishing. Mullins acknowledges that self-development is not simply progressive, but that the "various selves clash with each other."[167] Though joined together in the full human personality, short of Christian conversion these three selves cannot achieve a harmonious life.[168] In this transformation the limited "natural self" is superseded by the attainment of the "true self" through the powerful grace of God.[169] The human person is recreated; although there remains a continuity of consciousness, the motives, purposes, and energies achieve a new

[163] Mullins, *Christian Religion in its Doctrinal Expression*, 256.

[164] Ibid., 257.

[165] Ibid., 385; see 460. The resurrection body of the righteous in eternity is wielded as a "perfect instrument" of the soul (474).

[166] Ibid., 56.

[167] Ibid., 57.

[168] Ibid., 61.

[169] Ibid., 64.

"I" in place of the old.[170] Again we see Mullins's consonance with Augustine in the recognition that the sin-marred self is riven by contradictions.

This more dynamic and psychologically derived anthropology adds color to Mullins's distinctive account of soul competency. Mullins understands the natural self to be a fragmented personality that is healed and brought to a progressive realization of unity through regeneration and sanctification. Effectively, each Christian is made a new person through spiritual birth and then accepts the responsibility of maturation aided by divine beneficence. This transformative process *begins* at regeneration, rather than reaching its culmination.

Reading Coles alongside Mullins suggests a lacuna in the latter's thought that may be filled by turning to the radical-democratic theorist. Like Augustine before him, Mullins perceives that the self-realization of the newly created Christian occurs primarily by means of "this new power within."[171] Mullins simultaneously asserts, as noted above, the depth of God extending beyond the perception of any one human being, converted or not. If the development of the "true self" requires growth in Christian experience of a God who exceeds the individual's understanding, then such a self cannot feed solely upon an interior engagement with Being.

Coles has insisted that each self is fashioned through reciprocating encounters with different others who enact modes of being and doing transgressive of a self's prior perception. In a sense, the self passes through multiple "rebirths" or "conversions" as a person responds to the depth of the world. Mullins expresses a traditional Reformed anthropology that elevates a singular and decisive moment of rebirth that imparts salvation. The seminal, theological importance of this initial conversion need not be denied by introducing the notion of the continually reconstructed self. For a Christian appropriation of the artistic self, regeneration may still be interpreted as the necessary impetus that empowers the true self or competent soul for effective and practical transformation through engagement with difference.

In this case, the difference with which each self wrestles is the particularity expressed by each believer within the Christian community. Such diversity stems from the dispositions of each person's natural faculties as well as their narrative of experiencing God. All Christians bear a unique

---

[170] Ibid., 69.
[171] Ibid.

imprint of the journey of self-realization and sanctification, yet none ascertain with clear vision the fullness of what God intends. Being joined together in a spiritual union that is called, in the traditional language derived from the Apostle Paul, the "Body of Christ," each Christian is thus dependent upon one another to more fully discover what Christ intends for his very members. Each self requires other Christian selves for the sake of coming into the way of life proleptically received in conversion yet awaiting eschatological consummation.

This hidden potential in Mullins's construal of the redeemed self is obscured not only by his own prioritization of the personal relationship with God but also, I contend, by interpreters' willingness to overdetermine the valence of "competency." It must be noted that to speak in common discourse of a person's competence is not to claim infallibility or even excellence in a particular field of knowledge or practice. Rather, competence identifies that a certain threshold has been reached in which one is acknowledged as bearing requisite skills or capacities. When not defined as meaning an independent self-sufficiency, Mullins's doctrine of soul competency may be allowed to represent a dynamic model of Christians' graced privilege of discerning the divine will in tandem with, and reshaped by, interaction with fellow believers.[172]

The depths of life in Christ are more fully plumbed in community with others who testify to the reality of this Person as they experience him in the study of Scripture, in worship, and in service. Because a (re-)new(ed) personal identity is fashioned in the journey of sanctification, it is necessarily shaped and defined by engagement with the other Christian personalities. This realization demonstrates that it is impossible to exhaust religious self-formation in terms of a private, spiritual relationship between "the soul and its God."

The ecclesial mode of this dialectical selfhood-within-depth reveals an irreconcilable contradiction with Coles's post-structuralist vision of personal artistry. The concept of art, and what artistry entails, has itself changed over time in tandem with new perceptions of what is true and good. Charles Taylor writes in *Sources of the Self: The Making of the Modern Identity* that art was classically defined by its ability to imitate realities to

---

[172] See the discussion on a Christian minister's competence as a manifestation of grace for the purpose of serving as the Spirit's instrument in Colwell, *Promise and Presence*, 216.

which it signified. In the modern era, however, art has come increasingly to be understood as the artist's personal act of expression.[173] This perspective coincides with the expressivist turn in the notion of selfhood, which identifies each person as a unique being who is able to, and responsible for, generating one's own distinct "style" or "path" through life.[174]

Because of his anti-metaphysical commitment, Coles clearly defines self-artistry in expressive rather than imitative terms. There is neither divine will nor innate pattern of human nature that prescribes the bounded frame within which the individual artist may sketch. His radical-democratic project defends, therefore, the establishment of an ethics and concomitant societal structures which will support the pluralistic dynamic of personal self-realization. A Baptist vision of the artistic and "competent" self, however, can never accept the pure expressivism of Coles. A theological, Christocentric metaphysic bends the definition of art back toward the classical definition. Jesus declares in the Gospels that his followers must seek perfection (Matthew 5:48) and practice mercy (Luke 6:36) in imitation of God the Father. In the epistles, Jesus himself becomes the example to follow,[175] and the Apostle Paul also offers himself as one to imitate because he imitates Christ.[176]

In keeping with Mullins's stance, the recognition of human sin and finitude results in a skeptical valuation of Coles's artistic *ethos* as it is stated. The construction of the self is a haphazard and even a dangerous task without the guiding boundaries of what Charles Taylor calls the "framework" of moral judgments.[177] There can be no pure form of expressivity that operates without the imposition of a singular perspective. As much as Coles wants to derive his practice from anthropology, it has been the already-established principle of receptivity that has guided Coles to seek out the appropriate intellectual structure. Although Coles is resolutely anti-metaphysical, he has assumed a permanent and universal value that guides his exploration of the three thinkers in *SPO*. For Baptists, a thicker framework is seen as necessary, and this is found in the very Person who also exhibits the depth which may be explored in the journey of self-renewal. Christ is

---

[173] Taylor, *Sources of the Self,* 376f.

[174] Ibid., 374f.

[175] 1 Timothy 1:16; 1 Peter 2:21.

[176] 1 Corinthians 4:26. See Philippians 3:17.

[177] Taylor, *Sources of the Self,* 26.

both the frame and the canvas of the artistic project.

Conclusion

What have we learned about the anthropological theories that drive radical-democratic and southern baptist articulations of the political, and how do these relate to one another? Coles's exploration of self and the other in the thought of Augustine, Foucault, and Merleau-Ponty concludes with the articulation of a contingent selfhood that finds its richest possibilities for development through receptive engagement with the diversity of being as expressed in other human agents. This anthropology is used to defend a politics that not only respects but fosters creatively conflictive encounters between persons and communities of difference. His dynamic anthropology contrasts with a traditional, "static" model in theology of the human as the unity of permanent soul and mortal body. Mullins draws upon the traditional language to argue for the doctrine of "soul competency" as the essential center of Baptist thought. For Mullins, each Christian believer receives the dutiful privilege of directly relating to God and discerning the divine will.

Coles's argument for the artistic self offers a modification to Mullins's soul competency that fills in his own affirmation of interdependence in the Christian life. By construing Christ as the depth of Being which Baptists must explore together, or else be handicapped by the finitude of each person, the charge of excessive individualism levelled by critics may be overcome. An ecclesial orientation of soul competency is restored by placing its practice in the political and spiritual context of mutual Christian discipleship and discipline.

A Baptist stance in keeping with Mullins's respect for theological orthodoxy will not simply adopt the radical-democratic understanding of the artistic self *in toto*. Coles presents an "expressivist" rather than "imitative" notion of artistry that denies the existence of any transcendent or divinely given order which determines better or worse expressions of human personhood. While the Baptist practice of church demands an openness to Christ leading his people to new insight through the inspiration of the Spirit, that openness is also determined by the understanding of Christ given through the witness of Scripture as read and interpreted by the Church over time. Baptists remain committed to following Christ as an example of authentic human selfhood.

The encounter between radical democracy and Baptist theology provides a way forward for construing the significance of the spiritual-democratic process for the self-identity of Christians. Mullins presented soul competency as a summarizing statement of Baptist convictions concerning the sovereignty of God over each individual life as well as the freedom each person has for a form of self-determination under God. His individualistic account of the human encounter with God remained true to the voluntarist impulse of the Baptists while neglecting to adequately justify the purpose of gathering together in congregations. If there is no such thing as a static self, but a process of personal development dependent on interrelationships with different others, then a well-functioning self *needs* engagement with others for its very existence. Moreover, the fullness of Christ as the depth of Christian experience overflows beyond the capacity of any one individual to receive. Therefore, as each "artist" fashions his or her self in a unique instance of the imitation of Christ, this craft is enhanced through serious encounter with others engaged in the same project. Might then we speak of inter-competent selves fashioning each other in the work of sanctification?

As stated, this presents an idealistic picture of harmonious cooperation within a shared consensus about what such imitation means, yet radical democracy accepts conflict as a fundamental and ineradicable aspect of the democratic project. Baptists have not been so sanguine about conflict, however. Unity of doctrine and purpose has been designated a marker of God's favor. Disagreement has been explained as a product of sin or disbelief. Southern baptists have witnessed a series of controversies over the past century and a half but have not come to terms with dissent as a necessity of their ecclesiological convictions. I now turn to the question of whether radical democracy offers a means for constructively incorporating conflict into the spiritual-democratic process.

CHAPTER 3

RECEPTIVE GENEROSITY AND INTERDEPENDENT PERSONHOOD

The difficulty of Mullins's concept of soul competency, which has resulted in its increasing rejection by contemporary southern baptist theologians, is the apparent individualism that sidelines the essential value of the Church as the community in which selves are formed in the image of Christ as they are admonished and exhorted by one another through prayer, worship, the study of Scripture, and holy conversation. Coles offers a corrective anthropological discourse in naming how selfhood and identity are constructed, broken down, and refashioned in the continually unfolding encounter with Being. Mullins is right to stress that this encounter with Being includes an unassailable linkage of each believer with God. That is not Mullins's full or only word, given the locations in his writings where he points to the necessity of interdependence. In doing so, Mullins more faithfully reflects historic Baptist emphases. Contra individualizing trends, Baptists have articulated a communal Christianity in which selves support one another in the journey of discipleship. Especially because of their congregational polity, such gatherings are meeting points wherein diverse theological opinions, contextual interpretations of Scripture, and missional priorities will rub against one another, generating sparks that could start a fire. Difference is inescapable even in the most homogenous of churches. What is the significance of this fact for the community of believers, and how should difference best be expressed?

This chapter will explore how dissent is conceptualized in the work of Coles and among Baptists. Southern baptist life is torn between two attitudes toward dissent: the "more light" or mutability principle that considers theological conclusions to be tentative and open to contestation, and the concern for unity that employs confessionalism as a tool for doctrinal conformity. Because of this tension, dissent commonly manifests and is understood as the act of *private judgment* by individual believers. In other words, dissent is reduced to the independent development and expression of opinions by persons by themselves rather than in communal deliberation. While private judgment is a concept that extends to the earliest days of Baptists, by itself it is not enough to make for agonistic politics. So, while it is not improper, per se, over-reliance on private judgment as the mode of dissent has prevented difference from serving communally formative aims, and this against the intention of early Baptists who defended liberty of conscience. What is needed to enact the contestable church is a different mode of dissent beyond private judgment.

In Coles's book *Rethinking Generosity* (*RG*), he presents the theme of *receptive generosity* as the constitutive principle of his version of radical democracy. Receptive generosity identifies a politics of flexible interaction between the identical and the non-identical in which persons are willing to give and receive the critiques and insights that arise through vulnerable encounter. In the following pages, I will trace how Coles develops this concept through his readings of Kant, Adorno, and Habermas.

Coles's notion of receptive generosity finds its theological analogue in the writings of Carlyle Marney, a renegade Southern Baptist pastor from the mid-twentieth century. Marney's personalist theology requires a web of relationships as the precondition for achieving personhood, which is realized as one escapes inherited "structures of prejudice" and false images of self and other. For Marney, Christ is the template of a new humanity and the Church—the site where two or three or gathered, rather than the institutional frame—is the venue for overcoming falsehoods. So, to see ourselves and the world around us rightly we must enter into vulnerable relationships in which we risk the confrontation between our perceptions and those of others. Marney practically equates this pursuit of genuine personhood with the classical concept of the priesthood of all believers. The universal priesthood, seen in this way, has an inescapable interpretive element—interpretation not just of Scripture, but of the whole range of human experience and interpersonal encounters.

I suggest that Marney's thought unites Baptists and radical democracy concerning the necessity of conflict as vital for growth; for the former, it spurs spiritual maturation into the newness that Christ offers. A key point of creative tension here is the relative value of teleological orientation. Receptive generosity opens a space beyond Baptist thought and even Marney to remain engaged with voices, both internal and external to the tradition, which exceed consensual determinations. On the other hand, the conviction of a new humanity—indeed, a new heaven and a new earth—provides a roomy frame within which to receive difference in the trust that all our dialogues, disputes, and nagging questions are leading us

Receptive Generosity and Interdependent Personhood

somewhere. If we find a worthwhile ecclesial vision at the intersection of Marney and Coles, dissent among Baptists centers on the mutual interpretive insights of one's fellow believers, remains open to external voices, and retains the hope that the cycles of blindness and violence will come to an end in eschatological peace.

United in Truth

Throughout their history, Baptists have been of two minds regarding the value of dissent and diversity *within* their churches and denominations. As Barry Harvey has written, Baptists have been "vacillating constantly in an unholy and unhealthy rhythm between dogmatism and Sheilaism."[1] One tendency has been the enforcement and consequent celebration of uniformity in doctrine and practice. In the historical review presented in the second chapter, the typical southern baptist congregation of the eighteenth and nineteenth century vigorously policed its moral and doctrinal boundaries, brooking no opposition to what were deemed the clear mandates of Scripture. Church meetings were primarily oriented neither to administrative affairs nor to open deliberation of contestable concepts; rather, they were juridical proceedings intent on enforcing disciplinary codes. Only reluctantly and gradually toward the end of this period would Baptists abandon strict conformity to Calvinistic orthodoxy and certain moral taboos as a condition of church membership.

The church manuals of the mid-nineteenth century placed great stress on practices that would maintain unity and forestall the eruption of conflict. Pendleton writes in his *Church Manual* (1867) that "the peace, efficiency and usefulness of a church" requires substantial agreement on the teachings of Scripture. Even a diversity of opinions on trivial matters has stirred up trouble in hundreds of churches, he claims.[2] That Southern Baptists of this period accepted Pendleton's judgment is demonstrated by

---

[1] Harvey, "Where, Then, Do We Stand?," 368. "Sheilaism" is a term that has gained currency via Bellah, et al., in *Habits of the Heart*. They quote a young nurse who identifies her personal spiritual beliefs, utterly disconnected from any religious community, as "Sheilaism" and "my own little voice" (221). The term has since been adopted as shorthand to describe self-absorbed and individualistic modes of religious or spiritual expression.

[2] Pendleton, *Church Manual*, 16.

widely attested policies concerning the admission of membership candidates. Various polity manuals and systematic theologies insisted upon churches adopting regulations that would guard the harmony of like-mindedness. In his *Baptist Church Manual* (1853), Brown reproduces his edited version of the *New Hampshire Confession* as the first two-thirds of the booklet. Following this are his "Rules of Order," the first article of which addresses the reception of members. The text stipulates that the candidate must hold to "the views of faith and practice held by this [hypothetical] church" alongside demonstrating genuine repentance from sin. Such actions are not in themselves sufficient for admission, which is decided upon by the current membership as a whole. Brown sets forth the policy that no person shall be received if five or more negative votes are cast.[3] J.L. Dagg does not specify as strict a doctrinal standard as Brown in his recommendations set forth in the second volume of the *Manual of Theology* (1859). For him, the examination of a candidate's profession of faith centers on ascertaining affective and moral outcomes of conversion. The applicant must convincingly testify to the fact of a transformed life.[4] He sets a higher bar for admission, however, in that the vote of the congregation must be unanimous. Dagg's reasoning is that conflict is harmful to the character of a church: "Harmony and mutual confidence are necessary to the peace and prosperity of a church; and, if these are to be disturbed by the admission of a new member, it is far better, both for him and the church, that his admission should be deferred, until it can be effected without mischief."[5]

Hiscox, writing in his popular *The Baptist Directory* (1859), describes the stipulation of unanimous membership votes not only as desirable but to some extent practiced in actual church life.[6] P. H. Mell confirms in his *Corrective Church Discipline* (1860) that some Southern Baptist congregations maintained this rule. However, he also identifies an existent practice for overcoming the veto of a minority opposition. Those who disagree with an admission or excommunication are asked if they will acquiesce in the decision despite their opposition. If they decline, then the majority initi-

---

[3] Brown, *Baptist Church Manual*, 26f.
[4] Dagg, *Manual of Theology*, 268f.
[5] Ibid., 269.
[6] Hiscox, *Baptist Directory*, 79.

ates a patient effort to persuade them. Persistent opposition leads to a demand of submission and the exercise of discipline even to the point that the recalcitrant are ultimately removed from the church.[7] Interestingly, Mell identifies the will of the majority as the "right view" in the dispute. Those who resist consenting for the sake of unity are therefore judged as violators of Christ's intention for the church.

All these writers believed that the vigorous exercise of discipline was a fundamental practice for keeping Baptists together as regulated gospel churches. Unity depended on an enforced conformity to what was seen as the laws of Christ, but the postbellum period of industrialization and urbanization witnessed the gradual disappearance of church discipline. Admission procedures relaxed in the wake of revivalism, yet a lingering cohesiveness of theological convictions allowed some Baptist writers of the early twentieth century to praise a seemingly miraculous unity that, to their eyes, existed without the support of a formal structure. Two expressions of this confidence are voiced by Northern Baptist theologians. Robert Stuart MacArthur writes in *The Baptists: Their Principle, Their Progress, Their Prospect* (1911) that Baptists are better united in their beliefs and practices than any other Christian tradition in America, despite their lack of a compulsory creed.[8] Likewise, William Roy McNutt, in *Polity and Practice in Baptist Churches* (1935), expresses his doubts that other sizeable Christian communities can "display a vital and living unity than that which holds together Baptists."[9]

Mullins adds his assent in a chapter of *Axioms* that interprets the execution of Baptist ideals in extra-congregational organization. The key principle for him is voluntarism, such that the bonds within and between churches are built up through mutual cooperation and approval of shared aims. Any efforts to compel obedience inevitably generate strife.[10] Although Baptists have never submitted to a coercive authority, he remarks that they have remained remarkably united. He does not deny that schisms have occurred, but he claims that over time reunion has been effected

[7] Mell, "Corrective Church Discipline," 453.

[8] MacArthur, *Baptists*, 16.

[9] McNutt, *Polity and Practice in Baptist Churches*, 113.

[10] Mullins, *Axioms of Religion*, 212–15. Note Mullins's inversion of the values expressed in the polity manuals of the prior century. Whereas before, policing the boundaries of a shared theological vision was seen as essential to prevent conflict, now it is identified as an inevitable *cause* of conflict.

through "the quiet influence of personal conviction and spiritual and intellectual growth."[11] He is confident that the absence of imposing human wills allows unity to form under the guidance of Christ's will.[12] In these early twentieth-century writings, we see a reversal of the assumptions that guided the more disciplinary era of Baptist polity. Where before, it was necessary to maintain structures of enforcement so as to protect unity in the churches, these authors believed unity was maintained precisely *because* it was encouraged by example rather than imposed by ecclesial authority.

If such optimism were a widely accepted opinion among Baptists, it was soon tested and found wanting in the face of daunting twentieth-century conflicts. The challenges of modernity, manifested in the form of biblical criticism and the theory of evolution, catalyzed the bitter conflicts of the Fundamentalist-Modernist Controversy within several American denominations during the 1920s and 30s. Although Northern Baptists were particularly embroiled in the controversy,[13] Southern Baptists did not emerge from this period unscathed.[14] Breakaway bodies split from the former in the 1930s and 1940s while the latter remained largely intact, with no small measure of responsibility owed to Mullins.[15] Nevertheless, the same fundamental tensions would erupt with greater ferocity in the struggle for control of the SBC that began in 1979, resulting in the creation of two ecclesial networks in separation from the Convention. None of these splits has been reconciled into a new harmony as the enduring divisions put to rest notions of a (super-)natural unity welling up among Baptists.

The campaign that redirected the Southern Baptist Convention's theological orientation has tilted in the direction of greater conformity in doctrinal matters, utilizing measures of both recommendation and enforcement to achieve this goal. For Southern Baptist conservatives, it is a return to the recognition that conformity requires active measures. Baptist sociologist Nancy Ammerman's surveys of Southern Baptists during the height of the controversy found that self-identified fundamentalists and conservatives were far less likely than self-identified moderates to support

---

[11] Ibid., 216.

[12] Ibid., 219.

[13] Hudson, *Baptists in Transition*, 120f.

[14] J. J. Thompson Jr., *Tried as by Fire.*

[15] Ellis, "E. Y. Mullins," 14f.; Freeman, "E. Y. Mullins and the Siren Songs of Modernity," *passim*; Dilday, "Mullins the Theologian," 75–86.

strongly the toleration of different theological views.[16] The consolidation of control meant policy decisions could be enacted that drew firm boundaries against dissent. The *Baptist Faith and Message* was amended in 1998 to include an article on the family that insisted on a complementarian view of gender relationships in which the husband and father is the head of the household. When the confession was more thoroughly revised two years later, its article on the Church expanded to include a statement limiting the office of pastor to men.[17] Citing claims of anti-Americanism and liberalism in the BWA, and also angered by the reception of the Cooperative Baptist Fellowship, Southern Baptists voted to withdraw from the international Baptist body in 2004.[18] The conservative movement has also de-emphasized the concept of the priesthood of all believers and accentuated the authority of pastors, indicating an obvious preference for submission to vetted leadership over against collective deliberation.[19] More will be said about these trends toward authoritative pastoral leadership in the next chapter.

Sometimes the preferred parameters could appear remarkably quixotic from an ecumenical perspective. The conservative leadership has at times insisted that the penal substitutionary theory of Christ's atonement should be received as *the* correct, biblical understanding of the significance of the cross.[20] Disagreement over the acceptability of Pentecostal/charismatic practices resulted in the convention's International Mission Board banning missionaries who "speak in tongues" in 2005, and subsequently lifting the ban ten years later.[21] The recent surge of interest in Calvinism among Southern Baptists, especially among seminary leaders and students,

[16] Ammerman, *Baptist Battles*, 113.

[17] Article VI, *Baptist Faith and Message* (2000) available at "Comparison Chart."

[18] Alan Cooperman, "Southern Baptists Vote to Leave World Alliance," *Washington Post*, June 16, 2004, http://www.washingtonpost.com/wp-dyn/articles/A44658-2004Jun15.html.

[19] Shurden, *Not an Easy Journey*, 64–87; Humphreys, *The Way We Were*, 114f. and 120f.

[20] E.g., James T. Draper's comment at the 1988 SBC Pastors' Conference that substitutionary atonement should be on a list of necessary theological convictions, in Ammerman, *Baptist Battles*, 116. This is echoed by the "Report of the Presidential Theological Study Committee" that was approved at 1994 convention.

[21] See B. Allen, "IMB drops ban on 'private prayer language'"; Weaver, *Baptists and the Holy Spirit*, 350–53.

prodded some in leadership to declare Reformed theology anathema to "traditional" Baptist soteriology, leading to vigorous defenses both by Calvinist figures and by non-Calvinists who felt that the boundaries were now being drawn too narrow.[22] Moderate Baptists could readily construe these developments as the fulfillment of their prophecies that conservatives would turn on each other once they had gained power.[23]

Openness to New Truth

Alongside the principle of unity, early Baptists voiced a divergent strand of thought, which they shared with other dissenters from the established Church of England, and which has been articulated in multiple variations over the centuries. According to this perspective, the will of God is not identified solely with a secure deposit of revelation that can only be preserved and passed down to future generations. Rather, the message that has been granted once for all in Scripture may be plumbed to new depths through the activity of the Holy Spirit in a listening, discerning Church. This openness to further insight has been referred to as the "principle of mutability."[24]

An oft-quoted expression of this sentiment was stated by John Robinson, pastor of the English Separatist congregation in Amsterdam that would become the Pilgrims of Colonial America.[25] In his farewell sermon to the first group that boarded the vessel *Mayflower* in 1620, Robinson

[22] Gentry, "As Baptists Prepare to Meet, Calvinism Debate Shifts to Heresy Accusation." The statement is available in full at Michael Foust, "Statement on Calvinism draws approval, criticism," Baptist Press, May 31, 2012, http://www.bpnews. net/37939/statement-on-calvinism-draws-approval-criticism.

[23] Walter Shurden noted such predictions but portrayed them, as of 1993, as myths moderates told each other in the face of unity among conservative activists. See Shurden, "The Struggle for the Soul of the SBC, 281f.

[24] Leonard, *Baptist Ways*, 5. Leonard cites Andrews, "The Maine Wheele That Sets Us Awoke," 34. The phrase appears to be original to the seventeenth-century Scottish Presbyterian Robert Baillie, who writes critically about the willingness among Protestant Independents to rethink their beliefs. See Nuttall, *Holy Spirit in Puritan Faith and Experience*, 107.

[25] This congregation was effectively the same community as John Smyth's Separatist group. Resident near to one another in the same region of England, the churches maintained close contacts and together moved to the Netherlands to escape persecution. They split in 1609 over several differences of opinion, but before Smyth accepted believer's baptism (see Pearse, *Great Restoration*, 187–92).

Receptive Generosity and Interdependent Personhood

urges his flock to remain obedient to his instruction only insofar as he emulates Jesus Christ. They should embrace a receptive openness to God revealing truth to them by other means, for "the Lord hath more truth and light yet to break forth from His holy word."[26] Robinson joins together two convictions that appear at first glance to be polar opposites: complete submission to the authority of Scripture and a profound trust that further insight is waiting to be revealed. For Robinson, the paradox is resolved in the conviction that God is superintending the Church's ongoing journey of discernment, from age to age and in each gathered congregation.

That early Baptists in America shared this principle of receptivity is demonstrated by reviewing the texts of early church covenants. The Swansea Church in Rehoboth, Massachusetts, declared in its 1663 covenant that its members would practice Christ's ordinances "according to what is *or shall be revealed* to us."[27] In 1682, the Baptist church of Kittery, Massachusetts (now Maine) declared a covenant of faithfulness to God's commandments according to their present light of understanding as well as whatever "he shall please to discover & make known to us thro his holy Spirit according to the same blessed word."[28] This statement expresses a threefold conviction about discerning religious truth. First, the standard for judging valid belief is Scripture. Second, the meaning of Scripture is unveiled through what the Protestant tradition has identified, ever since the Reformers, as the illumination of the Holy Spirit.[29] Finally, this illumination is not limited to the re-presentation of established and universal meanings to each new individual or each new generation of Christians. Rather, the anticipation is set that a congregation gathered together around Scripture may discover as-yet unrealized significance to its words as it wrestles with novel contexts for enacting discipleship to Christ.

Similar expressions of receptivity to new truth, especially as a process of spiritual illumination of Scripture, are given in the 1665 covenant of

[26] Robinson, *Works of John Robinson*, 2:xlv.

[27] DeWeese, *Baptist Church Covenants*, 133. Emphasis added.

[28] Ibid., 134.

[29] E.g., the first article of the *Westminster Confession of Faith*, which was adapted as by English Particular Baptists as the *Second London Confession* in 1689 and by American Baptists as the *Philadelphia Confession* in the following century. The framers "acknowledge the inward illumination of the Spirit of God, to be necessary for the saving understanding of such things as are revealed in the Word..." (Lumpkin, *Baptist Confessions of Faith*, 250).

First Baptist, Boston, the 1671 covenant of the Seventh-Day Baptist Church in Newport, Rhode Island, the 1756 covenant of Middleborough Baptist Church in Massachusetts (written by Isaac Backus), the 1780 covenant of the Baptist church in New Durham, New Hampshire, the 1783 covenant of the Cherokee Creek Baptist Church in North Carolina (now Tennessee), and the 1785 covenant of Bent Creek Baptist Church in Tennessee.[30]

Early English Baptists also declared their openness in their confessions of faith. As a small and distrusted sect in a highly charged polemical environment, they were unsurprisingly inclined to strike an irenic tone with their fellow Protestants. The inaugural sentence of the *First London Confession* (1644) states that Baptists are frequently labeled heretics and creators of division in the church. In light of this objection, the framers present the confession as vehicle for "vindicating the truth of Christ" they proclaim.[31] They invite its readers to ponder the teachings promulgated in the document so they may conclude whether the charges made against the Baptists are false. They also declare their faith that the Lord will "daily" increase believers' recognition of truth.[32] As it stands, the first confession, grounded in the assumption that Baptists bear the true and faithful witness to the gospel, appears one-sided in calling for open-mindedness on the part of external critics. When a second edition of the text was published two years later, a conclusion was added after the articles. Here one finds a different sort of confession to the positive theological claims presented in the body:

> Also we confesse that we know but in part, and that we are ignorant of many things which we desire and seek to know: and if any doe us that friendly part to shew us from the word of God that we see not, we shall have cause to be thankfull to God and them. But if any man shall impose upon us anything that we see not to be commanded by our Lord Jesus Christ, we should...die a thousand deaths, rather than

---

[30] DeWeese, *Baptist Church Covenants*, 133f., 140, 146f., 149. This list is representative and not meant to be construed as comprehensive. These are all the covenants reproduced in DeWeese's book that explicitly identify the possibility that God will grant new theological insight to the community.

[31] Lumpkin, *Baptist Confessions of Faith*, 154.

[32] Ibid., 155.

Receptive Generosity and Interdependent Personhood

to doe any thing against the least tittle of the truth of God, or against the light of our own consciences.[33]

The Particular Baptists would issue another confession in 1677 with a conciliatory purpose. Desiring to demonstrate their common ground with fellow Calvinists, they slightly modified the Westminster Confession of Faith and adopted the altered statement as the *Second London Confession*. An appendix on the disputatious question of the proper subject of baptism concludes the text. Despite the fierceness with which the debate has been conducted, the appendix proclaims affection for and fellowship with fellow Protestants. The framers plead for concomitant respect via acknowledgment that the Baptist position is affirmed not as a matter of obstinate differentiation but as a principled commitment to Scriptural teaching as they understand it. They hold their belief concerning baptism without reservation, but also without unmoving certitude. Fellow "Servants of our Lord Jesus" are invited to demonstrate to the Baptists their mistake. In response, they will carefully consider the arguments and accept the doctrinal opponent not as an adversary but "our chiefest friend that shall be an instrument to convert us from any error that is in our ways."[34]

Neither confessions written in Britain after the establishment of toleration, nor confessions written in America for the next two centuries, reiterate this irenic tone toward fellow Christians. Baptists, though, would continue to stress the provisional and fallible nature of confessions, never ascribing to any one the authority to define permanent theological boundaries. Thus, when the drafting committee presented the *Baptist Faith and Message* to the SBC meeting of 1925, the report included an explanation concerning the roles played by confessions throughout Baptist history.[35] While any given confession may represent the general consensus of a group at the time of its adoption, it cannot be considered complete or infallible. The Bible is held up as the exclusive authority for religious matters, with confessions playing an auxiliary role as "guides in interpretation" that should never be employed to restrict freedom of inquiry. The preamble to the 1963 edition quotes in full the declarations concerning Baptist confes-

---

[33] Ibid., 149.

[34] Ibid., 275f.

[35] All the following references to the *Baptist Faith and Message* in any edition are taken from "Comparison Chart."

THE CONTESTABLE CHURCH

sions given in the original report and makes additional comments to emphasize the principle of provisionality. This committee declares, "Baptists are a people who profess a living faith." Such a faith is also stably rooted in Christ. Interestingly, the sole authority for theological truth is no longer identified as Scripture *simpliciter*, but "Jesus Christ whose will is revealed in the Holy Scriptures."[36] Here, the emphasis has shifted from the text to the divine person who stands behind and authorizes it. Moreover, this divine person is also the one who, through the agency of the Spirit, directs the Church in the present. For the 1963 framers, then, genuine faith entails "a growing understanding of truth."

Further evidence for a strong embrace of the mutability principle in this period is provided by a small pamphlet published in the very same year. Several Baptist denominations in the United States and Canada were cooperating in a five-year evangelism campaign, known as the Baptist Jubilee Advance, which would be completed in 1964.[37] The chairman of the committee overseeing SBC participation in the endeavor appointed a separate group to draft a statement of Baptist principles and purposes. The resulting document, *Baptist Ideals*, was published by the convention's Sunday School Board.[38] The tract's preface notes that Baptists throughout history have "reformulated their beliefs and reevaluated their practices." The first section in the body of the text addresses the question of authority. *Baptist Ideals* reiterates the ordering in which Jesus Christ is the ultimate authority and the Bible is secondarily authoritative by virtue of revealing the will of God in Christ. The second section focuses on human beings as individuals, affirming soul competency and liberty of conscience. Then, in the concluding section, openness to new truth is presented as a vital practice. "Every Christian group, if it is to remain healthy and fruitful, must accept the responsibility of constructive self-criticism."[39]

The principle of mutability was itself muted in favor of permanent conviction when the *Baptist Faith and Message* was revised again in the year 2000. This latest edition was fashioned in the wake of the recent conflict

---

[36] This despite having just quoted the 1925 statement that Scripture itself is the sole authority.

[37] Leonard, *Baptist Ways*, 408.

[38] Baptist Press, "5-Point Statement on Ideals Released."

[39] Ibid. for all the preceding.

124

over control of the Southern Baptist Convention as well as dramatic cultural shifts in the United States. In the middle of the 2000 preface, the 1925 statements about confessional faith are reiterated, yet this cited text is surrounded by declarations of continuity and solidity as confessionalism is steered back toward confidence in foundational verities. Citing 2 Timothy 1:14, the framers identify the responsibility of every Christian generation to guard the "treasury of truth." The notion of a progressive realization of truth is also undermined by the twice-stated affirmation of "eternal truths." The latter expression of this phrase is used to temper the theological dynamism of the 1963 preamble. "Our living faith," writes the committee, is not described as growing but as "established upon eternal truths." This most recent of the confessional preambles also insists that confessions, more than merely witnessing to cherished beliefs, have also been employed by Baptists as "instruments of doctrinal accountability."

This shift in tone would seem to be a decisive break with the Baptist heritage as expressed in the 1925 and 1963 preambles. It is frequently believed, as Lumpkin writes, that Baptist confessions are "simply manifestos of prevailing doctrine in particular groups."[40] It must be noted, however, that this account of confessions—only exemplary and never authoritative—is a historical misreading; there have been occasions when Baptists employed statements of faith precisely to command some threshold of doctrinal conformity. In 1856, James Petigru Boyce of Furman University declared that theological institutions needed to adopt statements of faith so as to prevent erroneous teaching. Boyce claimed that their use would be perfectly consistent with Baptist ideals.[41] Three years later, Southern Baptist Theological Seminary was founded with Boyce as its first president, and a statement named the Abstract of Principles was incorporated into its charter.[42] Although every professor was required to subscribe to the Abstract,[43] Professor John Broadus contended in a speech that students would be equipped to interpret Scripture with complete freedom of thought.[44]

---

[40] Lumpkin, *Baptist Confessions of Faith*, 17.

[41] Garrett, *Baptist Theology*, 145f. Garrett remarks that Baptist centers of higher education did not employ confessions at this time, but that Boyce's alma mater, Princeton Theological Seminary, utilized one.

[42] Leonard, "Types of Confessional Documents among Baptists," 38.

[43] Shurden, "Southern Baptist Responses to their Confessional Statements," 71.

[44] Leonard, "Types of Confessional Documents among Baptists," 38.

Walter Shurden describes how various Southern Baptist agencies or organizations, including all six seminaries, would adopt statements of faith and make them binding on constituents.[45] Other examples of confessional enforcement may be found in southern baptist life preceding the creation of the SBC[46] and extending into recent years, as previously noted.

Whereas confessions have been embraced as boundary-setting tools, other Baptists who stress the mutability principle and freedom of conscience have questioned the validity of confessions altogether. The Separate Baptists of Colonial and Early Republican America, more egalitarian and independent-minded than their Regular Baptist cousins, refused to draft confessions of faith and, when they united with the Regulars, undercut the regulative authority of the united bodies' adopted confessions.[47] One significant, early opponent of the confessional tradition was Leland. Writing in "The Virginia Chronicle," Leland recounts the adoption of a confession during the merger of the Regular and Separate Baptists of Virginia in 1787 and states his preference that their union had been achieved absent such a document. Leland's objection to confessions is twofold. First, they improperly mediate between the individual Christian and the Bible, the latter being the only authoritative text in religion. Moreover, they "check any further pursuit after truth [and] confine the mind into a particular way of reasoning."[48] Leland thus endorses not only biblicism but the "new light" hermeneutic that envisions a progressive understanding of Scripture, which is best practiced if it is not channeled by restrictive interpretive traditions.

Strict anti-confessionalism has remained a continuing voice in southern baptist life. For example, when the first *Baptist Faith and Message* was proposed and approved in 1925, a vocal minority contended that no single statement could honor the theological diversity within the Convention, nor that doctrinal disagreement may be resolved by its implementation.[49]

---

[45] Shurden, "Southern Baptist Responses to their Confessional Statements," *passim*.

[46] E.g., Leonard, "Types of Confessional Documents," 35, for the Elkhorn (Kentucky) Association in 1785.

[47] Lumpkin, *Baptist Foundations in the South*, 62f.; Garrett, *Baptist Theology*, 164; Shurden, "Southern Baptist Responses to their Confessional Statements," 69f.

[48] Leland, *Writings*, 114.

[49] Shurden, "Southern Baptist Responses to their Confessional Statements," 75.

More recently, many moderates disenfranchised by the conservative resurgence have looked askance at proposals by their peers to shift this branch of the Baptist family away from its anti-confessional stance to a "generous orthodoxy" that more closely resembles (but should not be equated with) the moderate confessionalism that characterized the SBC during the middle of the twentieth century.[50] Progressives in the Alliance of Baptists, meanwhile, have entirely displaced theological confessionalism with positional statements on sociopolitical issues.[51]

Fostering Dissent through Private Judgment

Despite its fractious diversity, Protestantism centers on a shared sensibility that Christianity has diverted down wrong paths and seemingly established judgments may be interrogated. Dissent has thus been a necessary tool to correct the errors to which the Church had been subjugated and under which it remains to the present day. This is true as a negative move (to guard against failures of faith and practice as they recur) or as a positive one (to discern and affirm the latest iterations of divine will for novel contexts). These twinned expectations—human frailty and new light—together relativize the authority of any given creed or ecclesial institution. Paul Tillich coined this acceptance of contingency the "Protestant principle."[52] The posture of openness characterizes the life of the Church on equal grounds with the posture of faithfulness.

Dissent from the community's current standards is the motive force for transformation, but where is that force best applied? Sometimes dissent

---

[50] A prominent example was the outcry directed against a proposed revision of the "foundational statement" for the Cooperative Baptist Fellowship of North Carolina. Opponents of the proposal exemplified the "more light" emphasis, expressing fears that the new statement would impose credalism and squelch the freedom of individual conscience. See B. Allen, "State CBF proposal sparks debate about Baptist identity," *Baptist News Global*, September 19, 2010, https://baptistnews.com/article/state-cbf-proposal-sparks-debate-about-baptist-identity/#.WVGFYmgrJPY. For a defense of the "generous orthodox" approach to confessionalism, see Freeman, *Contesting Catholicity*, 93–139.

[51] E.g., note the prioritization of social justice declarations in the Alliance's Covenant and Mission statement, available at "Who We Are," Alliance of Baptists, accessed December 16, 2022, https://allianceofbaptists.org/who-we-are/.

[52] Tillich, *Protestant Era*, 161–84.

is simply neglected or even suppressed, as has been shown. When it is allowed or encouraged, the most commonly articulated mode for expressing independent thought among Baptists is the concept known as *private interpretation* or *private judgment*. Rooted in convictions about both the liberty of human conscience and the freedom of God to speak to whom God wills, private judgment asserts that each Christian has the right and the responsibility to read and interpret Scripture for oneself, form opinions on theological and moral issues, and live accordingly.

The first Baptist theologian in the United States to name private judgment as a key principle is Francis Wayland. Writing in his *Notes on the Principles and Practices of Baptist Churches*, Wayland asserts "the absolute right of private judgment in all matters of religion" to be a perennial rallying-cry of the tradition.[53] The individual's evaluative faculty is exercised in relation to Scripture, (specifically, in Wayland's phrasing, the New Testament), which God has placed not in the hands of an elite but those of every human being. The responsibility falls on each person to study the New Testament and, discerning its truths, to shape one's life accordingly. For Wayland, the Bible communicates God's will in a plain manner, but still the Holy Spirit is present to assist every Christian who seeks understanding. He exudes confidence that anyone who searches for God's will in this manner "will not fail to discern it."[54]

While he may be the first Baptist in America known to employ the phrase, Wayland's confidence that each believer can discern divine truth through the personal reading of Scripture has antecedents as far back as the earliest years of the movement in England. C. Douglas Weaver and Scott Bryant quote multiple early English Baptists who proclaimed that all persons (or at least all men) should personally study the Bible under the Spirit's guidance and enjoy the liberty to preach their convictions.[55] One prominent example would be Helwys's argument against the Church of England hierarchy in *The Mystery of Iniquity*. Helwys is justly famous for opposing coercive obedience to the state religion and proposing liberty of conscience in its place. His critique pertains not only to the demarcations between church, state, and society, but also to the nature of authority

---

[53] Wayland, *Notes on the Principles and Practices of Baptist Churches*, 132.

[54] Ibid., 132f.

[55] Weaver, "Early English Baptists," 145ff; Bryant, "Early English Baptist Response to the Baptist Manifesto," 242–45.

Receptive Generosity and Interdependent Personhood

within the church itself. While Helwys rejoices that Bible and liturgy have been translated into the vernacular, he contends that this is but a half-step to realizing a more faithful Christian community. For although the common person may read Scripture, the bishops of the Church of England reserve to themselves the right to delineate permissible interpretation of the text, even to the point of imposing retribution on dissenters.[56] Helwys contends that the power of the Spirit working through Scripture has been curtailed by this restriction. He pleads with King James I that that all people be allowed independent discernment, reaching their own interpretations of Scripture and challenging church leaders on that basis.[57]

Several decades later, General Baptist leader Thomas Grantham, debating a (real or imagined) Catholic apologist, wrote in his *Christianismus Primitivus* that the authority for Christian faith and practice is Jesus Christ as he speaks in Scripture by the Spirit. As believers seek to discern this divine voice, they utilize what Grantham calls "a Judgment of Science" on religious matters. Every man may rely on this judgment to affirm or reject the prescriptions of others.[58] Grantham supports this right to a Judgment of Science over against authoritative figures by citing the Apostle Paul's encouragement of his Corinthians readers to exercise the faculty.[59]

Seventeenth-century Baptists on the other side of the Atlantic Ocean made similar appeals to personal discernment in their disputes with the Colonial Puritan establishment. William Turner, one of the founders of the First Baptist Church of Boston, asked his interlocutors, "Is it not a reasonable thing that every man have his particular judgment in matters of faith, seeing we all must appear before the judgment seat of Christ?"[60] Another founding member, Edward Drinker, declared the right of every Christian to decide matters of religious truth.[61]

The exact phrase "private judgment" is not uttered by any of these figures although Turner's wording is proximate. One can readily observe, nevertheless, that the conceptual content of Wayland's private judgment

[56] Helwys, *Mystery of Iniquity*, 43.

[57] Ibid., 44, 49.

[58] Grantham, *Christianismus Primitivus*, 4:1f.

[59] "I speak as to sensible people: Judge for yourselves what I say" (1 Cor 10:15, ESV).

[60] Qtd. in McLoughlin and Davidson, "Baptist Debate of April 14–15, 1668," 102.

[61] Ibid., 116f.

is identical with these early Baptists' convictions about ordinary believers' use of Scripture. The general points of agreement are that 1) the Bible is generally comprehensible to any reader, 2) especially when the Holy Spirit is humbly invoked, 3) so therefore each Christian has the right and duty to draw conclusions on the meaning and significance of biblical teaching for one's own life and for the community at large. These convictions recur among leading Baptist figures subsequent to Wayland who have reiterated private judgment as a fundamental principle. Augustus Strong calls it an inalienable liberty exercised by the whole church. He reiterates the insistence that private judgment does not exalt autonomous human reason, for the latter properly discerns the meaning of the text only insofar as it relies upon the indwelling presence of Christ.[62] Mullins avers that Jesus, wanting free followers rather than coerced subjects, invites persons to evaluate his teachings for themselves. Again, Mullins stresses that the human mind does not work unaided, but with a reasoning capacity enhanced by virtue of regeneration.[63] Contemporary theologian Molly Marshall writes that private judgment serves a constructive purpose for churches as it enables new insights inspired by the Spirit to permeate.[64] The examples from Baptist writings across the last two centuries can be readily multiplied.

Critiques of Private Judgment

While the principle of private judgment holds a longstanding pedigree in the Baptist tradition, drawing upon traces as far back as the initial decades of the movement in both England and America, it has nevertheless come under severe criticism in recent years. The *Baptist Manifesto* represents one prominent criticism. Citing 2 Peter 1:20-21,[65] the signatories decry private interpretation according to individual conscience as forbidden by Scripture itself.[66] Their concern echoes in precise terms their rejection of Mullins's soul competency, which was noted in the previous chapter. Much like that other contested concept, they assert that private judgment valorizes heroic

---

[62] Strong, *Systematic Theology*, 1:220.

[63] Mullins, *Freedom and Authority in Religion*, 326–30.

[64] Marshall, "Exercising Liberty of Conscience," 149.

[65] "[K]nowing this first of all, that no prophecy of Scripture comes from someone's own interpretation. For no prophecy was ever produced by the will of man, but men spoke from God as they were carried along by the Holy Spirit" (ESV).

[66] Freeman, "Can Baptist Theology be Revisioned?," 305.

individualism. Study of the Bible becomes "insulated" from the Christian community as each person pursues a free-rein hermeneutic. *Manifesto* co-author Freeman, writing an accompanying article in the journal *Perspectives in Religious Studies*, claims that private judgment is not an inheritance of the Reformation but a borrowing from the political philosophy of John Locke.[67] His implication is that Locke's ideas are a foreign admixture and not a complementary illumination of Baptist practices.[68]

Freeman is joined in his denunciation by fellow scholars who encourage the spirit and practice of "catholicity" among Baptists. Given this project, their criticisms of private judgment identify its potential to undermine receptivity to the weighty precedents of the Christian tradition, which has wrestled with interpretive and doctrinal questions well in advance of modern-day pietists reading Scripture for themselves. D. H. Williams, a Baptist patristic scholar and an early advocate of evangelical engagement with pre-Reformation theology, warns that the Bible, when treated in isolation from the Christian community past and present, becomes susceptible to idiosyncratic interpretations justified by the alleged inspiration of the Holy Spirit. Such a hermeneutical approach derives from the assumption that Scripture's purpose is to meet the needs of individuals, who thus can identify its import as capably as can a corporate body of believers. On the contrary, Williams insists, the text is best understood when read within a community of intentional religious discipline.[69]

Steven Harmon, another Baptist patristics scholar and ecumenical theologian, agrees that the thrust of private judgment is toward the separation of persons and congregations from the universal church's collective

---

[67] Ibid., 285 n. 35. In his "A Letter Concerning Toleration" (1689), one of Locke's arguments for restricting the magistrate's authority to civil matters is this exercise of human will. "And such is the nature of the understanding," he writes, "that it cannot be compelled to the belief of anything by outward force. Confiscation of estate, imprisonment, torments, nothing of that nature can have any such efficacy as to make men change the *inward judgment* that they have framed of things" (emphasis added).

[68] A different perspective on Locke is provided by Disciples of Christ theologian David M. Thompson, who notes that Locke did not assume that all religious opinions should be granted equal treatment, for he excluded atheism from official political toleration. Moreover, Thompson claims, Locke affirmed that "the community of faith would shape the consciences of its members" ("Conscience, Private Judgment and the Community of Faith," 10f).

[69] Williams, *Evangelicals and Tradition*, 99–101.

wisdom that has been passed down through the centuries. Because it is seemingly an ahistorical and anti-traditional method of theological inquiry, Harmon identifies it as particularly emblematic of American cultural influence.[70] Freeman and Williams reach the same conclusion: acceptance of private judgment demonstrates the combined influence of Enlightenment philosophies and frontier populism.[71] Williams cites as a representative voice a nineteenth-century Calvinist Baptist who commends the personal reading of Scripture in antithetical opposition to consultation of early church theologians, councils and synods, or the overall collective sense of the church.[72]

Walter Shurden, in his article responding to the *Baptist Manifesto*, expresses his incredulity at the rejection of private judgment. He rightly notes that Baptist history is replete with justifications for the practice and laments, "I am not sure I have ever seen a statement on the Baptist identity proposing the denial of private interpretation of Scripture prior to the *Manifesto*."[73] Shurden cites several supportive precedents from Baptist history, all of which predate Locke's writings, just as the examples provided above. Additionally, he rejects the notion that private judgment entails giving final authority to the isolated individual, and follows this with an important question for *Manifesto* communitarianism: on what basis is the community authorized to check individual interpretation, and how will it do so without falling into a form of authoritarianism?[74]

Disciples of Christ theologian David Scholer strikes a more conciliatory tone, suggesting that the centrifugal force of private judgment must be mitigated by demarcations of legitimate diversity. Each believer's act of biblical interpretation is an exercise of responsibility to the text but not control over it. The confessional boundaries of the community provide the restraining limits for the exercise of responsible interpretation.[75] Private judgment is thus acceptable as a tool for negotiating beliefs concerning

---

[70] Harmon, *Towards Baptist Catholicity*, 37.

[71] Freeman, *Contesting Catholicity*, 74–76; Williams, *Retrieving the Tradition and Renewing Evangelicalism*, 19. Both of them depend on the historical account provided in Hatch, *Democratization of American Christianity*.

[72] Williams, *Retrieving the Tradition and Renewing Evangelicalism*, 20.

[73] Shurden, "Baptist Identity and the Baptist *Manifesto*," 326.

[74] Ibid., 327f.

[75] Scholer, "Authority of the Bible and Private Interpretation," in *Baptists in the Balance*, ed. Goodwin, 190.

adiaphora within the framework of an orthodoxy that has been granted assent.

Shurden's pointed question about the authority of the community remains a thorny challenge to this proposal. Is it possible to erect an eliminative collective orthodoxy without begging the question? Despite the dangers of disintegration, the Protestant principle dissects claims of unquestionable authority with logical clarity. There is no consensually acknowledged court of appeal that can grant final judgments on where the boundaries stand, never to be shifted further. Unless, that is, one fideistically accepts a magisterium as in some way self-authenticating, but if there is no infallible guide to the placement of limits, then private judgment must be allowed to negotiate the terms of belief even at the now-porous edges.

The answer to this question is perhaps best provided by James William McClendon Jr., one of the *Manifesto* authors. McClendon proposes a significantly (and perpetually) reorienting perspective on theological authority and the value of personal discernment. Ultimately, God is the one proper authority to adjudicate doctrinal and ethical claims, yet God, in God's freedom, is not restricted to the confines of any finite locus of judgment, be that the text of Scripture, a Christian community, or the lone rebel who feels compelled to declare a new word of the Lord. McClendon suggests that all such other authorities, under God, must endlessly interact with each other, offering and receiving insight in the medium of their relationships. Using the image of a Ferris wheel, he proposes that the process of discerning truth must circulate between these centers, neither of which can claim a fixed location "above" the others.[76]

In short, the community needs its prophets, but prophets need a community of address to fulfill their own identity and mission. The danger of private judgment isolated from an understanding of communal contestation is that it, as the term suggests, *privatizes* dissent into the isolated expression of subjective opinion. It holds the danger of reinforcing a non-Christian notion of expressive selves who occasionally bounce off one another but do not truly enter into mutually interrogative and transformative relationships. Conflict and dissent must be constructively engaged as irreducibly relational expressions of being in order to serve the purpose of shared discernment in faithfulness to Christ. Coles's model of receptive

[76] McClendon, *Doctrine*, 454–88.

generosity articulates the value of granting space for dissonance which, when united with Carlyle Marney's understanding of Christian priesthood, offers an understanding of the contestable church as a space for shared spiritual growth and discernment *through* the conflict of encounter with others.

Romand Coles's Quest for a Receptively Generous Democracy

In *Rethinking Generosity*, Coles turns his attention from the interaction between the self and the vastness of being writ large to the immediate relationships between selves in their specific acts of encounter. The very first words of the book present a grim picture: "These are not generous times."[77] The candle that Coles lights in this dark—and henceforth a recurrent theme of his work—is the practice of "receptive generosity" as a necessary condition for the well-being of humanity. Oxymoronic in character, this phrase encapsulates the ethical dialectic that Coles outlines as either corrective or extrapolation to the ideas of previous philosophers. Properly expressed, generosity and receptivity are intertwined movements of engagement with different others. Their separation entails disaster for the productive possibilities of politics, whereas their conjunction rejects "both possessive individualism and ideologies of monological generosity" in the quest for a better dynamic of living together.[78]

Standing alone, the claim of generosity casts a disconcerting shadow. According to Coles, its most prominent articulations in Christian theology and rationalist philosophy build upon a presumed self-identical foundation. By "self-identical" Coles intends a being that exists fundamentally independent of external objects, such that its identity is based entirely on intrinsic properties and therefore is indefectibly impermeable to receiving difference internally. Such a self moves unidirectionally toward the other because it is capable only of generous extension. The two self-identical beings commonly portrayed in this fashion are God and the "transcendental subject" theorized by Kant.[79] Coles briefly reiterates his critique of Augustine of Hippo from *SPO*, noting as well this time that subsequent Augustinian thinkers fall into the same pit of celebrating creational diversity

[77] Coles, *Rethinking Generosity*, vii.
[78] Ibid.
[79] Ibid., 2.

Receptive Generosity and Interdependent Personhood

as the gift of God's *caritas* while simultaneously devaluing the alterity of persons external to the Christian community as marred by the privative nothingness of evil.[80] But Coles's critique of hubristic Christian blindness is only a preliminary exemplar in *RG*. Maintaining the resolutely post-theological orientation of *SPO*, Coles is still theorizing with the assumption that the "death of God" has been realized. He openly aims to foster a robust ethical vision absent God as the postulated fount of morality.[81] Nevertheless, he identifies his project as "post-secular" rather than "secular" in orientation. The idea of the secular, according to Coles's genealogical analysis, subsists in efforts to "place human beings...on the sovereign throne" of a now-withdrawing God.[82] To be post-secular, then, is to abandon this quest for sovereignty altogether for the sake of a less stable yet more hopeful future created by receptive generosity. The structure of *RG* argues toward Coles's post-secular construction of interdependent selves through his interpretations of Immanuel Kant, Theodor Adorno, and Jürgen Habermas.

The major impetus for Kant's philosophical project was to rescue confidence in Enlightenment rationality after the assault of David Hume's skepticism.[83] Hume analyzed the act of perceiving and concluded that it is impossible to observe anything about the substances that may lie behind perception.[84] The radical conclusion of Hume's argument holds that one can never assuredly demonstrate a correspondence between one's ideas and the objects those ideas claim to apprehend.[85] According to Coles, the most consistent extrapolations of this conclusion include the epistemic absence of an external world, a continuous self, and a God that would grant order to either of these realities.[86] The relevant implication for Coles's ethical concern is the tilt of Hume's skepticism toward undiluted receptivity. The knower can only know perceptions as they arise in awareness—that is, they are received—and not as they are given by an Other. While Coles does not

---

[80] Ibid., 2f. Coles cites his article where he criticizes contemporary English theologian John Milbank for repeating Augustine's error: "Storied Others and Possibilities of *Caritas*," 331–51.

[81] Coles, *Rethinking Generosity*, 6.

[82] Ibid., 8.

[83] Allen and Springsted, *Philosophy for Understanding Theology*, 155.

[84] Ibid., 143,

[85] Critchley, *Continental Philosophy*, 17.

[86] Coles, *Rethinking Generosity*, 10.

THE CONTESTABLE CHURCH

state this, it is expected that he would agree with the inverse consequence: there is no warrant for believing that the Other may be the object of one's generosity.

Kant answers Humean skepticism with what philosophers now refer to as his transcendental deduction.[87] A priori knowledge of the external world is possible because objects *as they are perceived* are shaped by our application of pre-existent categories of understanding which our minds supply. As a logical consequence, Kant presupposes that behind our sense of self is the (ultimately unknowable) transcendent subject that synthesizes impressions via the categories into consciousness and knowledge.[88] Coles writes that this transcendental subject "give[s] the conditions of knowledge and experience to which objects must conform."[89]

As Coles acknowledges, Kant's formulation of this subject in the *Critique of Pure Reason* entails the give-and-take of generosity between self and the world. The philosopher recognizes that unadulterated giving from the self cannot be trusted as anything more than arbitrary whimsy, yet Coles insists that Kant defangs the world-shaping power of otherness for the sake of the subject's sovereignty.[90] The gift of the other's existence is also a curse by bringing forth heteronomy that potentially undermines Kant's project and reinstates the skepticism of Hume.[91] How does Kant effect the coronation of his law-giving subject? This occurs via his well-known argument distinguishing *noumena*, or objects in themselves, and *phenomena*, or objects as they appear to us in our understanding. All objects generating the impressions of the subject's attention remain radically other and unknowable, but the categories inherent in the subject give order to sensibility's impressions and generate knowledge of objects as phenomena.[92]

"Yet the idea of an otherness," Coles writes, "that is *nothing but* a functional condition for the sovereignty of the subject is...not the idea of

---

[87] See Allen and Springsted, *Philosophy for Understanding Theology*, 159; Critchley, *Continental Philosophy*, 17.

[88] Critchley, *Continental Philosophy*, 17; Allen and Springsted, *Philosophy for Understanding Theology*, 160–61.

[89] Coles, *Rethinking Generosity*, 11.

[90] Ibid., 24f.

[91] Ibid., 27.

[92] Ibid., 28f.

Receptive Generosity and Interdependent Personhood

an other at all."[93] He finds that Kant cannot void the heteronomy of the other by reducing it to sheer indeterminacy, for such a proposition generates a tension in the philosopher's epistemology. Understanding has the task of "legislating" nature by categorizing the sensory manifold into objects of experience, yet the giving of a manifold through sensibility entails a prior determination of "parts" that allow synthesis in the first place. Otherwise, what appears in the sensibility is epistemically *nothing* altogether. There must be something given in the manifold that understanding consequently acts upon. Coles spies a contradiction at the heart of Kant's project: an otherness that is simultaneously out there "in itself" yet given form out of nothingness only by receptivity.[94]

The implications of this abstruse epistemology for political ethics may not be readily apparent, but for Coles the modernist paradigm that owes much to Kant has been afflicted by homeomorphic dilemmas. Political liberalism of various stripes has grounded its legitimacy in its tolerant welcome of diverse perspectives. However, a genuinely dialogical encounter with otherness all but surely leads to transformation and therefore disproves the singular sovereignty of any such political configuration. Coles names the two paths at the fork to be a radicalized abandonment of sovereignty and an exclusionary declaration of the "nothingness" of the other. Kant's epistemology is a "foundational narrative" that culminates in such real-world problems as the mistreatment of Native Americans by the European settlers and their descendants.[95]

In the *Critique of Practical Reason*, the challenge of receptivity appears as a radical contingency that threatens to undermine any attempt at constructing a universal, rational morality. To give the law of morality properly, the subject must refuse receptivity to determine and act upon universal law.[96] Coles raises the critical question that arises more naturally in the contemporary postmodern context, but the force of which Kant already recognized. Is this supposedly objective sovereignty of the subject nothing more than an arbitrary reification of unacknowledged limits of one's conditioning?[97] According to Coles, few have found Kant's answers

[93] Ibid., 31. Emphasis original.

[94] Ibid., 31–35.

[95] Ibid., 36. A more direct line of influence may be traced by examining Immanuel Kant's views on non-Europeans as inferior races (see Carter, *Race*, 79–123).

[96] Coles, *Rethinking Generosity*, 40f.

[97] Ibid., 41f.

137

THE CONTESTABLE CHURCH

to this problem tenable. More importantly for Coles's project, Kant's persistence in shoring up the narrative of the autonomous lawgiver leads him to smuggle receptivity back from its exile. The journey begins with Kant accepting that reason is responsible for tending to the needs of the self, among which stands happiness. While happiness cannot serve as the basis for the structure of practical reason, it is an aspect of the highest good and is a deserved reward for ordering one's life according to morality.[98] The will may be capable of giving itself the moral law, but not happiness itself, and thus Kant postulates God as the all-powerful and rational being from whom happiness may be received.[99] He also correlatively grants immortality as the necessary condition for progress toward complete obedience to the moral law.[100] Coles notes the paradox that ensues as receptivity returns by the hand of God:

> What begins as an unconditional rejection of receptivity-as-contingent-desire ends in the need to postulate an ultimate harmony between our self-giving moral autonomy and the pleasurable reception of the heteronomous world...Self-giving sovereignty must give itself generous otherness to sustain its unconditional rejection of the contingencies involved in receiving heteronomy.[101]

Coles spies further gleanings of a more engaging generosity in the *Critique of Judgment*, wherein Kant wishes to evaluate aesthetics through his proposed faculty of judgment.[102] Coles mines Kant's discussions of the concept of the sublime, as well as the production of fine art by genius, to present an alternative dimension of relationality in Kant. The sublime is, for Kant, the experience of an object that exceeds comprehension and is effectively unbounded.[103] While Kant had given imagination the task of synthesizing impressions into the unity of experience in the First Critique, he now acknowledges a wildness of nature that exceeds the subject's grasp. But the unity of experience is a necessary condition for the unity of the

[98] Ibid., 42f.
[99] Ibid., 44f.
[100] Ibid., 47.
[101] Ibid., 46.
[102] Scruton, *Kant*, 97.
[103] Ibid., 109; Coles, *Rethinking Generosity*, 56.

138

Receptive Generosity and Interdependent Personhood

sovereign subject, exposing it to entanglement with uncontrollable contingency.[104] Furthermore, Kant describes the comprehension that translates multiplicity into unity to be a form of violence committed by the imagination. Although this is required to intuit a world structure out of the succession of impressions, Kant seems to take leave of his account of the legislative self and suggests instead a pre-synthesis encounter with the other as a range of possibility. The apprehension of this manifold, writes Coles, is "simultaneously a *reduction*."[105] Reason grants a unified order through the violence of rejecting or editing the extensive range of possibilities experienced in the encounter with the other.

If the sublime reveals a boundlessness of a reality that exceeds the categorizations of understanding, then the expression of genius via aesthetics offers a vehicle for probing the phenomenal boundaries. Kant identifies fine art as the product of genius and defines the latter as "the talent that gives the rule to art." Coles immediately notes the dissonance between this claim of nature's generosity and the key theme of the autonomous subject. The artist's originality is made possible by a prior receptivity.[106] Equivalent to "spirit" (*Geist* in German), genius "animates" the mind through relationship to external objects, empowering the give-and-receive at the horizon between what is present to one's cognizing and what remains beyond.[107] Furthermore, Kant accepts a social dimension to genius, naming the arousal of this principle in one mind as inaugurated through the encounter with genius in other minds.[108] This portrait of genius dethrones the subject and "locates the animation of our mental powers in a dialogical giving and receiving within ourselves and with others."[109] Identifying the inextricable interrelationship of aesthetics and epistemology, Kant affirms that all cognizing must navigate the terrain between limitation and expansion, with the result that self and experience arise together through "open and unending articulation."[110]

Kant gestures toward this realization in his essay "What is Enlightenment?" wherein he sees the advance of reason occurring not through

[104] Coles, *Rethinking Generosity*, 56–58.
[105] Ibid., 58f. Emphasis original.
[106] Ibid., 61.
[107] Ibid., 61–63.
[108] Ibid., 65.
[109] Ibid., 66.
[110] Ibid., 67.

139

individuals thinking freely but through a public enlightening itself as an interactive, social project.[111] Here, Kant celebrates independent thought beyond the confines of pre-determined rules that maintain immaturity. He calls for the comparison of judgments that may result in a sense of the community (*sensus communis*). According to the dominant strands of Kant's philosophy, reason will shape this process toward inevitable consensus.[112] It is here that Coles considers the shape of this consensual judgment if Kant's transcendentalism is rejected. First, the inquiry into others' modes of arguing rebounds as an investigation of one's perceptual limitations. Second, the recognition of one's debt to the social context for the animation of genius invites the generosity to receive others in their very otherness, allowing them to provoke with difference. Coles reinterprets *sensus communis* as the cultivated awareness of these tensions that is life-giving for the individual and the community. Here freedom is imagined not as unconditioned autonomy but as the exploration of possibility, animated through the process of giving and receiving.[113]

Not all is well as subjective sovereignty gives way to receptive engagement with the objective other. Coles turns to Theodor Adorno in the second chapter of *RG* as a means, he states explicitly, of balancing Kant's optimistic narrative of mutual enlightenment with darker shades of tragedy.[114] Adorno (1903–1969) was a German philosopher and a member of the first generation of the philosophical Frankfurt School. Disillusioned both by the authoritarian outcome of the Russian Revolution and the conditions of modernity at large, Adorno was one of the originators of the critical theory school in political philosophy.[115] Directing philosophy to the goal of human freedom, critical theory has refused to secure this goal to any fixed institution or ideological system. Rather, closed structures of determination are ruthlessly critiqued and openness to new possibilities is continuously engendered.[116] This resistance to reified formulation culminates for Adorno in his concept of "negative dialectics," which is an inversion of G. W. F. Hegel's proposal that the dialectic of ideas proceeds progressively toward synthesis. Rather, the negation of ideas is intrinsically

[111] Ibid., 69.
[112] Ibid., 70f.
[113] Ibid., 71–74.
[114] Ibid., 74.
[115] Critchley, *Continental Philosophy*, 73, 88, 112.
[116] Bronner, *Critical Theory*, 1f.

Receptive Generosity and Interdependent Personhood

valued and repeated continuously, perhaps endlessly, to prevent human autonomy from being subsumed by confident overdeterminations.[117]

Adorno is pessimistic about overcoming injustice and violence to achieve genuine human freedom, and as such he is considered a "dark" thinker. Postmodernist analysts, on the other hand, fault Adorno for never rejecting the possibility of rational reconciliation among discourses and perspectives,[118] but Coles interprets Adorno in contradiction to widespread opinion concerning Adorno's unrelenting gloominess.[119] Coles identifies in Adorno a portrayal of enlightenment as a form of receptive generosity and an understanding of both thought and ethics as being dialogical in character.[120] For Coles, standard readings do not appreciate Adorno's insistence that negative dialectics is an activity or practice whose end is in the performance itself and not in codified theses. Coles writes, "Given Adorno's claim that all declarations about the world are nonidentical to that which they seek to identify, thinking must be the endlessly renewed activity of moving beyond one's current conceptualizations."[121] In other words, Adorno remains faithful to the conception of critical theory as a method that ruthlessly interrogates all systems in the name of freedom. Adorno is consistent on this to the point of arguing that negative dialectics must, as ongoing event, surpass its own conceptualizations through the encounter with non-identity.[122]

Coles construes negative dialectics as an ethical vision and as a process of receptive suffering that evokes new possibilities as it brings to light forms of suffering that have remained hidden. While this activity "endlessly solicit[s] receptive generosity," it also names the tragedy that occurs whenever identities are enclosed as a result.[123] The acknowledgment of the ethical may itself become problematic if declarations engage proponents in the maintenance of doctrinal specificity and thus remove them from continuing in receptive generosity. Coles sees Adorno negotiating this tension by developing his thought in a "constellational" manner; that is, by

[117] Adorno, *Negative Dialectics*. See Held, *Introduction to Critical Theory*, 200–22.

[118] Held, *Introduction to Critical Theory*, 79f.

[119] Coles, *Rethinking Generosity*, 75. In this endeavor, he is not alone. See Sherratt, *Adorno's Positive Dialectic*.

[120] Coles, *Rethinking Generosity*, 76.

[121] Ibid., 80.

[122] Coles, *Rethinking Generosity*, 81.

[123] Ibid.

aligning declarations in an imagined constellation of ideas that overlap and prod one another. Against Habermas's reading, Coles finds that Adorno pursues his "morality of thinking" as a reconsideration of enlightenment freed from the practice of domination.[124]

Coles turns to *Dialectic of Enlightenment,* which Adorno co-authored with Max Horkheimer, to interpret their prefatory remark that "myth is already enlightenment; and enlightenment reverts to mythology."[125] Coles reads their claim as an assertion that "mythical closure," that is, the framing of knowledge in determinate and definitive structures, is an intrinsic element of the process of enlightenment. The pursuit of accurate insight entails the creation of "myths" that shoulder both falsehood and truth, and this becomes the condition of subverting correlative hubristic dangers for a more generous engagement with the world.[126] For Adorno and Horkheimer, modernity equates the unknown with that which is to be feared and intends to address this fear by achieving total understanding. Contrarily, their alternative construal of enlightenment accepts that the other is always epistemically *nonidentical,* or both itself as the object of recognition as well as the excess beyond the grasp of cognition. The dialectic, then, is an unending activity of language at the edge of knowledge, never entirely free from the mythical but always dialogically exploring what remains beyond conceptual identification.[127]

Acknowledging epistemic limits, Adorno adopts a *"style of thinking animated by concerns that demand a difficult receptive engagement with otherness."*[128] Adorno maps the terrain of this engagement by exploring the relationship between identity and non-identity in *Negative Dialectics.* Every thought, as an attempt to comprehend the world, simultaneously cloaks aspects of the world in concealment, leaving it consistently nonidentical despite the thinker's best efforts.[129] Concealment is not always unjust, but every person's particularity generates significant blindness and injustice. Reflecting on this truth of human experience is to become aware of how one is implicated in the damage that ensues,[130] but there is no

[124] Ibid., 81–83.
[125] Adorno and Horkheimer, *Dialectic of Enlightenment,* 84.
[126] Ibid., 85.
[127] Ibid., 85–87.
[128] Ibid., 93. Emphasis original.
[129] Ibid., 94.
[130] Ibid., 97f.

Receptive Generosity and Interdependent Personhood

"identical self" that stands apart from relationship with non-identity; instead, the self exists *through* a relation to difference that transcends calculated identities of other-awareness.[131] This finite positioning would generate unsurmountable forms of suffering were there not, Adorno claims, a capability of thought to recognize the contradictions between its truth claims and ongoing concealment, and consequently shift perspective back and forth between internal coherence and external wildness.[132] Adorno contends that this dialectic of consciousness, while never capable of escaping finitude, affords human beings the most opportunity to lessen the suffering that blindness entails.[133]

So, the morality of thinking is indeed, Coles claims, not simply an exercise of epistemic humility but a practice of *caritas* toward other human beings that epitomizes receptive generosity. The capacity to recognize the specificity of the other and, in turn, to participate in "real giving" by seeking the joy of the other, is the shape of this generosity. One's generosity cannot be based on a claimed undistorted perception of one's object, which is impossible, nor should generosity be reduced to satisfying wants that have been generated by the consumer culture Adorno critiques. Rather, authentic generosity both responds to the current reality of the other and invites the other to enhance their receptive generosity toward the world. The gift is necessarily agonistic, for the invitation toward receptivity includes critically challenging others at their present limits.[134] Receptivity also requires the respectful maintenance of distance between self and non-identical others, lest the abstractions of totalizing thought drain the world of its "color."[135]

Could we ever reach definitive conclusions through which the non-identical has been identified and violence has abated? It is possible to eisegete Adorno as a visionary utopian, and Coles cites passages that raise the prospect of complete peace and enlightenment. It appears contradictory to utter such evocations in tandem with the pursuit of negative dialectics, but the paradox is resolved by recognizing Adorno's constellational practice as a manifestation of his morality of thinking. Because concepts are partial

[131] Ibid., 99.
[132] Ibid., 99–101.
[133] Ibid., 101.
[134] Ibid., 104–106.
[135] Ibid., 106f. The metaphor of color is drawn by Coles from Adorno, *Negative Dialectics*, 405.

THE CONTESTABLE CHURCH

representation of the nonidentical object, they must be gathered together and juxtaposed in order to determine their meanings, reveal their shortcomings, and through their tensions suggest new directions for thought.[136] Adorno exemplifies this by simultaneously imagining the transcendence and the persistence of violent encounters. Placed together as two poles of thought, the hope for redemption and the resignation to finitude transfigure one another by reversing their directional tendencies. Brought down to earth in movements of thought, eschatological vision shifts from a surreal longing to an animating discontent that struggles against the tragedies of existence. Meanwhile, the acknowledgement of one's conceptual transgressions abandons a restrictive sense of futility when aroused by the notion that the destructiveness of relationality is surmountable.[137] The opposing concepts restrain and uproot one another in the negative dialectic.

For Coles, Adorno engenders a dialogical practice in response to the indeterminacy of the non-identical. The object, elusively evading comprehensive definition, evokes both philosophy and art in a continual epistemological movement between approaching and withdrawing from otherness. Adorno does not reject the ideal for consensus, but rather relativizes it as one dimension of the relationship with non-identity. The ineliminable contestations between self and other, and the constraints of situated finitude, implicate dissent as an equally permanent aspect of dialogical encounter. Every act of consensus entails some subjugation of specificity and possibility, whereas every act of dissent includes the yearning for a fuller reconciliation among diverse subjects. Agonistic generosity cultivates dialogue in the tension between the two ideals.[138]

The term "dialogue" is employed to cover many forms and mediums of exchange and many types of objects as interlocutors, whether personal, collective, or even material and abstract. Coles expounds upon Adorno's concept of non-identity to illuminate elements of the common-sense understanding of dialogue as interpersonal encounter. Intersubjective communication is permeated by non-identity, which proclaims not only the distance between subjects but the *interior* distance between envisioned self-identity and the shadowed recesses of one's very being. Receptive generosity leads a communicant to reject the "face" that presents a person's

[136] Coles, *Rethinking Generosity*, 109–11.
[137] Ibid., 111–17.
[138] Ibid., 126–28.

144

Receptive Generosity and Interdependent Personhood

immanent self-understanding and risk articulating a portrait that may not itself be received.[139]

Habermas was a student of Adorno and Horkheimer and became the standard-bearer of critical theory in the second generation. He is perhaps best regarded for his writings on communication theory, which have shaped theoretical developments in deliberative democracy.[140] For Habermas, human beings are fundamentally constituted by communication, such that engaging in communicative activity is not a matter of voluntaristic election.[141] What makes an action genuinely communicative, and correlatively reciprocal, is the acknowledgment of the other's social identity as an individual offering that which is to be understood. When dialogical partners agree on the rules of discourse, identical meaning of terms and values arises.[142] This proper end of "pure reversibility" is achieved, or at least approached, via the cognitive ability to "shift position" in perspective, imagining the communicative process not just in the first but in the second and third persons. Coles considers this understanding of communication to be a "pressurized framework" that constricts the available energy that can be devoted to wrestling with non-identity.[143]

Everyday speech-acts serve the pragmatic ends of normal life and best achieve these ends when they are based on the goal of agreement concerning what is objective and normative. The employment of open criticism grants legitimacy to agreements that generate collective action. Here again is pressure applied to reach decisions, but Habermas sees the demands loosened in the alternate speech forms of poetry and argumentative discourse.[144] The latter holds to the problem-solving goal and the consensual ideal of everyday communication while relieving pressure by "extending the clock" into infinity.[145]

The consensual ideal generates two principles at the heart of Habermas's discourse ethics. The "principle of discourse ethics" proper declares

[139] Ibid., 128f.

[140] On Habermas's influence, and the debate between deliberative and radical democracy, see Kapoor, "Deliberative Democracy or Agonistic Pluralism?," 459–66.

[141] Coles, *Rethinking Generosity*, 139.

[142] Ibid., 140f.

[143] Ibid., 142.

[144] Ibid., 143.

[145] Ibid., 146f.

that "only those norms are valid that meet (or could meet) with the approval of all affected in their capacity as *participants in a practical discourse*." The assumption of justification depends on the "principle of universalization" that says "all affected can accept the consequences and the side effects [a norm's] *general* observance can be anticipated to have for the satisfaction of *everyone's* interest."[146] In short, genuine agreements are those that achieve the consensus of all participants, who also have acknowledged the terms of implementation. Against critics of these principles, Habermas lodges the charge of a performative contradiction because the very pursuit of persuasive argumentation assumes the goal of unanimity.[147]

Against Adorno, Habermas does not implicate reason in the tragedy of particularity. Rather, alienation stems from others construing their relationships in terms of opposition. Agonism is the lamentable condition to be supplanted by the quest for rational consensus. Because of humanity's essentially communicative nature, persons are characterized by the commitment to seek agreement. It is an ontological surd that humans agree to agree, or at least approach ever closer.[148]

It is important to recognize that Habermas consistently presents consensus as an asymptotic ideal and not a concrete condition for the realization of discourse ethics. He accepts the persistence of conflict such that the general interest may not harmonize optimally for each participant. Thus, he envisions his principles of discourse ethics as the tools to foster fair compromise. Coles finds that discord lacks a positive valence for Habermas, being a deficient form of relationality that is managed at worst and overcome at best.[149] On the other hand, Habermas's understanding of the ability to shift between perspectives, noted above, leads him to see self-identity as originating in the subject perceiving itself from the other's point of view.[150] Communicative relationality allows selves to recognize their own reality, and the realities of others, as autonomous beings, consequently assuming self-ownership through the arising of these recognitions

---

[146] Qtd. in ibid., 147. Original source is Habermas, *Moral Consciousness and Communicative Action*, 64–66. Emphasis original.

[147] Coles, *Rethinking Generosity*, 147f.

[148] Ibid., 150.

[149] Ibid., 151f.

[150] Ibid., 153.

Receptive Generosity and Interdependent Personhood

and of the demands made through interpersonal encounter.[151] It is by becoming accountable to the community that the self individuates as a responsible person capable of making choices free of blind habituation. The pressure of agreement should never be employed to override these developments in one's dialogical partners.[152] Rather, the self must maintain openness to others' critiques in the continual unfoldment of coexistence and communication.

Coles returns to Adorno to critique Habermas's communicative theory. He begins first by reviewing what Habermas has to say about the dimensions of existence that lie outside the domain of intersubjectivity. Habermas divides the world at large into "outer" or non-human nature and "inner" nature or the occulted aspects of the human psyche. With regard to the former, Habermas perceived no relationship to nature beyond the ends of instrumental control. Unlike Kant, he contends that human beings experience the otherness of nature through the laws that it supplies while affirming that our recognition of this actuality grants us our sovereignty. Because no other relationship with nature is possible, nature has no interrogative role in discourse.[153] Concerning the interior of the human person, Habermas critiques Freud and claims that the impulses and drives of the unconscious are not extralinguistic elements of psychology. They are rather motives and concepts that have been detached from the communicative realm by social power pressures and need only be retrieved by an internal application of the language of public communication.[154]

Coles responds that Habermas ignores his own acknowledgment of philosophy's inevitable finitude. His quasi-transcendentalism is more asserted than argued, and his linguistic constitution of the subject is defended by a pragmatic epistemology that says no needs are experienced that are not interpreted with language.[155] But, echoing Freud and a previous critic of Habermas, Coles notes the problem of equating knowledge with being. Moreover, as physical beings, humans participate in what Adorno calls "somatic moments" or openness to the world through our embodiment, which extends beyond linguistic conceptualization. Our

[151] Ibid., 154, 156.
[152] Ibid., 157f.
[153] Ibid., 160f.
[154] Ibid., 161–63.
[155] Ibid., 163–65.

senses generate a perceptual field bearing characteristics that are not exhausted by language. Language-based cognition and the bodily world are inescapably non-identical. The soundings of the latter's depth by the former are open to correction and reinterpretation.[156] Coles does not provide any examples, but one that comes readily to mind is the perception of the Earth's rotation. For observers here on the ground, the Sun appears to rise and set in a journey around the sky, and so this common-sense judgment was granted for generations. The truth concerning the movement of celestial objects eventually became apparent through more rigorous observation and calculation, extending the domain of language to the point of taking in the solar system.

For Adorno, it is this unending, questioning engagement with nature that helps human beings to make sense and find purposes for their lives, and the means by which our judgments are formed, broken apart, and reshaped.[157] If human thriving is based on dialogical encounter with the non-identical, then negative dialectics provides "an ethical-aesthetic sensibility," says Coles, that protects the edge where encounters take place.[158] This attitude contrasts with Habermas's interpretation of the human condition as constituted by pressure, be it the pressure of resource scarcity in persons' relationship with nature or the social pressure of coordinating collective action.[159] It is through Adorno's morality of thinking that Coles finds a depressurization of relationships with the other. Thought resists forceful impositions, breaking through the immediate to consider new possibilities for understanding the world and acting. While thought exhibits its own limiting compulsion to enclose identifications, it is nonetheless capable of self-critique. Coles argues that Adorno does not deny or eliminate pressure from the dialogical process, but rather constrains it as one aspect of relating to both nature and society.[160]

Raising the question of practical import, Coles contends that the inescapable presence of non-identity de-centers the noble but fallible goal of consensuality. Rather, life is best lived in the tension between pursuing unanimity and receiving otherness with epistemological and ontological

---

[156] Ibid., 165f.
[157] Ibid., 167.
[158] Ibid., 168.
[159] Ibid., 168f.
[160] Ibid., 170–72.

humility.[161] Habermas's discourse ethics tolerates agonism insofar as it may be subdued and directed toward universalization of norms, but Adorno's universalism of respectful receptivity encourages the exploration of possibilities beyond established rules and conventions. Coles argues that this sensibility broadens the range of diversity brought into the dialogue and heightens the sense of caution applied to all formulations of identity.[162] Paradoxically, Adorno's vision remains both hopeful and tragic in that it seeks ever-increasing interactions between non-identical beings while acknowledging that all determinations partake in violence because of their limiting contours. Coles suggests receptive generosity as the ethic that powers thoughtful human action in this ongoing dialectic without conceivable conclusion.

The Ground and End of Generosity

Coles offers a dynamic and inspiring vision of the generous encounter with difference, and one that is helpful for Baptists who seek an affirmative understanding of conflict in discernment. The path of his intellectual pilgrimage through the thinkers discussed in *Rethinking Generosity* highlights prominent issues in Baptist faith and practice. First, the tension between the idea of subjective sovereignty and the social construction of enlightenment in Kant parallels the divided Baptist mind over mutual accountability in community versus the privileging of private judgment. Second, both ends of the Baptist spectrum described above are strangely oblivious to the tragic in their midst, despite traditional teaching on human sinfulness. Baptists who stress their unity in truth express an overconfidence that dissent can be sublimated through proper teaching and mutual goodwill. Baptists who stress the mutability principle, especially as it is fulfilled through private judgment, lack the resources to address the alienation and egoism that emerge as individuals offer forth personal opinion as a means of self-satisfaction rather than as humble gift to the community in which it will be evaluated. Finally, in critiquing Habermas via Adorno, Coles helpfully problematizes the Baptist temptation to curtail conflict within a spiritual-sounding pressure toward consensus. It is increasingly common to valorize consensus decision-making over against, say, majority voting, especially when consensus is held up as a marker of early Baptist polity and

[161] Ibid., 173f.
[162] Ibid., 176f.

thus as something to consider recovering.[163] While replacing simple voting with consensus-based deliberation may be an improvement in Baptist polity, doing so without consideration of the "pressurization" away from insights will be damaging to the collective ability to hear the Spirit through individual voices in the congregation.

Baptists will also do well to critically examine the persistence of Coles's secularity in *RG* and the impact it has on his conception of the relationship between teleological and ateleological impulses in political life. Advancing a theme articulated in his prior work, *SPO*, Coles continues to pose Christian theism as a foil to his vision of dialectical inquiry toward common goods. His generosity toward Christianity is not entirely absent, for he acknowledges that his account of *caritas* is indebted to the theological narrative even though he intends to transcend the latter.[164] But this receptivity is attenuated because it is precisely the intellectual demise of the sovereign, creation-ordering God that Coles takes to be the welcome opportunity to ethic that becomes characteristic of his contributions to political theory.[165] God has inspired, throughout history, a blind generosity without receptivity that has taken shape in conquests, holocausts, and persecutions. Here again one witnesses Coles's pragmatist consequentialism: the case against God depends not on ontology, but implication. The claim that God's self-identity as the source of moral value is incompatible with God's receptivity of creational otherness will be critiqued below via Marney's account of human responsibility. In the meantime, three concerns will be raised about the validity of basing receptive generosity on naturalistic assumptions. Two are briefly reviewed while the third forms the basis for engaging Marney on the orientation of generosity and dissent toward the realization of newness.

First, Coles demonstrates an inconsistency by ruling out God as a possible basis for constructing the *ethos* of receptive generosity. According to his narrative, the term "God" only names a determinate formation of ontological concepts and doctrines bound together in dogmatic formulation. Adherents grasp this constellation as the framework for the orderly arrangement of all objects and others, making "identical" judgments as to

---

[163] E.g., Leonard, *Challenge of Being Baptist*, 44.
[164] *Self/Power/Other*, 3.
[165] Ibid., 23.

Receptive Generosity and Interdependent Personhood

their worth with respect to this account of reality. So, God, though conceptually infinite, is contained by the finite expressibility of theological reason. Coles's own proposal of receptive generosity hinges on the notion that natural reality as such exceeds reason and language, never to be delimited by categorical determinations. Because he needs description to remain ever imperfect, he enlists Kant's awe before the sublime and Adorno's respect for the extra-linguistic character of all things in order to invoke the moral call of constant revision and contestation.

If the natural world, mapped in reductive terms by the sciences and more immediately by our personal perceptions, may solicit such hesitating wonder, on what basis does Coles reject a transcendent reality that invites the same, one that simultaneously appears within and extends beyond frail formulations? His justification stems from a pragmatic but misleading dismissal of Christian discourse as a restrictive teleological cage that traps the imagination within the identical. Briefly, it will be enough to note the strong *apophatic* stream of Christian theology that emphasizes the mystery of God beyond human capacities to comprehend. According to the classical concept of the *analogia entis* (analogy of being), articulated most fully in the work of Thomas Aquinas, the being of God is both similar to and non-identical with the being of the created order. Christian theology therefore lives within a tension that names both God in revelation and God in profound otherness, with the result that language can only describe God in a limited, analogical fashion.[166] Although Baptists are not known for their philosophical theology, the basic principle of God's "hiddenness" to human understanding can be found especially in Baptists' early confessions.[167]

The second concern voices the much-discussed question of post-theological ethics. To his credit, Coles recognizes the force of the charge that

[166] Boersma, *Heavenly Participation*, 70–74.

[167] E.g., The inaugural article of the *First London Confession* of 1644 begins, "That God as he is in himself, cannot be comprehended of any but himself, dwelling in that inaccessible light, that no eye can attaine unto, whom never man saw, nor can see..." (qtd. in Lumpkin, *Baptist Confessions of Faith*, 156). In the same work see pp. 198, 252, 298. Coles does come to see the importance of the apophatic dimension as the impetus for Christian generosity at the edges, particularly as this is expressed in the writings of Rowan Williams, the prolific theologian and Archbishop of Canterbury from 2002 to 2012. See Hauerwas and Coles, *Christianity, Democracy, and the Radical Ordinary*, 174–94.

God's death creates a moral vacuum in which valuations of the good are privileged despite lacking adequate justification. He consequently concludes the chapter on Adorno with what he acknowledges to be all-too-brief response to this concern as expressed by Charles Taylor in *Sources of the Self*.[168] Here again one witnesses Coles's pragmatism driving his argument. Through the eyes of Adorno, we can see there is "something greatly worthy of our embrace" that arises through or is enhanced by negative-dialectical activity; namely, intelligence, freedom, and the "richness of being."[169] The first atrophies apart from receptivity, the second is inseparable with it, and the third would be otherwise occulted by enclosed systems of thought. The sense that these ends are best achieved through engagement with otherness is an experiential faith that testifies to what generosity has achieved and voices hope that it will generate yet new possibilities at the tensional edges. Coles advances the claim with admirable humility, offering the suggestion that receptive generosity contains "animating power" but that it remains very much untried.[170]

This answer to theological accounts of ethics via Taylor raises the question of meta-ethical commitments that determine receptivity's limits. Surely his peers in the academy and grassroots activism alike can be largely expected to affirm the importance of intelligence, freedom, and diversity, but why, indeed, are these compelling moral plumb lines in the first place? In his corpus, Coles insists not only on these, but on other moral claims with an implicit realism about their objective status. So, for example, social arrangements and dispositions beyond the pale include slavery and hierarchies based on race, gender, and national origin.[171] Reasonably, one can rule out of place values that contradict the salutary functioning of receptive generosity, such as the violent ambition of the self-made pagan critiqued by Augustine and seconded by Coles in *SPO*. The possibility of contradiction means that the ethics of receptive generosity are not simply inculcated in the performance or realized as its conclusion, however tentative. The dialogical practice is necessarily informed by a pre-existing vision of the good, even if that vision must embed itself within an agonistic relationship between concept and expression to be perceived with greater clarity and

---

[168] Coles, *Receptive Generosity*, 134.
[169] Ibid., 135f.
[170] Ibid., 136f.,
[171] Coles, *Beyond Gated Politics*, 39.

depth. Otherwise, if there are no presumptive moral facts or values, can any be realized at the end of a process which, in point of fact, has not end?

The aim here is not to stray into a discussion of the philosophy of ethics far in excess of my present purposes. Rather, the question at hand is the consistency of Coles's presentation of receptive generosity as it operates at the very edges between agreed understandings of the good and radical others with powerfully contradictory visions. On the one hand, Coles densely and convincingly argues for an ethical orientation toward welcoming the non-identical in transformative encounter. On the other hand, in his books Coles frames these arguments in sharply convictional, forceful, and quite negative assessments of discourses and arrangements of power that he finds antithetical to the radical democratic project.

What is being put to the question here is the third concern that will animate the following discussion: whether Coles is right to insist, as he does in *RG* and throughout his writings, that it is possible to balance the ateleological and the teleological in perpetual interaction, one always folding into the other to prevent either violent negation of difference or an incapacity to achieve a functional politics. If anything, Coles emphasizes the ateleological in his explication of the practice of radical democracy while stressing the teleological in his rhetorical gestures against anti-democratic forces he sees in the world. But might not the latter reproduce new forms of blindness against visions of the good because they have been labeled and dismissed according to his reference frame? Meanwhile, is the former ultimately nihilistic, for what hope can be sustained in an unending and ultimately unresolvable process?

While Coles provides a worthy and important critique of theological dispositions toward closure that oppress the emergence of challenging and prophetic perspectives, many Baptists might look upon radical democracy and wonder about the ground and the end that support receptive generosity. For them, compassionate openness to difference will be rooted in the gospel, but they, too, have been torn between the teleological and the ateleological in a manner not far different from Coles. Perhaps the way forward is not to aim for an uneasy balance, but for a teleological orientation that both inspires receptivity and directs it toward a resolution that remains outside our reach. This mode of actuating dissent can be seen in the writings of the southern baptist pastor-theologian Carlyle Marney, to whom we now turn.

Personhood and Contestation in Carlyle Marney

Although he is not well-remembered at present, Marney (1916–1978) was one of the most prominent pastor-theologians in mid-twentieth century America. Born and raised in rural east Tennessee, Marney received his higher education at Southern Baptist schools and pastored prominent Southern Baptist churches. Well-regarded as an eloquent preacher who distilled his vast learning in a folksy, appropriately Southern vernacular, he travelled the country to give invited sermons and lectures. While the sketch of his resume implies a figure comfortably ensconced in the establishment, Marney was considered a rogue by the Southern Baptist leadership and conservative elites. Having abandoned his own conservatism while a student at the Southern Baptist Theological Seminary, Marney criticized the parochialism and theological narrowness of the denomination in turn. Early in his career he sought to be an agent of reform within the Convention while also participating in the ecumenical movement and developing close contacts with mainline Protestants. Deeply concerned about social issues as well, Marney pressed the Church on racial reconciliation and for meaningful engagement with the problems of poverty and class stratification. The inertia he witnessed on all fronts inculcated in his later years a growing pessimism about the institutional structures of Christianity and a deepening universalist vision of humanity. After leaving Myers Park Baptist Church due to health concerns, Marney founded a retreat center in the mountains of western North Carolina known as Interpreter's House. Its purpose was to be a place of rest, healing, and renewal for ministers and others who felt wounded in their vocations of service. Animated largely by Marney's charismatic presence, Interpreter's House closed upon his death.[172]

Marney's biographer identifies him as both a "pilgrim" and a "boundary person" whose ideas and self-identity evolved in response to a lifetime of crossing borders between cultures, sensibilities, and thought systems.[173] His very marginality is likely the key to his current obscurity; lacking any natural constituency or institutional base his works have not been readily disseminated. All but one of Marney's books are now out of print.[174] His public sermons and lectures, which were key vehicles of his thinking in his

---

[172] For this outline of Marney's life, see Carey, *Carlyle Marney, passim.*
[173] Ibid., 16.
[174] The exception being *Priests to Each Other.*

Receptive Generosity and Interdependent Personhood

later years, remain unpublished. Although his education and ministerial career were conducted entirely within the Southern Baptist fold, Marney eventually de-emphasized the labels of "Baptist" and even "Christian." His new understanding, as he related it during a series of lectures at Myers Park in 1974, was that "humanity" is the only true noun and more specific terms are simply qualifying adjectives.[175] Yet, paradoxically, it was through this cosmopolitanism that Marney also renewed his commitment to the traditional language and symbols of the Christian faith.[176] His dialectical tension between the particular and the universal, between new directions and well-trodden paths, makes him a fitting figure to assist in the exploration of a radically-democratic Baptist ecclesiology. Therefore, if the last chapter sought to rehabilitate an establishment figure who has been increasingly marginalized, this present effort attempts to recover a marginal figure and demonstrate his relevance for those who still wear the label "Baptist," whether with confidence or hesitation. This recovery will proceed by tracing his understanding of personhood as an interdependent phenomenon, its development into his concept of the "new humanity," and the significance of this vision for Christian community. This movement can be traced through four of Marney's principal works: *Faith in Conflict* (1957), *The Recovery of the Person* (1969), *The Coming Faith* (1970), and *Priests to Each Other* (1974).

Marney's first book, *Faith in Conflict*, is an apologetic for Christianity amidst the challenges of science, evil, prejudice, and death. In this beginning of his corpus, he takes up the theme of human personhood that will remain his central concern for the rest of his life. Here, it serves as a key element in the defense of the faith. Marney writes in his first chapter on science that discoveries and theories tend to revolve around great personalities.[177] Furthermore, the entire enterprise is dependent upon human scientists as much as the existence of a tool is justified by the craftsman. Both facts indicate that "[p]ersonality is paramount."[178] In the chapter on evil, Marney states that the answer to this problem is personal; the Person whom Christians claim as the center of history.[179] The incarnation is God's

---

[175] Ibid., 110.
[176] Ibid., 107.
[177] Marney, *Faith in Conflict*, 21.
[178] Ibid., 23.
[179] Ibid., 70–73.

155

involvement in personhood, sharing the experience of being, like all persons, "Unique, of another origin, a microcosm, capable of entrance into infinity; he is individually unrepeatable, always subject, never object; he is a category of value, a primary whole, indestructible, an irreplaceable form...."[180] But this high praise for persons is nothing like a more confessional version of Kant's subjective sovereign. When Marney celebrates the person, he does not mean a figure that stands alone as the master of its own fate and the bearer of self-generated value and values. In the last chapter on death, Marney draws a distinction between individuality and personality. The former is a distortion of humanity's true purpose. Human personality, on the other hand, is dependent upon the aptitude for community. He identifies it as a "task to be achieved" as the self creatively explores its potential in company with others and in the face of encroaching death. Every human not properly a *being* but is unique as a process or, in Marney's terms, an *event*.

The programmatic statement in the preface of *The Recovery of the Person* (hereafter, *RP*) reads, "The church is the womb within which persons happen and recognize one another."[181] Here one finds an optimistic claim for "church" that lacks the qualifications to come in later writings, but for now, at least, the ecclesial community is the declared ground for personhood. That assumption in place, the critical issue for Marney is not the meaning of the church, but the meaning of person. His insistent claim is that to be a person is to be involved in relationship, and that one's personhood is fashioned and refashioned through honest exchange with others. "The only value we have," he says, "is the personal in relation."[182]

That the dialogue between selves be *honest* is essential for achieving whole personhood. Each individual bears the tragic marks of finitude in the form of one's own myth created through localization in a particular setting, but experiencing life together with another cultivates the opportunity to share one's myth, hear a new myth, and shift one's perceived situatedness back and forth between them. Forsaking this process leaves an individual to be hoodwinked by one's own mask, thereby abandoning personhood for an ignorant loneliness.[183] As Marney also notes in *Priests to*

---

[180] Ibid., 74f.
[181] Marney, *Recovery of the Person*, 9.
[182] Ibid., 20.
[183] Ibid., 136f.

Each Other (*PO*), inherited cultural myths may also distort the Church's faithfulness. Such honesty must extend to collective distortions of the gospel, especially in the American context.[184]

In *RP*, Marney begins to consider the implications of personality for his projected "new human race." Declaring a "humanistic" orientation toward theology, Marney sees knowledge of God as built on one's experience with fellow human beings. This knowledge is therefore not the theoretical product of cognition, but an outcome of active morality as one takes responsibility for the condition of the world.[185] He goes so far as to contend that biblical propositions concerning God are derived through the authors' understanding of human beings.[186] This anthropocentrism appears to lead Marney to the brink of advocating a kind of deism, in which reason discerns an otherwise absent God exclusively through his handiwork. It is not until the second part of *RP* that Marney incorporates a theology of revelation into this account. Critiquing both Friedrich Schleiermacher and Karl Barth for inscribing God as too incomprehensibly transcendent, Marney contends that God exhibits a personhood analogous to that of human beings. This personhood is demonstrated through the incarnation, for in Jesus Christ God appears wearing a face.[187] Revelation offers no exception for Marney to the notion that God is known through personality, for Jesus is the very person in whom God supremely communicates himself.

Marney writes in *RP* that the biblical hope of renewal is based on identifying oneself with this particular man who was himself obedient to death on a cross. Through this identification persons come to recognize their innate freedom and responsibility as agents.[188] The influence of Jewish philosopher Martin Buber is made apparent as Marney declares the cross to be, for Christians, the hyphen of I-Thou where "we receive our I-ness by receiving his Thou-ness."[189] The portrait of human wholeness given in Jesus Christ engenders the new race as persons-in-becoming confront the darkness they bear in themselves. Marney writes in *The Coming*

[184] Marney, *Priests to Each Other*, 48, 55.

[185] Ibid., 36f.

[186] Ibid., 62.

[187] Ibid., 96. Marney draws upon the church father Irenaeus of Lyons for this image.

[188] Ibid., 99–109; 145–49.

[189] Ibid., 146.

Faith (*CF*) that redemption entails recognition of one's limits and the "primal powers" of sinfulness. It is not possible to undertake this examination in isolation; rather, one confesses this depth before others so as to be heard and loved. The confessor switches places to hear and love others in their journey of redemption.[190]

The church as a genuine community, then, is not primarily for Marney a setting for proclamation or a catalyst for missionary endeavor, but the fellowship of hearers enabling each other's personhood in the journey to wholeness. Practicing listening and acceptance, participants in this community become resting places for one another as they unburden themselves of their limitations.[191] The mutual interchange of hearer and heard fosters true *koinonia*, which means "to know each other in common. The possessed is possessor, the given is giver, the heard is hearer, and the brother is a means of grace."[192] As Marney explains in *CF*, ministry and mission to the world are realized as the fruit of this central practice. The church is a house of healing that makes ministers of its members and then sends them out to save.[193]

Marney briefly mentions Martin Luther's teaching about believer priesthood in *CF*, but it is not until his final book that he elaborates his ecclesiology in terms of this doctrine that has become so central to Baptist identity. In the introduction to *PO*, he identifies the conviction driving Christian community as being "that the Man Christ can make us whole," and in consequence the church may become a "well society" that engages its surroundings with responsible discernment—"aiming to keep the world out and bring the world in."[194] The priesthood of believers is the mode of relationship in which this wholeness emerges. Marney's account of how priesthood operates demonstrates that it is a synonym for personhood. He restates his belief that God has placed responsibility for the creation of a better world in human hands.[195] But our habit is to evade responsibility, and one method to that end is to define irrevocable answers to the questions of our existence.[196] Among these answers is the self-image one holds,

[190] Marney, *The Coming Faith*, 142–44.
[191] Marney, *Recovery of the Person*, 157f.
[192] Ibid., 158.
[193] Marney, *The Coming Faith*, 158f.
[194] Marney, *Priests to Each Other*, 3.
[195] Ibid., 64.
[196] Ibid., 66f.

Receptive Generosity and Interdependent Personhood

which is the same as the individual myth Marney names in *RP*. The prescription is identical as well: Christian growth requires the "nerve to submit" to the correction of self-image through the wisdom of the church. This is a means to answer Christ's call to deny oneself.[197] For Marney, though, the church that engages this work is not necessarily a formal, organized body. Due to an invasive idolatry, the institutional church must be set aside:

> *The correction of our images of the self in Christ has to happen among my friends who care about Christ—my real church.* I wish to God I could just say "corrected by the church," but the modern church is the religious institutional encasement of our submission to the images of our society. So, I have to ask you to submit to the judgment of a different church, that small and intimate one, that personal one composed of whatever little group in Christ you are beginning to be able to trust.[198]

Marney speaks of God being silent and leaving the work of shaping the new humanity in the hands of selves accepting the challenge to become persons. Traditionally, the fundamental orientation of priesthood is that the priest is a mediating agent between God and human beings. The priesthood of believers is a way of naming how each Christian has the privilege and duty to discern how God is inviting him or her to serve the church. Has Marney wholly abandoned the "vertical" dimension of priesthood, setting the examination and critique of the various self-images entirely in the "horizontal" exchange between the willing actors? It is easy to read him this way, but there are a few moments in his writing where he asserts God's involvement in the personal dialectic. Marney, in *RP*, identifies the Holy Spirit as an active participant in the relationships that make up the Christian community. Because the Spirit becomes a part of the inner life of each Christian, persons become means of grace. God is not entirely absent but manifested in the mediatory sacrament of human beings, and so "we meet God in each other."[199] In *PO*, the correction of one's self-image, when practiced among those for whom Christ is important, is a correction that occurs in Christ. Marney has insisted that Jesus is the bar at which the standard for human wholeness is set, but no one can clear that bar by singular effort. Ultimately, one's self-image must be submitted

---

[197] Ibid., 68.
[198] Ibid., 69. Emphasis original.
[199] Marney, *Recovery of the Person*, 154.

THE CONTESTABLE CHURCH

to Christ for correction, but unless he is met in a setting where "two or three are gathered,"[200] then the Christ to whom one is submitting may be yet another image. Perhaps this false Jesus simply mirrors the mode of life with which a Christian is comfortable.[201] If Christ is active in the power of the Holy Spirit to make human beings whole, our best hope for hearing him speak is practicing a priesthood of mutual accountability.

Envisioning Interdependent Priesthood

Marney's outline of personhood as a process of becoming whole through relations with others, manifested in the church as a Christ-centered priesthood, offers a theoretical bridge between Coles's vision of receptive generosity and traditional Baptist perspectives on priesthood as mutual discipline and service. Points of contact with each will be presented in turn. Finally, a synthesis will be offered in the reappraisal of believer priesthood as receptive generosity oriented toward the eschatological consummation of human aspirations.

Marney's anthropology narrates a developmental account of selves who *become* insofar as they practice openness in their encounters with others. "Individuality" is not the preferred outcome of a life, for it names a distortion of human potential by an inward turn toward one's inherited or self-generated mythology. Authentic community offers the opportunity to surmount these limitations. The notion of crafting one's personhood through engagement with the broader realm of beings echoes Coles's articulation of the artistic self as described in the previous chapter. However, similarly to Mullins, Marney also implies a more "substantial" account of human beings. Even though our personhood is a process, Marney suggests at times that this process is grounded in a stable substrate. His repeated emphasis on "becoming whole" indicates a sense that human beings who seek personhood are entering a work of healing and not *de novo* creation. He also describes personhood in *koinonia* as the process for removing the masks that obscure our true faces.[202] Unlike Coles, Marney is happy to propose a divine blueprint for each life—an intended wellness that has been obscured rather than an open-ended, polysemous canvas upon which the self may be painted.

[200] Matthew 18:20 (NRSV).
[201] Marney, *Priests to Each Other*, 69f.
[202] Marney, *Recovery of the Person*, 157.

Receptive Generosity and Interdependent Personhood

A radical-democratic response to Marney may be that he has simply restated in different terms Augustine's notion of the "confessing self" which Coles critiqued in *SPO*. Both figures identify a depth to the self that must be plumbed in order to overcome sinfulness and realize one's divine calling. This similarity of approach is not at all surprising, given that Marney accepted Augustine as a central figure in Christian theology. Moreover, he expressed his profound indebtedness to Martin Luther, who himself relied heavily on the Bishop of Hippo.[203] Will Marney lead those who follow him into the same dilemmas of confessional imperialism which Coles has named?

Two further parallels with Coles's thought counteract this potential. First of all, Marney declares an inescapable tentativeness about theological claims. All of them originate with, and are subject to the conditions of, human thought. There are no fundamentals that may be excused from the potential for correction. The great tragedy of humanity is contentment with conceptual limits, refusing the opportunity to stretch beyond inherited frames of reference.[204] But our finitude is paired with the freedom of God's speech as a living word, such that Christians are "right to expect him to speak" in new contexts.[205] His favored image of the church as a "pilgrim people" is not only moral but intellectual. Religious convictions must be open to "continuing conversion," for, according to Marney's personalism, they are held in relation to Christ as a living Person whose life is ever excessive of comprehensive grasp.[206] Theological agreements, like political decisions and settlements, are ever subject to new insight, whether drawn from old voices in revision or new voices entering the conversation. Marney rebukes the woundedness of Christianity when its adherents refuse to accept wisdom and learning from any source, naming in particular the scientific revolutions generated by Copernicus, Darwin, and Freud.[207] His dialogical openness provides a rejoinder to Colesian concerns about Christian "jealousy" foreclosing engagement with the other.

Second, Marney echoes Adorno's tragic awareness of the suffering generated by our perspectival restrictions. His experience as a sojourner

[203] Carey, *Carlyle Marney*, 60.
[204] Ibid., 68.
[205] Marney, *Recovery of the Person*, 49.
[206] Marney, *Priests to Each Other*, 105.
[207] Marney, *The Coming Faith*, 16f.

wandering farther into exile from the Southern Baptist mainstream colors his account, as for him the inevitable violence of difference manifests most clearly in structures that restrict human imagination and agency. "Institutional repetitiveness" establishes routines that cut off the possibility of redemption,[208] and every philosophy, science, or worldview can become an opiate that turns humanity away from its responsibility to participate in its own liberation.[209] Marney justifies his turn to the "little church" for salvation because the institutional church embodies our surrender to images of self and world thrust upon us by society.

Marney also brings to the fore two key theological convictions for Baptists. First, his ecclesiology, as critical as it may be of institutional scaffolding, re-presents the Free Church vision of communities gathered together by Christ so that persons may form and be formed by one another in the quest for wholeness. In chapter 1 we noted the historical importance of mutual accountability and discipline for southern baptists. Church covenants have declared the commitment that members will "walk together" in the journey of faith, continuously circulating among themselves encouragement, teaching, and correction.[210] This is the notion of the priesthood of believers, which Marney so capably argues is a doctrine about how believers serve the fellowship by sharing their experience and understanding of God. Marney stresses, however, the conflictual rejoinder that may also occur when that understanding becomes the subject of critique.

The inescapability of boundaries to our awareness and tensions in our relationships leads Marney to stress the eschatological orientation of Christian faith. His image of the Church as a pilgrim people reflects the "new light" conviction noted earlier in this chapter. Baptists do not ascribe infallibility or definite authority to any ecclesial organization, stressing the relative character of all expressions of faithfulness and their exposure to extension or correction in the future. Hope lies in a gift not yet fully given: the fullness of the Kingdom of God revealed in what Marney describes as the new humanity. Marney agrees with Baptists and with historic Christianity in general by finding a goal to history in the person of Jesus Christ.[211] Though he has advocated an ateleological process of dialogue

---

[208] Marney, *Recovery of the Person*, 158.

[209] Ibid., 165.

[210] See DeWeese, *Baptist Church Covenants, passim*.

[211] Marney, *The Coming Faith*, 73.

Receptive Generosity and Interdependent Personhood

within the gatherings of the "real" church, he frames this by the *telos* found in a transcendent God who can and will save humanity from itself and its exhausted powers.[212] Something greater awaits humanity, which we can never know fully, let alone enact it, but we can long for and live in the light of it.

The commonalities between Coles and Marney invite Baptists to welcome tensional disagreement as an element of faithful accountability through the priesthood of all believers. Christians can only serve as priests to one another—that is, representatives of God's grace and truth in this moment—if this priesthood operates in a receptively generous manner. On the one hand, and this is the part that comes most easily, we are to *give* our insight and the fruit of our experience, sharing freely with our fellows gathered to worship and hear the wisdom of the Spirit. We speak of what we know from our immersion in the narrative of Scripture as it relates to our praying, working, playing, and all that life entails. Our discernment we offer that others may sift, evaluate, and accept as it resonates with their own life of faith. On the other hand, we are to *receive* the same from others, sitting with what we hear, asking questions, and pondering the significance. This is not a simple one-for-one exchange, however, and it may often be anything but peaceful. Coles and Marney alike contend that the other's gift may wound us, for it may be a judgment that exposes the non-identical rift between the image and the self as it is experienced from the outside. The reader may note the exceptionally striking parallel here between Adorno's agonistic rejection of the interlocutor's "face" and Marney's notion that the church should be the venue for becoming unmasked by fellow believers.

In short, Baptists need one another to function as priests, not simply because a priest has no meaning without a flock to serve, but because each person's representation of God-and-self carries limitations and obscurations which cannot be self-examined in isolation. The process of discernment produces not only conflict with competing ideas but dissenting portraits of the ones who offer them. This insight demonstrates the insufficiency of private judgment beyond even the criticisms noted above and further justifies the importance of dialogue taking place in communal settings of trust and vulnerability. Private judgment is not "wrong" or to be disallowed, for there are times when the sole individual may become a

[212] Ibid., 50; Marney, *Recovery of the Person*, 78.

163

prophet who makes plain the failures of the community to embody the gospel. Although it is useful, private judgment is not the primary mode of expressing disagreement for the church that seeks to discover together the mind of Christ in the power of the Spirit. First of all, it conceptualizes dissent as an opinion formed separately from participation in the community and subsequently shared. An emphasis on private judgment can lead to a portrait of the church as a debate society in which preformed and settled opinions are presented, brought into conflict, but never meaningfully deliberated upon. Moreover, private judgment fails to account for dissent as an exercise of the community correcting one's own perceptions of what and how one believes. Baptist must practice dissent not just from each other's opinions, but from any proponent's presumption to be transparent to oneself or to the process by which one's judgment was formed.

Marney and Coles together invite Baptists to shift disagreement away from an individual's self-assertion *over against* the church to an *ethos* of listening, testing, and weighing different voices freely *within* the church. As noted at the beginning of this chapter, southern baptists have wavered between a refusal to ascribe a positive valence to conflict, on the one hand, and on the other they have celebrated the free multiplication of opinion without recourse to sustained dialogical processes in which judgments become steppingstones on the path toward common determinations of faithfulness. The schism that erupted in the latter twentieth century sorted southern baptists generally into two camps. Although this typology simplifies the internal convictional texture of the different wings, conservatives who remain in the Southern Baptist Convention can be said to favor the principle of unity around a shared moral and theological confession. Moderates and progressives affiliated with the Alliance of Baptists and CBF commend diversity of expression as an integral component of the Baptist way of being the Church. A radical-democratic Baptist ecclesiology proposes a third way that joins these tendencies as two sides of the same coin. Accepting the necessity of the "ateleological" dimension to mutual discipleship, this vision calls Baptists to engage in receptive generosity through intentional exercises of attention and discernment. Drawing from Coles, southern baptists can realize the interdependence of the ateleological and the teleological, reconciling them, as Marney does, within a properly eschatological reference frame. Unity in truth is indeed a mark of the Church, but this is ever an aspiration and not an accomplishment, something which is sought for in "already but not yet" moments when the

Spirit opens our eyes to see one another and the work of God in our midst. Dissent serves the function not of reinforcing some abstract ideal of human rights, but of inspiring the community to reconsider the meaning of its work and witness as it continues its wilderness wanderings.

Once again, the clear difference between Coles's project and a Baptist version of radical democracy is the place held by the teleological in the communal imaginary. From this point of view, Coles's attempts to juxtapose the ateleological and the teleological in a balance is too unstable to sustain the common life. Coles wants to have his cake and eat it, too—set definite limits and values for a democratic culture but also pursue a relentless outreach to the non-identical. There can be no working around this difference: southern baptist dissent will be expressed as an instrument of retexturing the expansive narrative of God in Christ bringing about the redemption of the cosmos. Baptist teleology is not only theological and quite specifically eschatological. The vision of the future toward which God is leading humanity is the roomy frame within which conflictual dialogue occurs, guarding against fissiparous division through a shared image of our destiny. Dissent, though, is not foreclosed precisely because this future is, as Marney reminds us, beyond our ability to grasp. We cannot comprehend what the end will be beyond the images that transfix and transform us.[213] This awareness, at its best, *drives* Baptist responsiveness to difference. Thus, Baptists engage the ongoing conversation of what it means to live now in anticipation of what is to come, seeking ever to renew our understanding of what will last.

Although Coles and Baptist radical democrats may continue to disagree on the relative emphasis of the teleological and the ateleological, both would agree that the attitude of receptive generosity, while itself an intrinsic good, serves the purpose of facilitating communal discussion that eventually resolves into determinate (though ever vulnerable) judgments about the identity to be held and the actions to be taken. Radical democratic organizations are not book clubs or mere social gatherings—they set pri-

---

[213] Here there is a parallel with McClendon, who, drawing upon Ludwig Wittgenstein, describes biblical eschatology as a collection of "concrete end-pictures" that are not so much objective accounts of what will be but offer a mode of "seeing-as" that is interpreted within specific contexts and with the function of transforming a person's life (*Doctrine*, 75–93).

orities, pursue goals, and enact programs. But to not be hung up on continual reconsideration and conversation requires some instantiation of authority wherein ateleological generosity funnels into certain convictions and actions. The question of the shape of this authority, and how it manifests in particular practices among Baptists, will be the focus of the final chapter.

CHAPTER 4

AUTHORITY AND TRADITION

The cultivation of difference is an intrinsic good for both radical democracy and Baptist ecclesiology, for conflictual encounter offers an the emancipatory yet difficult path by which communities of discourse travel on the way to making decisions about the goods proper to shared flourishing. Radical democracies and local churches are not aimless discussion circles; rather, inspired by an ungraspable ultimate *telos*, each tradition intends determinate judgments in the here and now, recognizing that these are fallible and open to correction. Nevertheless, moments of decision must be discerned and enacted. The necessity of reaching decisions in a participatory polity invites reflection on the construction of authority that facilitates the reaching of conclusions, however tentative they may be, in and through processes of negotiating difference. Democratic governance, in its various permutations, must define both the locus of the authority that decides as well as the shape of authorization, or the means through which the holder(s) of authority legitimately resolve the questions circulating within the body politic.

Political democracy and Baptist ecclesial practice were both developments that emerged in opposition to ancient modes of authority that vested decision-making in an elite minority, be it hereditary autocrats and/or wealthy landowners for temporal affairs or bishops and archbishops for the religious domain. In theory, all citizens share sovereignty in a democratic society. For Baptists, the true sovereign is Jesus Christ as head of the Church, but the responsibility for discerning and implementing his will devolves to the gathered church. In older patterns of authority, the elites largely dictated their judgments and expected obedience from the rest of society. In democratic cultures and churches, decisions achieve legitimacy when they are perceived to be the outcomes of fair and accessible processes of discussion in which members have been able to freely participate. Contemporary political-liberal and democratic societies authorize decision-making through processes of voting and representative government. Through these means, it is theorized that "popular sovereignty" achieves a relative if imperfect manifestation. However, political theorists are increasingly attentive to the problem of "postdemocracy," or the conditions in Western nations that have attenuated the involvement of the general public in political activity. In such circumstances, bare proceduralism can mask resurgent elitism behind the façade of thin democratic practice.[1] But both radical democrats and Baptists are concerned with cultivating a form of political life that roots authorization in robust and distributive modes of participation by "ordinary" persons.

This chapter will examine how Baptists may authorize contestation and its resolution through two interconnected social practices so that the dialogical process is oriented toward making faithful common judgments under the rule of Christ. The term "social practice" here designates a complex, shared activity or set of activities that strives for certain goods through definite means ordered according to standards of conduct and excellence.[2] Practices provide a framework for intentionally directed common life while also possessing the flexibility needed for practitioners to adapt them to changing circumstances and contexts. The definition of a social practice is broad enough to encapsulate both general categories of human endeavor that may otherwise be called "fields," such as medicine, law, and architecture, as well as quite specific forms of human action such as the practices that mark the life of a congregation, e.g., Bible study, worship, and prayer. Larger practices frequently contain means that are practices in and of themselves. For example, surgery is one of the ways through which the practice of medicine intends the health of human beings.

The two interrelated practices, found both in the writings of Coles and in southern baptist thought and activity, are here denoted as *episkope* and *traditio*. *Episkope*, a transliteration of the ancient Greek word meaning "oversight," denotes modes of guidance or leadership that direct the community toward certain goals. In ecumenical Christian usage, *episkope* has multiple dimensions and can refer to the agency of established church leaders as well as the responsibilities of all the people. Although Coles does not use this specific term, he addresses very similar questions of shared leadership in radical democracy. *Traditio*, the Latin word from which we derive "tradition," carries a significant double meaning that will be explored in depth below. In brief, both Coles and recent Baptist theologians

[1] Ward, *Politics of Discipleship*, 63–72.
[2] Drawing upon McClendon Jr., *Ethics*, 172–76; idem., *Doctrine*, 28; Dykstra and Bass, "Times of Yearning, Practices of Faith," 6–8.

168

have employed *traditio* to express the active "traditioning" process in which a particular community carries forward the inheritance of its past but also reinterprets and redefines what has been received to meet the demands of the present moment.

Traditionally, the minority elite exercise leadership (*episkope*) as they determine the best way to guide the community through the dissemination (*traditio*) of established practices, rules, customs, obligations, policies, and procedures. So, to give a notable example from Christian history, Ignatius of Antioch, the famous first–second-century CE bishop and martyr, contended for a church polity in which the deposit of faith is preserved by bishops who serve under and stand in the place of Christ, and who communicate that deposit through their subordinate priests and deacons to the rest of the faithful, who apart from the authorized officeholders are to "do nothing."[3] But the participatory governance of radical-democratic and Baptist communities rejects the concentration of final, determinative authority in the hands of the few, even if they were elected and hold a "representative" role. Each person has equitable standing to participate in the decision-making process and novel insights that break from past conclusions are explicitly welcome. *Episkope* and *traditio* now bear a fruitfully ambivalent meaning in the ateleological openness to exchanges between inter-competent and interdependent selves that has been traced in previous chapters.

The arguments to follow will re-envision the matrix of shared authority between the pastorate and the "laity" by articulating a reciprocal process of overseeing and traditioning. This fresh interpretation of mutual responsibility provides a solution to a dilemma of pastoral authority that has plagued Baptists throughout their history while reclaiming the centrality of communal Scriptural hermeneutics. A comparison with Coles's presentation of *episkope* and *traditio* will offer insights on how to strengthen capacities for handling disagreement as integral components of cooperative discernment.

Because *episkope* is historically tied to distinct officeholders, but leadership has such an uncertain character in democratic polities, we will begin with a historical survey of southern baptist beliefs concerning pastoral authority. This review demonstrates another tension running through Baptist history regarding the extent to which the pastor's position calls for

---

[3] Ignatius of Antioch, "To the Magnesians" 7.1, 247.

169

obedience on the part of church members. The two sides of the spectrum are methodologically united in their quest to determine how the clergy may exercise authority *over* the rest of the community, but the consensus of opinion also holds that ministerial authority serves the function of "equipping" the laity to be active participants in Christian service. The duty to strengthen "ordinary" believers' competence in the practice of faith implies a more permeable, interactive quality of pastoral authority exercised in the midst of mutually enhancing relationships. This insight will invite us to consider Coles's model of leadership derived from the example of the Student Nonviolent Coordinating Committee in the 1960s and presented in a chapter of *Christianity, Democracy, and the Radical Ordinary*. Coles also understands that *episkope* aims at the empowerment of others, but he realizes, more clearly than have southern baptists, the consequences for a democratic theory of leadership; namely, leaders exist to create more leaders.

Coles's analysis of the aforementioned civil-rights group demonstrates that habituating members to a community's narrative and practices is necessary to maintain cohesion. This fits a common view of traditioning as training persons to incorporate the received wisdom of the past. Nevertheless, the proliferation of *episkope* broadly distributes the responsibility for guiding the community in the present and increases the likelihood that discrepant visions of the good will arise. Instilling the tradition in others allows discordant interpretations to emerge more vigorously. Coles explores the productive paradox of *traditio* in depth throughout his book *Beyond Gated Politics* (*BGP*), arguing for a practice of traditioning in which participants simultaneously intend to extend and subvert what has been passed down. *Traditio*, then, is the active pursuit of the friction between the teleological and the ateleological in order to reconceive the significance of identities, values, and convictions for new contexts.

This complex interpretation of *traditio* can also be found in the writings of a theological movement known as Baptist catholicity. This assemblage of scholars and ministers is urging Baptists to rethink their identity as emergent from, dependent upon, and necessarily interactive with the larger Christian or "catholic" (universal) tradition. Critics frequently misinterpret "Bapto-Catholics" as attempting to constrict theological diversity by demanding allegiance to narrow creedal parameters. This chapter will conduct a close reading of southern baptist theologian Steven Harmon who, in his seminal work *Towards Baptist Catholicity*, argues for a dialogical *traditio* model of engagement with the breadth of Christian faith and practice, one that mirrors Coles on many points.

A Baptist conception of *traditio* will hold that every Christian participates in carrying forward or reconsidering the doctrines and habits that have defined the faith. Consequently, every Christian participates in *episkope* as well. Harmon consequently argues, in a chapter of his book *Baptist Identity and the Ecumenical Future*, that Baptists and other Free Church Christians grant authority in theological and moral reasoning to the entire community of disciples. Here we see again the necessary entwinement of the two practices: oversight occurs through traditioning and the act of traditioning fosters oversight. Baptists closely tie these practices to the reading of Scripture, so finally we will turn to communal interpretation of the Bible as the key means by which Baptists may correlate them. This historic practice manifested not in the form of private Bible reading but in interactive habits of shared investigation and interpretation of Scripture for the advancement of Christian faithfulness.

Turning back to the tension named at the outset of this chapter, it will be argued that a radically-democratic Baptist ecclesiology envisions the authority of pastors activated in the interplay of *episkope* and *traditio* as they both convey the received theological heritage and catalyze the reinterpretation of that heritage by the gathered body as it seeks the mind of Christ through the Holy Spirit. The purpose of the clergy becomes not teaching the Word of God but *teaching the people how to teach one another* the Word of God. Finally, addressing Coles's project in return, we will see that Baptists' *radical* (to the root) focus on reading Scripture together suggests another correction to Coles's ateleological emphasis, exemplifying a practice that centers and coheres the community without restricting its discernment to previous models of faithful witness.

The *Episkope* of Pastors in Baptist Thought

The notion of episcopal authority localized in a distinctive office derives from the New Testament depictions of organization in the early church. The two most prominent terms denoting leadership are *presbuteros* and *episkopos*, which are most literally translated as "elder" and "overseer," respectively, but more loosely as "presbyter" (later, priest) and "bishop." Contemporary scholarship generally agrees that there was some variation

171

in New Testament patterns of ministry and authority, as witnessed, for example, by additional functions and titles given in the various Pauline lists of gifts imparted to the church by the Holy Spirit.[4] But the later New Testament texts suggest that this diversity consolidated into a common pattern of two defined offices: the elder-overseers who led the churches and the deacons who played an auxiliary role.[5]

Beginning in the second century CE, ecclesial polity began to shift toward the "monarchical episcopate," in which bishops were distinguished from presbyters and elevated above them as the chief spiritual authorities and administrators charged with defining the doctrines, practices, and customs of the churches. Bishops also began to exert authority over multiple churches in a given region, appointing the presbyters to manage individual congregations.[6] By late antiquity, the recognizable hierarchy of bishops, priests, and deacons, officeholders legitimated by apostolic succession and granted the authority to govern the churches, administer the sacraments, and discipline the faithful, was well established.

The Protestant Reformation opened the door to questioning this ancient system and various new sects and movements began experimenting with governance structures that they believed were faithful to the New Testament witness. As early Baptists read Scripture, they noticed both the presence of overseers in self-governing churches as well as the capacities ascribed to all disciples to prophesy, discipline, exhort, and discern truth from error, the mind of Christ from the habits of the world. So, like their antecedents in English Separatism, they crafted a participatory, congregationalist polity in which the people set apart elders to oversee their common life.

What does it mean to grant *episkope* to the appointed leaders in a church structure that was formed in explicit rejection of the old hierarchies? From the beginning, the Baptist understanding of pastoral authority has possessed an ambivalent character. On the one hand, Baptists have expressly denied that ordained ministers are elevated to a rank of formal and sacramental authority that separates them from the laity. On the other

---

[4] The consensus derives from the seminal arguments for diverse New Testament ecclesiology in Käsemann, "Unity and Diversity in New Testament Ecclesiology," 290–97; and R. E. Brown, "Unity and Diversity in New Testament Ecclesiology," 298–308.

[5] Merkle, "The Scriptural Basis for Elders," 245.

[6] Dever, "Elders and Deacons in History," 231f.

172

hand, Baptists usually affirm that the ministry exercises a vital role for the well-being of churches. The perplexing question has been just what the parameters that define this role are.[7] What power can be placed in the pastor's hands if the whole community bears the responsibility to discern the divine will and practice the gifts of ministry?

This tension characterizes Baptist writings throughout the past four centuries. John Smyth insisted, as the Separatists had done, that "ministerial power"—that is, the right to receive and excommunicate members, preach the gospel, and administer baptism and the Lord's Supper— properly belongs to Christ, who delivers this authority into the hands of each gathered community of saints. The entire body retains the responsibility of discipline but normally delegates the ministry of word and sacrament "to the Elders or Bishops."[8] In the absence of appointed officeholders even the "two or three" persons of Matthew 18:20 may validly conduct all the duties of a church.[9] Yet the elders have particular responsibility to "govern" a church by ensuring that its actions are performed in good order and to "feed" its people through the proclamation of Scripture.[10] Even so, the latter was no exclusive prerogative. His church's worship services were characterized by open discussion as to the meaning of a biblical passage, followed by a series of sermons delivered by men who felt led by the Spirit, and were granted permission by the group, to speak.[11] There was no clear demarcation in the tasks assigned to pastor and congregant.

Two divergent approaches to pastoral *episkope* have sought to cut this Gordian knot and have appeared throughout southern baptist history. Grenz categorized this division as a contest between "semi-Presbyterianism" and "democratic congregationalism." The former grants principal decision-making authority in a local church to the pastor and/or a body of elders. The latter prioritizes the determinative authority of the entire community.[12] The basic question at stake is the location of the final authority

---

[7] Bebbington, *Baptists through the Centuries*, 178f.

[8] Smyth, "Parallels, Censures, Observations," 2:386–406.

[9] Ibid., 2:428; Smyth, "Principles and Inferences Concerning the Visible Church," 1:258; "A Declaration of Faith of English People Remaining at Amsterdam," in Lumpkin, *Baptist Confessions of Faith*, 120.

[10] Smyth, "Principles and Inferences Concerning the Visible Church," 1: 259–61; "A Declaration" in Lumpkin, *Baptist Confessions of Faith*, 121.

[11] Ellis, *Gathering*, 46f.,

[12] Grenz, *Theology for the Community of God*, 554.

for ordering the common life of a church, which consequently shapes the formulation of pastoral authority.

Baptists who emphasize the prerogatives of the people as a whole agree with Smyth that pastors support the well-being of a congregation but are not essential for a gathering of Christians to be genuinely church.[13] According to Reynolds, pastors "rule" insofar as they teach lay persons to obey the commandments of the Kingdom of God. Believers should be ready to examine such teachings for themselves and not betray their calling through unconditional submission.[14] So why should the interpretations and exhortations of ministers be heeded, if it cannot be so simply in virtue of their office?

Because Baptist pastors lack formal authority, it has been suggested they therefore exercise a *moral* authority over the membership. Ordained to a position of public service, pastors experience the distinct opportunity of modeling appropriate Christian behavior. Exemplifying the virtues concomitant upon all believers grants them the right to be heard, if not the presumption of correct judgment. For the proponents of this version of Baptist *episkope*, there can be no other charge to pastors when authority finally rests with the people. Johnson, the first president of the Southern Baptist Convention, describes ruling elders as a "council of advisers" for the church. If they and the community came to disagreement over an interpretation of the Bible, then they should "separate in love."[15] Later polity-manual authors of the nineteenth-century agree: an honorable life lived before the eyes of the laity accords pastors an earned, persuasive influence.[16] Dagg, in his volume on church order, poses the objection that such a governing structure grants the minister insufficient authority to enforce the dictates of Scripture. Such a weak office would be overwhelmed by the votes of ignorant, ordinary Christians. Dagg responds that his "moral power" is enough for a minister to lead his church. He expresses confidence that one who is demonstrably holy and compassionate, and who brings to mind the weighty matters of salvation, can possess a nearly limitless influence. Dagg also grants that the opposite scenario may occur: the

---

[13] See Reynolds, "Church Polity," 349; Hiscox, *New Directory*, 83.

[14] Reynolds, "Church Polity," 356, 398f.

[15] Johnson, "Gospel Developed through the Government and Order of the Churches of Jesus Christ," 193, 195.

[16] E.g., Hiscox, *New Directory*, 100f.

Authority and Tradition

people are right, but the minister is claiming an unearned entitlement.[17]

The other approach to the question of pastoral oversight in the church has found the above objection to be more forceful than Dagg considered. Benjamin Keach, an early English Particular Baptist, insisted that congregants must obey an elder unless they had clear and just cause not to do so. Obedience should be given not only to pastoral teaching regarding the clear commands of Scripture, but even to particular calls to action. If a pastor invokes "any extraordinary Duty," such as seasons of focused prayer or fasting, then the people should yield to this injunction.[18] Later prominent Baptist figures, such as Englishman John Gill in the eighteenth century, would set forth similarly high views of pastoral leadership.[19] According to historian Leon McBeth, such views were not merely the detached theorizing of a clerical elite, but reflected actual practice among contemporary Baptists in America, for whom lay deference to their ministers was quite pronounced.[20]

Because of their origins in and theological affinity to the Puritan-Separatist movement, some early Baptists vested decision-making authority not in a single pastor but in a council of elders. In this respect, they found biblical warrant for two orders of elders: the "ruling elders" who governed the church and the "teaching elders" who bore the added responsibility of preaching and administering the ordinances.[21] This polity never achieved majority status among English or American Baptists, but in the latter case it appears to have been most widespread from the mid-eighteenth century to the early part of the nineteenth century. Prominent advocates for the model included Griffith[22] and Morgan Edwards.[23] Debates arose in associations and individual churches, with some deciding in favor of ruling elders.[24] It is difficult to determine what mandate ruling elders held. In Griffith's case, for example, his description of ruling elders is very brief and comes shortly after more egalitarian statements regarding the

---

[17] Dagg, *Manual of Theology, Second Part*, 277f.

[18] Keach, "Glory of a True Church and its Discipline Displayed," 68.

[19] Shurden, "Priesthood of All Believers and Pastoral Authority in Baptist Thought," 136f.

[20] McBeth, *Baptist Heritage*, 248.

[21] Merkle, "Scriptural Basis for Elders," 251.

[22] Griffith, "Short Treatise Concerning a True and Orderly Gospel Church," 98.

[23] Wring, "Elder Rule and Southern Baptist Church Polity," 201.

[24] Ibid., 199–201; Mark E. Dever, "Baptist Polity and Elders," 19.

175

self-governance of the church.[25] Lacking coherent articulation in statements by denominations or exemplary theologians, it is likely that the office was subject to idiosyncratic formulation in various locales. Nevertheless, some such as Reynolds recognized ruling eldership's potential for undermining congregationalism through a concentration of power in the hands of a few.[26]

The belief that either a single pastor or a body of ruling elders should exercise centralized and determinative *episkope* in a congregation began to accumulate widespread currency in the Southern Baptist Convention in the latter decades of the twentieth century. Ammerman notes that vigorous public debate over pastoral authority arose in the SBC in the mid-1980s.[27] This was but one aspect of what historian Leonard called the "clergification" of the SBC. In the sole-pastor variation of autocratic leadership, the ordained minister is the "undershepherd" who is the direct subordinate of Christ in the church and the person who orders and ministries and teachings according to Scripture.[28] Some conservative leaders employed more explicit language. The prominent pastor of the First Baptist Church of Dallas, W. A. Criswell, insisted that a pastor is a "ruler" of the church. Another minister, Jerry Sutton, favorably compared the authority of the pastor to the husband and father in a patriarchal household.[29] While even the majority of conservative southern baptists at this time did not accept that a pastor wields final authority, 34 percent of fundamentalist pastors surveyed by Ammerman thought so. Unsurprisingly, theological moderates almost uniformly rejected the notion.[30]

While taking root among right-wing southern baptists, this perspective was at least partly inspired by the Church Growth Movement (CGM), which has claimed pastoral rule as a key factor for vital and expanding congregations.[31] One prominent advocate for Church Growth principles

[25] See the discussion of Griffith in chapter 1.

[26] Reynolds, "Church Polity," 251f.

[27] Ammerman, *Baptist Battles*, 87.

[28] Leonard, "Southern Baptists and the Laity," 641.

[29] Ammerman, *Baptist Battles*, 87.

[30] Ibid., 89.

[31] McSwain, "Critical Appraisal of the Church Growth Movement," 532. For an introduction to the movement from an insider, see Glasser, "Church Growth at Fuller," 401–420.

within the SBC has been Thom Rainer, a former CEO of LifeWay Christian Resources. In his *Book of Church Growth*, Rainer repeats the common CGM claim that the pastor functions to discern the "vision" or mission God is giving to a local church. He does so through a process of prayer and inquiry into himself and his context. The pastor must then articulate the vision and direct the congregation to actualize it.[32]

Another well-known proponent of strong pastoral authority is Richard Land, former director of the SBC's public policy body, the Ethics and Religious Liberty Commission (1988–2013). In a *Theological Educator* exchange with a Southern Baptist pastor, Land rejects the designation "authoritarian" as pejorative, insisting instead that pastoral leadership is "authoritative." Such leadership seeks to persuade and influence but commands a level of unilateral power beyond visible exemplarity.[33] The pastor must not be "arrogant or dictatorial" and must be open to correction by the members of his church.[34] For Land, the authority of pastor over people is realized in the moment of conflict between them. What is to happen if they disagree with one another? In that case, the pastor makes the decision, and the people submit. Land contends that no "great, God-honoring church" exists in which the congregation leads instead of the pastor.[35]

While the moral-influence and the authoritative models of pastoral authority differ on the manner in which it may be exercised, they agree on the *function* of that authority. The role of the pastor or body of elders is not primarily to make administrative policy decisions although the authoritative model tends toward concentrating such power in the hands of lead-

---

[32] Rainer, *Book of Church Growth*, 185–93. Rainer's co-author in another volume, noted CGM advocate C. Peter Wagner, remarks that one demonstrated trait of megachurches worth emulating is strong leadership, which entails the pastor outlining a vision and convincing the congregants of its divine origin. Wagner insists that the "authority of the pastor is unquestioned" in such churches, implying that this is the most successful pattern of church governance (Towns, Wagner, and Rainer, *Everychurch Guide to Growth*, 66f.).

[33] Land and Langley, "Pastoral Leadership," 75. The stability of his convictions is indicated by the reproduction of this article in *Journal for Baptist Theology and Ministry* 3/1 (2005): 74–80.

[34] Land and Langley, "Pastoral Leadership," 76, 78.

[35] Ibid., 79f.

ership. Nor do Baptists, unlike the episcopal communions such as the Roman Catholic Church or Eastern Orthodoxy, prioritize sacerdotal actions such as presiding over baptism and the Eucharist. By and large, Baptists have believed that the ordinances or sacraments could potentially be conducted by any member in good standing, but for good order's sake their administration is reserved to the ordained ministry.[36] Although making decisions and leading the rituals of faith are important aspects of the pastor's duties, the question of authority results in much difficulty because *episkope* serves first and foremost to position the pastor as a *teacher* of the congregation.[37]

Baptists have frequently seized upon the biblical metaphor of the leader as a shepherd feeding or tending the rest of the church as his flock. In the post-resurrection narrative of John 21, Jesus has Peter reaffirm his love for his master three times—a reversal of the latter's previous denials of any relationship with the man arrested as a blasphemer and subversive. Jesus calls upon Peter to demonstrate this love in his sacrificial service to future disciples: "Feed my sheep" (v. 17).[38] Moreover, in the first epistle attributed to Peter, the author exhorts his fellow elders to shepherd their flocks voluntarily and with pure intent. They must not covet material gain for their work nor should they "lord it over" their congregants. Although he prods the younger members to accede to the authority of the elders, he also insists that each one relates to the other with humility (1 Peter 5:1-6).

Polity manuals of the eighteenth and nineteenth centuries quoted or alluded to the 1 Peter passage quite frequently, focusing particularly on the admonishment to leaders not to be domineering.[39] While largely rejecting a polity of pastoral commandment and lay obedience, the same manuals also elevate the shepherding metaphor. The pastor's chief authoritative function is to feed the flock by means of interpreting Scripture and identifying its significance for the church at present. Griffith writes that the pastor must foremost "preach the word of God unto them, thereby to feed

[36] Maring and Hudson, *Baptist Manual of Polity and Practice*, 181, 193f.

[37] Steven Harmon calls the pastor's magisterial responsibility an "actualization of episcopacy" (*Baptist Identity and the Ecumenical Future*, 129n60).

[38] Keener, *Gospel of John*, 2:1235–37.

[39] See examples in *Polity*, ed. Dever, 98, 121, 190, 316, 351, 473, 550.

the flock."[40] Identical sentiments are expressed in the Charleston Association's *Summary of Church Discipline*[41] and Reynolds's *Church Polity*.[42] Contemporary Baptists have repeated the proposition that pastors/elders have the primary responsibility of teaching and preaching Scripture.[43] Preaching unfolds the meaning of the text and equips believers to shape their lives accordingly.[44]

But there is a destabilizing element conjunctive with the pastor's episcopal authority. Because of their participatory congregationalism, Baptists have stressed the involvement of the laity beyond the passive reception of instruction and sacraments from a domineering leadership. The "gathered" church is constituted not in a hierarchical fashion as Christ calls bishops who appoint successors and priests and whose consecration sets them apart as conduits of divine grace. Rather, its members find themselves called together by Christ into a community that, in the traditional language of many Baptist covenants, agrees to "walk together" in mutual discipleship. The identity of the church is dependent on a "regenerate" people and its mission and ministry is placed in their hands. As such, Baptists have interpreted the pastor's teaching role as a dynamic catalyst for other believers to embrace the gifts of the Spirit they have been given in order to proclaim the gospel in word and deed. Wellum and Wellum insist that the Bible must not be delivered to a congregation only through the mediation of "experts." Rather, all persons are to study Scripture for themselves while being supported by those recognized as gifted teachers.[45] Similarly, Davis writes that overseers must train members to act independently in the practices of discipline, reconciliation, and forgiveness, rather than seeking the intervention of church leadership.[46]

To borrow Mullins's terminology, it is the work of the pastor to heighten the "soul competency" of the Christians under one's care, providing them the tools to practice a deeper level of Christian discipleship in response to the guidance and empowerment of the Holy Spirit. Baptist

[40] Griffith, "Short Treatise Concerning a True and Orderly Gospel Church," 97.

[41] Ibid., 121

[42] Ibid., 351.

[43] Merkle, "Biblical Role of Elders," 251.

[44] Towns, et al., *The EveryChurch Guide to Growth*, 100.

[45] S. J. Wellum and K. Wellum, "Biblical and Theological Case for Congregationalism," 72f.

[46] Davis, "Practical Issues in Elder Ministry," 306.

defenders of democratic congregationalism stress that the minister's ideal aim is fostering the maturity of the congregants to discern and implement the Church's mission in their context, and this to the point that the responsibilities of ordained leadership are truncated. Southern Baptist theologian James Leo Garrett Jr. contends that congregationalism is more adept at developing strong, active participants than other polities, pointing to the evidence of significant lay figures in twentieth-century SBC history.[47] At the outset of that century, Strong wrote in his *Systematic Theology* that the pastor's duty is to develop the Church's self-governance such that it could "manage its own affairs." He likened the pastor to a capable mountain guide who assists climbers to the summit.[48] The pastor's *episkope* thus functions best when it activates the *episkope* of other believers.

That mutual, interconnected *episkope* lies at the heart of Baptist ecclesiology may be demonstrated by a review of church covenants, which are declarations of communal fidelity to which members agree to uphold. A frequent expression found in these covenants is the declaration to "watch over" one another, literally re-presenting the meaning of *episkope*.[49] Such oversight typically refers to a commitment of moral accountability in which Christians promise to support one another in doing good and resisting behavior antithetical to the gospel. So the 1727 covenant of the First Baptist Church of Newport, Rhode Island, avers that congregants will "watch over Each others [sic] Conversation & not Suffer Sin upon one another...to stir up Each other to love & good works."[50] Given the Baptist insistence on deriving moral and theological norms from Scripture, however, the covenants include a subtext that members should be well-versed in the Bible and capable of conveying its significance. This is shown in the 1738 covenant of Tulpohokin Baptist Church in Pennsylvania, which calls upon congregants "to admonish, exhort, and watch over one another in love, and also to reprove according to gospel rule."[51] But sometimes the covenants may state outright that collective *episkope* requires a widespread aptitude for reading Scripture. Thus the 1785 covenant of

---

[47] Garrett, "Affirmation of Congregational Polity," 54.

[48] Strong, *Systematic Theology*, 3:908.

[49] Many examples of the phrase can be found throughout DeWeese, *Baptist Church Covenants*, e.g., 137, 138, 139, 148.

[50] Ibid., 136.

[51] Ibid., 138.

Bent Creek Church in Tennessee declares that the church will enact disciplinary judgments "according to the best light we have or shall have from the holy scriptures."[52]

Moreover, the episcopal authority of the laity extends even to admonishing and correcting the appointed overseers if the people judge they have strayed from gospel faithfulness. Reynolds adamantly insists that believers must oppose any attempts by leaders who, through ambition and corruption, "invade their just rights" and claim "a divine right of jurisdiction."[53] One of those rights, as demonstrated in the previous chapter, is to draw one's own hermeneutical conclusions pertaining to Scripture, and Davis concurs that "it is the congregation's responsibility to ensure that the elders' teaching, modeling, and ministry leadership are plausibly biblical."[54]

The Baptist conviction that the pastor's authority functions to equip other Christians to do the work of the church highlights the seemingly intractable tension in the understanding of ordained leadership. On the one hand, the pastor is regarded highly as an agent of interpretation and proclamation who safeguards historic theological commitments and declares the meaning of Scripture for the present time. On the other hand, the pastor possesses no formal means to command assent, for final earthly authority rests upon the whole community. The pastor cannot claim the sanction of an infallible, hierarchical magisterium and is, at least in theory if sometimes not in practice, susceptible to discipline and contestation by others.

The moral-influence and authoritative models share the same weakness in their attempts to resolve this tension. Both views endeavor to define how it is that the pastor can be *heard* and *obeyed* by church members, but proponents of neither position articulate what it means for the pastor to hear and respond to the perspectives of the laity. The explications of both views are quite clericalist, intending to convey the mode in which the pastor has been granted to practice a unidirectional authority. Crassly stated, what does it take to get the people to do what the pastor says? On the moral-influence view, one builds up spiritual "capital" through attractive words and deeds demonstrating the virtues of Christian faithfulness. On the authoritative view, one lives in an exemplary fashion as well but

[52] Ibid., 148f.
[53] Reynolds, "Church Polity," 351f.
[54] Davis, "Practical Issues in Elder Ministry," 306.

THE CONTESTABLE CHURCH

calls upon a set of biblical texts that seem to stress submission to goad the people into an appropriate form of deference. While they differ on the extent to which the pastor exercises independent judgment and decision-making, they agree that the key to resolving the problem lies in some form of assertion of authority from above.

One recent ecumenical document presents a more nuanced take on Baptist *episkope* that names the productive tension of mutual oversight between the leadership and laity. During the years 2006–2010, representatives of the BWA and the Pontifical Council for Promoting Christian Unity, an administrative department of the Roman Catholic Church, met for the second series of bilateral dialogues.[55] Each year's meeting focused on a particular theme, such as the relationship of Scripture and Tradition or the place of Mary, the mother of Jesus, in the life of the Church. Pertinent to this chapter's discussion was the topic of year four, "Oversight and Primacy in the Ministry of the Church," for it was in this conversation that the representatives explored convergences and disagreements on the patterning of *episkope* in Christian communities. A drafting committee produced a summary report of the conversations, titled *The Word of God in the Life of the Church* (hereafter *WGLC*). This report is structured into five sections reflecting the five yearly themes. Each section presents consensus statements in bold type followed by more detailed analyses of both shared affirmation and continued disagreement.[56] The drafting committee included Paul Fiddes, the Baptist co-chair of the dialogues, and Steven Harmon, the southern baptist theologian whose work will be discussed below. Harmon has affirmed that the claims made in *WGLC* regarding Baptist convictions are congruent with his personally held perspectives.[57]

What, according to *WGLC*, can be said about the structuring of *episkope* in Baptist churches? When Baptists have reflected theologically on pastoral ministry, they have recognized that this particular office possesses the function of *episkope*.[58] Simultaneously, each congregation holds the authority to oversee its own affairs because it "shares in the threefold office

---

[55] The first round of conversations took place in 1984–1988.

[56] For the preceding, see the preface in "The Word of God in the Life of the Church," 28–34.

[57] Personal communication, August 25, 2016. Other southern baptists contributed to the dialogues that precipitated the report, including Curtis Freeman and Timothy George, Dean of Beeson Divinity School in Birmingham, Alabama.

[58] "The Word of God in the Life of the Church," 37f.

of Christ as prophet, priest and king."[59] Pertinent responsibilities include appointing officeholders, celebrating the sacraments/ordinances, and determining the structures of community life. This arrangement of shared power is further complexified by the Baptist representatives' assent to an agreed formulation of *episkope* expressed trilaterally not only in personal (pastoral) and communal (congregational) dimensions, but collegial as well. The latter aspect acknowledges the mutuality of oversight shared by multiple officers, whether the college of bishops in the Roman Catholic Church or multiple pastors and/or deacons in a local Baptist church.[60] For Roman Catholics, canonical teaching locates final juridical authority in the bishop.[61] The dialectic is not so cleanly resolved in Baptist ecclesiology, as has already been noted in this chapter. Not only is ultimate earthly authority for discerning the mind of Christ vested in the gathered congregation, but Baptists have also insisted that pastoral *episkope* is beneficial, but not required, for a community to be truly and wholly church.[62]

Given these tensional overlays of *episkope*, what then is the pastoral role? First of all, *WGLC* identifies a Baptist-Catholic agreement that the oversight of officeholders serves to equip the larger community as participants in Christ's ministry to the world.[63] The mode of supply, the representatives also mutually affirm, is through *traditio*—defined particularly as the preservation and teaching of the apostolic faith that has been handed down. Even so, Baptists continue to insist that such oversight is not the exclusive prerogative of the clergy. The priesthood of all believers means, in the language of early Baptist covenants and confessions, that believers "watch over" one another, and that the continuity of the faith is placed in the hands of the entire fellowship.[64] In radical-democratic terms, this deliberately unresolved interface invites Baptist congregations and their ministers into a receptively generous and potentially agonistic communion. "It is a mark of Baptist covenant ecclesiology," states *WGLC*, "not to define in a legal or canonical way the respective authority of the minister and the whole meeting, but to leave the relationship as a matter of trust in each

[59] Ibid., 39.
[60] Ibid., 44f., 94.
[61] Ibid., 95.
[62] Ibid., 97.
[63] Ibid., 91.
[64] Ibid., 92f., 100f.

other and obedience to the rule of Christ."[65] Yet another agreed statement declares that the pastoral *episkope* bears the particular charge of fostering Christian unity.[66] The minister applies a centripetal force to hold the community together in and through its deliberations toward shared wisdom.

Baptists hold to paradoxical convictions regarding the authority of pastors to nurture the community and the authority of the community to govern itself. The Holy Spirit may speak through he preached word, the private word of encouragement or rebuke, or the combined words of the many in ecclesial gatherings. Consequently, the Baptist practice of *episkope* should not be reified into a fixed constitutional formula that lays out predetermined boundaries for when, where, and how oversight belongs to the leadership or to the people. Mutual oversight demands patient attentiveness to the perspectives of fellow believers and a supple responsiveness to changing conditions, competencies, and capacities. By the end of this chapter, we will sketch more fully what this may look like. At this point, though, we will turn to Romand Coles's account of radical-democratic leadership to discover parallels to Baptist concerns and solutions as well as potential insights for advancing Baptist notions of *episkope* toward the horizon that has been placed in view.

The Distributed *Episkope* of Radical Democracy

Throughout his corpus, Coles rarely articulates the modes or institutional structures in which his theoretical commitments may become embodied. Although he has been deeply involved in practical action and community organizing throughout his academic career, his account of radical democracy is predominantly abstract. Nevertheless, his later books devote more attention to expressing his vision via selected examples of the receptive generosity *ethos*. In the work co-authored with Hauerwas, *Christianity, Democracy, and the Radical Ordinary*, Coles calls attention to the exercise of leadership within two prominent social-justice organizations.

First, Coles examines the life and work of an African American radical democrat in the chapter, "'To Make This Tradition Articulate': Practiced Receptivity Matters, Or Heading West of West with Cornel West and Ella Baker." Baker, a lifelong activist, was one of the founders of the

---

[65] Ibid., 92.
[66] Ibid., 98.

Authority and Tradition

Student Nonviolent Coordinating Committee (SNCC), a prominent organization of the civil rights era.[67] Baker helped shape SNCC's radical approach to authority that set it apart, at least for a while, from other groups struggling for Black equality.

Coles demonstrates that divergent models of leadership in the movement were derivative of contrasting realizations of power and authority in Protestant, African American churches. The pastors who founded and directed the Southern Christian Leadership Conference (the organization of which Martin Luther King Jr. was the head) incorporated their understanding of the church as an institution managed by from the top down by ordained male leadership. Baker, on the other hand, practiced church in the manner of the autonomous women's auxiliary associations that inaugurated and conducted a wide variety of the "hands-on" ministries of their faith communities.[68] Consequently, Baker advanced an alternative perspective on leadership as self-distributing through the educational empowerment of more and more participants. SNCC thereby exemplified the radical-democratic understanding that a key function of leadership is to create more leaders.[69]

According to Coles, Baker built a culture within SNCC to "nurture the dialogical autonomy of the younger people."[70] Such formation was rooted in a "politics of exemplarity" in which leaders modelled openness to new perspectives and teachers asked questions and listened for insight rather than dictated the curriculum of movement organization. Baker personally instantiated her politics and received praise for living by these guidelines as she worked with the group's young volunteers.[71] The receptivity fostered within SNCC was extended to the wider Black community; activists were sent out with the stipulation that they were to learn from the ordinary poor they met just as much as they were to instruct.[72] Coles identifies SNCC's work as rooted in "empowering flows" in which those possessing crafted skills of democratic leadership and action entered impoverished, oppressed areas to locate persons of potential, nurture their

---

[67] See Ransby, *Ella Baker and the Black Freedom Movement.*

[68] Hauerwas and Coles, *Christianity, Democracy, and the Radical Ordinary,* 55f.

[69] Ibid., 59.

[70] Ibid., 63.

[71] Ibid., 64.

[72] Ibid., 67.

THE CONTESTABLE CHURCH

formation, and encourage them to do the same for others.[73]

Yet this inspiring and important civil-rights organization quickly departed from its initial vision, as disillusionment fed increasing alignment with Black power militancy and socialistic revolutionary fervor. A widespread movement that arose at the beginning of the 1960s was essentially dead by the close of the decade.[74] Coles rightfully notes that multiple causes lie behind SNCC's transformation and collapse, not the least of which being the tremendous pressures exerted by entrenched, structural racism.[75] But he also contends that this experiment in radical democracy fostered two related failings in overreaction to unreceptive expressions of power its leaders rejected. The first of these, Coles writes, was a "hyper-anti-ideological stance" that diminished SNCC's capacity to articulate theological and philosophical sources of guidance. Consequently, the practices SNCC elaborated were not accompanied by sufficient discursive interpretation to prevent their co-optation within alternate conceptualizations of political power—principally, domination, violence, and exclusion. The practices lacked orientation because they had become disconnected from the living tradition(s) that had sustained them.[76] For the most part, Coles's proposed means of addressing this drift is to integrate critical scholarship and theorizing more closely with on-the-ground social action. Prophets in the academy and on the street will find mutual benefit in attending to one another's insights in the exchange of abstract reflection and immanent narrative.[77]

The disorientation of a radically democratic community cannot be solved by an unmediated exchange of information between scholarship and movement activists as a singular, corporate entity. In a more cursory, single-paragraph analysis, Coles names the second failing of SNCC as "insufficient attention to explicitly formulating visions and practices of leadership that might enhance its capacities to bring a 'new thing' to flourish and endure in the world." Quoting the postmortems of leading figures, Coles identifies education as a key practice of leadership. Authority is exercised in educating those who enter the community to understand the

[73] Ibid., 70.
[74] On the collapse of SNCC see Marsh, *Beloved Community*, 111–24.
[75] Hauerwas and Coles, *Christianity, Democracy, and the Radical Ordinary*, 73f.
[76] Ibid., 75f.
[77] Ibid., 76–79.

Authority and Tradition

historical roots of its struggle for justice, training them to engage in the arts of democracy that have defined the community, and instilling in them the patience and hope needed to face the inevitable challenges that arise.[78]

Coles supplements this all-too brief analysis of leadership with the subsequent chapter, "Of Tension and Tricksters: Grassroots Democracy between Theory and Practice." He points out that all efforts to generate new, valued political arrangements bring up questions regarding the nature and exercise of authority.[79] So what forms of authority support the advance of the radical-democratic vision? He rejects illusions of "ultra-democracy" in which leadership phases out, to be replaced by an entirely egalitarian and unanimously participatory polity. However much radical democracy reaches for the ideal of greater involvement and interaction between diverse individuals and groups, communities will inevitably fail to reach consensus, evoke varying rates of participation by their members, and overlook certain instances of exclusion or imposition. There is thus a need to cultivate leaders who develop the skills of politics that are "attained only through long-term practice and reflection." Groups squander their capabilities if they do not foster the leadership of those who have gained competence in the practice of democracy. Coles identifies the Industrial Areas Foundation (IAF) as a model for developing grassroots, radically democratic leadership.[80] Rather than structuring a hierarchy exercising legal-rational authority, IAF empowers persons who demonstrate the appropriate qualities necessary to further the goals of community organization. As was the case with Baker and SNCC, the goal is to encourage even more participation and leadership, enhancing the democratic character of the network and its affiliates.

Nevertheless, a tension arises between the widespread engagement of many parties and respectful deference to persons elevated to authority. This tension evokes greater significance in the recognition that participants in radical democracy represent a fraction of the larger society. What right does a movement claim to be democratic when so few of the public are involved? In part, this problematic element is addressed by political theorist Hannah Arendt's suggestion that political spaces are open from the bottom, guided by the willingness to bring others in and bound by the

[78] Ibid., 77f.
[79] Ibid., 302.
[80] Ibid., 303.

sense of responsibility for those who abstain from political activity.[81] So there exist parallel challenges characterizing both the relationships between the activists of the organization and the community as a whole as well as the relationships within the organization between the mass of participants and the leaders who demonstrate more extensive capacities, knowledge, and wisdom.

So, how should the relationship between leaders and their movements be expressed? First, Coles says authority in a radical-democratic community means the voices and views of leaders carry added weight in comparison to ordinary members. In IAF, this is especially the case when decisions are made to fill vacant leadership positions.[82] But as this authority serves the goal of enhancing the capacities of all, it possesses a mutable nature, decreasing over time as equality increases, yet never reaches a utopian consummation.[83] Authority orients itself to "transgressing the boundary" between the political and apolitical, encouraging more and more people to make themselves present and develop their talents. Leaders are raised up precisely to "work the limit" and solicit new perspectives that reshape IAF's mission over time. Leaders increase in authority insofar as they share authority, bringing in the disengaged and helping the engaged to achieve further resourcefulness and intelligence. The future of radical democracy, Coles considers, will be dependent on organizations' ability to successfully navigate these tensions with a simultaneously authoritative and authorizing leadership.

Coles's account of leadership given in these chapters may be summarized in three main points. First, contra an assumption that persons who hold a passing familiarity with radical democracy might make, Coles dismisses the notion of a flattened, anarchic body politic. However formal or informal its constitution may be, leadership is a vital necessity. This is due in part to the complexities of directing collective efforts; some will inevitably be more active and interested, will be able to devote more time and energy, and will be more accomplished in such requisite skills as communication, coalition-building, envisioning, planning, and training. Coles, though, does not value leadership merely as a prudential tool to be em-

[81] Ibid., 304.
[82] Ibid., 305.
[83] Ibid., 306.

ployed because other options are lacking. Rather, leadership gives intentional, positive shape to the continual re-imagination of radical democracy. Secondly, therefore, leaders bear a dual function of *conserving* and *curating*. On the one hand, leaders sustain in the present what has been retained from the past because it is judged integral to the community's identity and mission. Stories, ideas, practices, and themes—as well as the physical artifacts, bodily postures, and social-psychological liturgies that encode them—are retained, interpreted, and communicated to the whole community, especially to its newest members. On the other hand, the leaders' positions and roles are not static, for they serve the function of enhancing others' capacities that they, too, may exercise initiative and oversight. Such empowerment—we can also say equipping—operates beyond the obvious need for continuity in an office as one generation of leadership replaces another. It is an extension of the notion of leadership so that a greater share of the polity can act with authority as more persons develop their particular gifts and utilize them in distinct areas of the community's work. Radical-democratic leadership is properly identified as an educative exercise, both in the sense of passing on the content of an inheritance and in training others for active participation. The third point flows from this perspective: authority most properly belongs to those who not only possess democratic skills in themselves but who are best able to educate others in those same habits and practices. Authoritative leadership is not a "zero sum game" in that some must lack it if others have it; instead, the recognition given to a leader is confirmed by the growing abilities of participants who have been under the leader's tutelage.

The convergences between Coles and southern baptist expressions of *episkope* should strike the reader as obvious. Baptists have stressed the importance, if not the absolute necessity, of official leadership for the well-being of the church. Pastors and elders offer a guiding hand through personal example, purposeful conversation, and thoughtful preaching and teaching. Baptists have defined the pastor's charge as equipping other believers, by which they mean advancing their understanding of and participation in the life of discipleship. The best *episkope* is the kind that resonates throughout the body and reverberates back upon its points of origin, but Coles conceptualizes the empowerment function of *episkope* more radically than Baptists have done so, at least explicitly. Leaders not only preserve the space wherein participants may develop and voice new perspectives and convictions; their proficiency shows itself in actively stimulating the emergence of that which had not before been imagined, indeed that which they themselves could not imagine. Leaders dare others to dream the future in novel dimensions. In Baptist terms, they go searching for sources of new light. For Coles, *episkope* cannot exist without the practice of *traditio*, and it will now be demonstrated that this is another convergence and generative possibility between southern baptist theology and radical democracy.

The Practice of *Traditio* in Radical Democracy

An inherent and productive tension lies at the heart of Coles's shared leadership model. As demonstrated in the previous chapter, Coles's radical-democratic vision accentuates and arguably prioritizes an ateleological openness to the new that exists alongside established trajectories of practice and principle. The empowerment of a large percentage of a group with the arts of leadership bears the quite welcome and intentional consequence of expanding the imaginative mental landscape. More voices speak more possibilities into being, many of which will modulate or perhaps deconstruct the orientations and desired outcomes heretofore supported by the polity. Conflict arises in the juxtaposition of two different ends: preservation of an identity-forming inheritance and responsiveness to changing contexts and demands.

Coles explores this struggle as a key theme running through *BGP*. In the introduction, Coles stresses that democracy is a dynamic process:

> Democracy has never been a safe, transparent possession; rather, it has been a practice largely in search of itself, struggling beyond pasts and presents in which it was unrealized…and in the face of futures threatening to retrench its achievements and aspirations. Democracy happens primarily as a generative activity in which people seek to reinvent it in challenges and contestations concerning the question of what it might become. Democracy is *democratization*.[84]

Awareness of this reality demands an *ethos* of dwelling in the tensions between competing values and perspectives, and Coles focuses especially on the clash between honoring received tradition and seeking reformation as circumstances call for innovation. This push-and-pull is etymologically encoded, for the Latin word *traditio* is at the root both of "tradition" and

---

[84] Coles, *Beyond Gated Politics*, xi. Emphasis original.

Authority and Tradition

of "treason." Each moment in the process of handing down a legacy exemplifies this ambivalence: to what extent will this bestowal entail continuity or evolution? Such questions are unavoidable, for every tradition is inextricably haunted by indeterminacy. This characterization of tradition exemplifies yet again the exchange between teleological and ateleological receptivities.[85]

After two chapters in which he makes the case for the unreceptivity of political liberalism, Coles explores the meaning of *traditio* through dialogue with two Christian thinkers: Catholic moral philosopher Alasdair MacIntyre and Mennonite theologian John Howard Yoder. Both figures clearly insist on the inescapable necessity of tradition while, at the same time, both understand tradition must move forward in time through contestations over its character and content.

Coles relates the common misinterpretation that MacIntyre is simply a sectarian who urges withdrawal to "isolated, homogeneous, and inwardly turned local communities."[86] To the contrary, he writes, MacIntyre "is best read as a theorist concerned with what it might mean to live well in the borderlands."[87] Even if this reading of him were inaccurate, MacIntyre's well-known critique of modernity in *After Virtue* presents the case that the discordant edges are well-nigh impossible to avoid. For most of us, these edges can be located internally. The collapse of a shared, ordering *mythos* in the West has resulted in the proliferation of radically disjunctive visions of the good, and these visions are often inchoate or incoherent because moral views are crafted in an abstracted manner as premises are lifted here and there from the remnants of lost or fading traditions.[88] MacIntyre proposes, in response to this morass, the cultivation of traditioned communities where ideas and practices are aligned.

MacIntyre does not make tradition into a static bedrock that cannot be moved. Rather, he contends that traditions are partly constituted by a

[85] Ibid., xiii–xv.

[86] Ibid., 79. A summary of Coles's engagement with Yoder, which occurred before more recent discussions about the ethics of retaining Yoder in current scholarly discourse, is integral to the argument that is developed in this chapter. Many readers will surely be aware that Yoder exploited concepts such as vulnerability and the otherness of the Church to rationalize sexual violence. See introduction, p. 18.

[87] Ibid., 80.

[88] Ibid., 81–83.

THE CONTESTABLE CHURCH

perpetual argument regarding how they are to be realized.[89] Consequently, traditions do not begin and heretofore remain in a state of unified coherence; such is rather the horizon toward which they point. The shared *telos* of a tradition guards against relativism and gives sustenance to contestation, for if individual claims to truth and goodness are too independent of one another there will be no shared premises that make a meaningful argument possible. Therefore, traditions grow along a path of developmental circularity in which new determinative judgments both build upon prior visions while reshaping the community's understanding of that toward which it journeys.[90] Such growth is facilitated in part by vulnerable dialogue with others who fall outside the traditioning community.[91]

Despite his sympathy for MacIntyre, Coles spies problematic resistances to the very vulnerability MacIntyre has declared vital for the health of a living tradition. Unsurprisingly, the issue at hand is a prioritizing of the teleological dimension over the ateleological. MacIntyre portrays a tradition as capable of increasing in self-confidence as a "successful form of enquiry" because its developed claims build up a resistance to valid criticism.[92] The danger, for Coles, is that this confidence may shift from a retrospective orientation—thus far all challenges have been answered—to a prospective orientation—it is expected, but not assumed, that all future challenges will be overcome. Coles questions whether this is sufficient. Shouldn't traditions accept not merely the possibility but the *probability* that their formulations will continue to demonstrate inadequacy before the task of framing reality?

Even more worrying for a radical democrat is MacIntyre's contention that this surging confidence warrants the exercise of exclusionary disciplines in order to define the zone of fundamental consensus, policed by authorities established to banish extraordinary dissent.[93] Coles does not deny the necessity of authority, which stands as the opposite pole in democratic paradox to the predisposition toward encounter with one's others. Nevertheless, MacIntyre's comfort with institutions of declarative judgment highlights the weakness of his teleological emphasis. This posture of

[89] Ibid., 85.
[90] Ibid., 90f.
[91] Ibid., 93f.
[92] Ibid., 101.
[93] Ibid., 104.

solidifying the boundaries may engender an affective response that perceives danger emanating primarily from the world out there, where dissent has turned into heresy, and less so internally as "teleologies, authorities, and disciplines" curtail openness to new possibilities.[94]

In contrast to MacIntyre, Coles sees in Yoder a Christian thinker who shifts tradition into the more ateleological mode of *traditio*. Yoder offers "a vision of dialogical communities that brings forth very particular and powerful practices of generous solidarity precisely *through* creative uses of conflict," forging a receptivity both to dissent within the Church and outsiders beyond it.[95] Yoder's thought bears a number of similarities to MacIntyre. He eschews universal reason, contending that the Church engages in dialogue with the world through and because of its claim of Christ's lordship, and he orients the process of contestation on a vector facing the eschatological *telos*. The arrow does not fly straight, however. The Church must be continuously prepared for *radical* reformation, in the literal sense of the original Latin meaning of "root."[96] In the face of new contexts and the different responses they evoke, the Church must return to its roots, which here means not a pristine doctrine to be restored but an embodied, communal re-reading of Scripture under the guidance of the Holy Spirit.[97]

Vulnerability is critical for a Yoderian reformation because attentiveness to external voices helps the Church to reimagine its practices and reconsider its edges.[98] The Church's witness is contextually discerned and dependent on coming to understand the perspective of the other, so the very mission of the Church in testifying to its Lord is predicated on receptive encounters.[99] For Yoder, then, "the outside is often not purely other."[100] This is not to say that all the Church's others have equitable claim on the conversation. Inevitably, certain perspectives must be found incompatible to the embodied narrative of the gospel, and Yoder concedes that his dialogical model of communal discernment must develop criteria to define such heresies. *Even then*, when a competing view must be declared out of bounds, vulnerability toward those understood as treasonous

[94] Ibid., 106.
[95] Ibid., 110.
[96] Ibid., 112–15.
[97] Ibid., 115f.
[98] Ibid., 119–22.
[99] Ibid., 124–26.
[100] Ibid., 128.

to the gospel must still be practiced, even if intimate fellowship can no longer be maintained.[101]

In a brief section at the close of this chapter, Coles pushes back against Yoder's gospel-centered generosity.[102] Concerned about the language of Christ's "jealousy" as Lord, he asks if this proclamation bears intrinsic closures against the generative receptivity Yoder has so admirably sketched out. While perhaps Yoder has extended tradition much farther toward the other, is the newness of encounter devalued by a centripetal pull of characteristic Anabaptist separatism? Or rather, does the Christian confession of the crucified and risen Jesus contain ineradicable vices? Coles wants to know if believers can embrace receptive generosity with such fullness that they will allow critique to reach the very heart of the narrative by which they live. That is not the last word, however, for Coles quite rightly flips the gaze and asks if radical democrats themselves must embrace a certain "jealousy" to sustain their vision. Might not their practice of generosity need certain limits of negation that better enables them to resist destructive modes of power? Here, however briefly, Yoder's vision leads Coles to ask if he has prioritized ateleology to the detriment of his democratic project.

Further on in *BGP*, Coles turns to feminists of color, particularly Gloria Anzaldúa, for a far less problematic portrait of *traditio* in practice.[103] He introduces her work in the context of a critical animating question in democratic theory; namely, the "legitimate scope and modes of disagreement and difference."[104] One oft-repeated solution establishes not-to-be-questioned parameters that set the boundaries for disputation. Political liberalism, for example, has sought universal guidelines by which pluralism and individual freedom may be maximized, all the while bracketing questions of ultimate meaning and truth. Coles, alongside other radical democrats, has sharply critiqued liberalism for circumscribing contestability within assumptions that have been elevated to the status of first principles. He reads Anzaldúa as presenting an alternative orientation to disagreement through the idea of the "new mestiza"—the creative mixture of cultures, identities, and aspirations that arises when essentialist definitions of

---

[101] Ibid., 129f.
[102] Ibid., 135–38.
[103] See Anzaldúa, *Borderlands*.
[104] Coles, *Beyond Gated Politics*, 185.

Authority and Tradition

race or nationality are abandoned.[105]

Coles highlights Anzaldúa's orientation by juxtaposing it with the political philosophy of the American historian and social critic Arthur Schlesinger Jr.[106] Schlesinger spoke similarly of American society as a "mixed race," by which he meant the assimilation of individuals from varied national and cultural backgrounds into a single new community united by core liberal values and oriented toward future possibilities. Schlesinger consequently rejected "multiculturalism," which he reduced to a form of tribalism in which politics is centered on the assertion of parochial differences over against each other.[107]

Anzaldúa shares some fundamental convictions with Schlesinger and the political liberal project writ large, such as equality and freedom, but Coles notices her work does not aim to establish set principles that will dictate in advance the safe space for accommodated diversity. Where Schlesingerian liberalism envisions a once-and-done crossing that creates the new, American breed of human, Anzaldúa's mestiza *ethos* flows through "perpetual wanderings" across borders. As a Chicana woman, Anzaldúa testifies to her people's physical experience of repeated migrations around the border region due to fluctuating economic and political circumstances. What has been a compelled form of nomadic existence now inspires her ethical-intellectual striving for deliberate and repeated crossings past social and ideological borders.[108]

Feminists of color such as Anzaldúa have not found a settled home in any collective identity, so the "new mestizas" divide their loyalty among the cultures from which they learn and to which they give themselves. Anzaldúa names this posture "nepantilism," from an Aztec word that means being "torn between ways."[109] She invites participants in democratic culture never to rest on a mythical stable ground, but to accept the constancy of flux between positions and forms. There, she writes, energy arises "from continual creative motion."[110] Coles demonstrates that Anzaldúa ar-

---

[105] Ibid., 185–88.

[106] See Schlesinger, *Disuniting of America: Reflections on a Multicultural Society*, and *The Vital Center: The Politics of Freedom*.

[107] Coles, *Beyond Gated Politics*, 189f.

[108] Ibid., 191f.

[109] Ibid., 192, quoting Anzaldúa, *Borderlands*, 78.

[110] Anzaldúa, *Borderlands*, 80.

ticulates a distinct mythos. Hers is not a Kantian position of universal reason, but a particular culture that fosters its own narrative and values although these are dynamic values of vulnerability, ambiguity, and movement. What she advocates is a dynamic *traditio* negotiation of tradition, one in which, Coles writes, "both traditional and treasonous yearnings and possibilities are entangled with one another."[111] But *traditio* doesn't just happen. It requires a community's formation *of* habits and continual formation of its members *in* those habits. Thus emerges, yet again, the tension between teleological and ateleological urgencies, but Anzaldúa is aware that this paradox defines her project and is the engine that drives the democratic process. By implication, the reader is made to see that this is the same inescapable paradox for Coles as well. The teleological and ateleological facilitate one another—or perhaps it can be said that they participate in one another.[112]

In his following chapter, Coles considers how the practices of the Industrial Areas Foundation, a grassroots network of community organizations in the United States and several other Western countries, exemplify a "nepantilist" democratic *traditio*.[113] IAF's success at creating stable coalitions among marginalized constituencies, Coles notes, stems from an emphasis on building relationships between diverse communities.[114] He identifies three crucial practices that drive IAF's receptive empowerment of participants, which may be labeled *listening*, *traveling*, and *tabling*.[115] According to Coles, democratic theorists commonly utilize the metaphor of "voice" to describe political communication and participation; thus the cliché, "Let your voice be heard." This semantic posture in effect occludes orientations toward receptivity. IAF, on the other hand, accentuates actions that increase capacities for listening to diverse others, such as the organizing tactic of "one-on-ones."[116] Listening integrally relates to traveling, which quite literally means movement of persons into spaces and communities with which they are unfamiliar so as to increase their capacities for understanding new perspectives. Consequently, IAF practices the

[111] Coles, *Beyond Gated Politics*, 193.
[112] Ibid., 199.
[113] Ibid., 213.
[114] Ibid., 215.
[115] Ibid., 216.
[116] Ibid., 219ff.

"continual movement of meetings and members around the various neighborhoods and institutions of an urban area."[117] The final practice, tabling, reorients another socio-political metaphor regarding the "table," which is an established arrangement of power. Questions based on this metaphor may include, "Who has a seat at the table?" or, "What does this person/organization bring to the table?" Turning the noun into a verb, Coles invites readers to imagine not a stable, fixed table, but shifting power dynamics in which those who travel from setting to setting exchange places, being central and authoritative in one space and being on the edges in another.[118] IAF demonstrates tabling by not merely raising turnout at typical public "tables" such as the meetings of municipal councils, but also by hosting "public accountability meetings" where government officials and the media are invited to witness or participate in an event with an agenda and structure decided on and presided over by members of the general public.[119]

All three practices serve the purpose of expanding receptivity, and as such they push against the limits set by liberal democracy. Given the contexts where IAF affiliates organize marginalized persons for grassroots action and given the dominant strands of democratic theorizing against which Coles is arguing, it is unsurprising that his examples of "on-the-ground" *traditio* in action are all ateleologically oriented. In stressing listening over voice and traveling and tabling over against stable social arrangements, Coles means to break open democratic imagination beyond the strictures of proceduralist respectability in which it has been entangled. Nevertheless, it should be noted that Coles identifies no practices that manifest democratic "jealousy" or a teleological tending of identity or inheritance. Baptists have much to learn from these practices of enhanced vulnerability to difference, but perhaps their own theory and practice of *traditio* can speak a word back to Coles about an attentiveness to the center of one's community that also remains generous at its edges.

Traditio in Bapto-Catholic Thought

Coles's nuanced appraisal of tradition's import for democratic movements resonates with an emerging school of thought among contemporary Baptist theologians. In the latter part of the twentieth century, figures in both

[117] Ibid., 224f.
[118] Ibid., 230ff.
[119] Ibid., 233.

the United States and the United Kingdom began to argue that Baptists should embrace a "catholic" *ethos* rooted in the wider Christian heritage, represented both by the diversity of traditions in the present and by two millennia of faith and practice. In the United States, the advocates of "Baptist Catholicity" (identified variously as "Bapto-Catholics" or "catholic Baptists") largely arise from the theological moderates who exited the Southern Baptist Convention in the wake of its rightward ideological shift although that is beginning to change.[120]

What is the Bapto-Catholic vision? In his seminal essay, which coins the terminology of "catholic Baptists," Freeman defines this sensibility as an openness toward the Holy Spirit's transformative activity "in and through the whole church."[121] Freeman calls Baptists to a critical engagement with tradition: they ought to listen attentively to the voices of Christian history but also cautiously, juxtaposing their ideas with central Baptist beliefs so that the gift of Baptist particularity is not submerged in a reductive ecumenical homogeneity.[122] A catholic Baptist spirituality acknowledges the unity, holiness, and universality of the Church that has together confessed the apostolic faith.[123]

A more comprehensive introduction to this theological project is provided by Steven Harmon in *Towards Baptist Catholicity: Essays on Tradition and the Baptist Vision*. As the subtitle indicates, the concept of tradition is the central axis around which the various catholic Baptist ideas gather. Practices such as sacramentalism, creedal confession, and liturgical renewal derive from the thing most necessary; namely, "a retrieval of the ancient ecumenical tradition that forms Christian identity" and which may yet reimagine Baptists' collective identity.[124] Harmon lists seven marks of

---

[120] This chapter will focus exclusively on Bapto-Catholic theologians rooted in that particular socio-religious context. "Moderate" catholic Baptists have in turn influenced some conservative southern baptists such as the founders of The Center for Baptist Renewal (http://www.centerforbaptistrenewal.com/). See Emerson and Stamps, eds., *Baptists and the Christian Tradition*. Works representative of British Baptist catholicity include Holmes, *Listening to the Past*; Fiddes, *Tracks and Traces*; and Colwell, *Promise and Presence*.

[121] Freeman, "Confession for Catholic Baptists," 85.

[122] Ibid., 86.

[123] Ibid., 87–94.

[124] Ibid., xix.

Bapto-Catholic theology, three of which explicitly refer to tradition: tradition as a source of theological authority, liturgy as a context for formation by tradition, and the constructive retrieval of tradition.[125]

Moderate southern baptist critics of the Bapto-Catholic paradigm have expressed concern that characteristically Baptist practices of dissent and the liberty of individual conscience will be squelched by the incorporation of tradition as a weighted authority for defining Christian faithfulness. The majority of negative responses so far have been directed at the *Baptist Manifesto*, which Harmon did not co-write or sign but which he subsequently affirmed and has reproduced as an appendix in *Towards Baptist Catholicity*.[126] In his critique of the *Manifesto*, Robert P. Jones refers to debates regarding the nature of Baptist identity when he declares that "tradition has no inherent authority *qua* tradition." It is, instead, an accumulation of ideas that form the starting point, rather than the summation, of the theological enterprise. Hewing closely to the "more light" *ethos* identified in the previous chapter, Jones names this method the "Baptist principle of revision."[127] Jones accuses the *Manifesto* of being insufficiently expressive of the Baptist heritage, raising his concern that the former's communitarian emphasis betrays the assumption of a "homogenous Christian story" and a monolithic orthodoxy that can barely tolerate reforms or alternative visions.[128] The Baptist historian C. Douglas Weaver echoes this fear in his review of *Towards Baptist Catholicity*. While recognizing that Harmon affirms the contestable character of tradition (more on that below), by his reading Harmon is given to emphasizing the unity of the Church's witness during the patristic period and the necessity of achieving unity in the present. Thus, according to Weaver, Harmon "restricts dissent if it leads to division." He also contends that Harmon limits the proper exercise of dissent to communities and never to individual voices.[129]

But Mark Medley, himself identified with the Bapto-Catholic movement, helpfully distinguishes the "practice of tradition" from the critics' assumed definition of a static, binding corpus of teachings passively transferred across the ages. In a journal article, Medley surveys the writings of

---

[125] Ibid., 6–17.

[126] Ibid., 215–23.

[127] R. P. Jones, "Revision-ing Baptist Identity," 37.

[128] Ibid., 48.

[129] Review of *Towards Baptist Catholicity*, 106f.

Roman Catholic theologians Terrence Tilley and John Thiel to explicate their bifurcated concept of tradition both as that which is transmitted (*tradita*) and as the process of transmitting (*traditio*), the latter of which Medley says subsists in the tasks of stewardship, interrogation, and invention.[130] While tradition does form the convictions and actions of adherents, the process of *traditio* entails reshaping the tradition as it is received, lived, and communicated.[131] Because tradition manifests in a process simultaneously continuous and discontinuous, *traditio* "must be understood as the negotiation of stewardship *and* interrogation *and* invention, invention *and* interrogation *and* stewardship" in a process open toward the promised but unrealized eschatological fullness.[132] These skills indicate that tradition involves remembering what has been handed down, asking questions and making judgments about its soundness, and finally the "betrayal" of reconfiguring the tradition imaginatively.[133] To practice tradition is to enter with others into a creative performance that is guided but not simply delimited by the virtuosity of previous artists.

Congruent to these modern Catholic theologians and to Medley, Harmon stresses throughout *Towards Baptist Catholicity* that a Baptist retrieval of the greater Christian tradition means entering an ongoing interpretative process that stretches across time and space. Mention has been made of the first Bapto-Catholic distinctive; namely, tradition as an authoritative source. In his discussion, Harmon cites Grenz[134] on tradition as a "hermeneutical trajectory" and Medley[135] on tradition as a critical engagement with the Christian inheritance.[136] When discussing the Bapto-Catholic marker of the community as a locus of authority, Harmon (again citing Medley) refers to the distinction between *traditio* and *tradita*, prioritizing the work of the community as "actively traditioning" over simply and statically conserving a settled doctrine.[137]

Harmon develops his distinctively Baptist approach to the authority of tradition in the third chapter of *Towards Baptist Catholicity*. Here, he

---

[130] Medley, "Stewards, Interrogators, and Inventors," 70–73.
[131] Ibid., 74.
[132] Ibid., 81f.
[133] Ibid., 83–91.
[134] See Grenz and Franke, *Beyond Foundationalism*, 93–129.
[135] Medley, "Catholics, Baptists, and the Normativity of Tradition," 119–29.
[136] Harmon, *Towards Baptist Catholicity*, 7.
[137] Ibid., 13.

contends with the ironic Baptist tradition of denying a role for tradition in ordering Christian faithfulness. He explicitly identifies his project as postmodern "hermeneutic of tradition" that is necessary in the wake of modernity's intellectual collapse.[138] Harmon demonstrates that Baptist anti-traditionalism is untenable for two reasons: first, the Scriptural canon itself has been defined via tradition, and second, Baptists inevitably read that same Scripture through various traditional lenses, including that of Nicene and Chalcedonian orthodoxy. In both cases, Baptists are often unconsciously yet inextricably inheritors of and participants in traditioning streams.[139]

The lion's share of this chapter surveys a variety of scholars and their proposals for the constructive retrieval of the patristic tradition.[140] It is here that Harmon demonstrates his sympathies for the receptive-but-critical dialectic of *traditio*. When he reviews the paleo-orthodoxy of Methodist theologian Thomas Oden, Harmon chides him for a misleading portrayal of early Christian consensus that obscures the diversity and particularity exhibited by the primary sources.[141] He approvingly cites Karl Barth's contention that tradition may be defined as a communal confession of faith that is necessarily fallible and contestable, being that it is subordinated to the Word of God.[142] He quotes MacIntyre's definition of a living tradition as "an historically extended, socially embodied argument...in part about the goods which constitute that tradition."[143] Harmon elucidates the advantages of MacIntyre's definition over static concepts of tradition: a refusal to idealize the past, the essentiality of argument among committed participants, and an embodied character that cannot be reduced to propositions to be contemplated. Turning to French philosopher Paul Ricoeur, Harmon traces his hermeneutical stages of first naivete, criticism, and second naivete, in which one moves from literal acceptance of a tradition to

---

[138] Harmon, *Towards Baptist Catholicity*, 40. Harmon uses the term "postmodern" to indicate a cautious and partial agreement with recent critiques of modern philosophical strivings for, or claims of, a neutral and objective practice of reason free from contingent conditioning (ibid., 6n14. See J. K. A. Smith, *Who's Afraid of Postmodernism?*).

[139] Ibid., 43–45.

[140] Ibid., 46–63.

[141] Ibid., 48f.

[142] Ibid., 51.

[143] Ibid., 53; MacIntyre, *After Virtue*, 222.

critique and finally to a renewed appreciation of its capacity to convey meaning. Harmon calls on Baptists to practice theology undergirded by second-naivete approach to tradition that balances receptivity and doubt.[144]

The chapter's discussion includes several other theologians, and Harmon offers various other proposals for a Baptist retrieval of tradition apart from elucidating its inherent contestability. As he synthesizes the influence of these various thinkers to construct his postmodern hermeneutic of tradition, he presents the essential role of argumentation as one of three defining motifs.[145] Dissent has no intrinsic value, being necessitated by the Church's inability to achieve the full unity that is its eschatological orientation, yet dissent has a place in that journey if it becomes conversation and not mere disagreement. Noting criticisms addressed to the *Baptist Manifesto*, Harmon contends that the document implicitly supports hospitality toward even a single contrary voice, but agrees that it would be helpful to more plainly affirm "the indispensability of the dissenter for the communal argument."[146] Even those dubbed "heretics" can be considered participants in the tradition, and though their opinions may be ruled out of bounds the interpretive community must always attend to dissenters who seek the common good just as well as the majority. Moreover, Harmon admits that his hermeneutic lacks criteria for determining when a disagreement may suffer the drastic sentence of heresy. This conceptual lacuna fosters a hazy liminal zone where certain persons and communities are neither clearly held within nor abstaining from the tradition, but the critical posture of Harmon's hermeneutic encourages the adoption of a charitable ear toward those on the edge and even well beyond. The voices at the heart of the tradition will inevitably receive the most attention, but, as the *Manifesto* itself insists, no source is to be excluded a priori from the *traditio* process.

Harmon returns to the theme of the contested tradition in three other sections of the book. In his seventh chapter, he discusses twentieth-century Swiss theologian Karl Barth as an example of Protestant retrieval of patristic theology. Contra his contemporary peers, Barth argued that the theological enterprise begins by attending to the Christian community,

[144] Harmon, *Towards Baptist Catholicity*, 55f.
[145] For the following, ibid., 66–69.
[146] Ibid., 67.

principally in the faith it confesses. Consequently, Barth intensively studied the Church Fathers as he worked on his own constructive theology.[147] Harmon reviews the biographical and textual evidence for Barth's interest in patristics before noting some exemplary principles that Baptists might adopt. The last of these is Barth's critical hermeneutic of tradition, which exemplifies the dynamic movement of *traditio*. Re-envisioning the Church's confession here and now entails both receiving the confession from others as well as hearing the Word of God afresh and confessing what one has discerned. "Barth regarded this tradition as neither fixed nor infallible," writes Harmon, "and he was free to take issue with various developments in the tradition—but only after first having heard fully the tradition handed over to him in and by the church." The best approach to appropriating the tradition is not repetition but rather moving the argument forward.[148]

Then, in the ninth chapter, Harmon considers how *traditio* might assist Christian centers of higher education navigate difficult conversations regarding the integration of faith and learning. Proponents urge an interdisciplinary methodology that incorporates theological reflection into all academic disciplines and thus explores the necessary relationship between the Christian confession and "secular" human knowledge.[149] Three factors cause this issue to be particularly heated: theological controversy, political division, and mutual suspicion between theology/biblical studies faculty and those of other disciplines regarding their approach to or conclusions about religious doctrines.[150] Harmon's response to these fears begins with an echo of the radical-democratic *ethos*, calling constituents of Christian higher education to dwell in the tangled thickets of contestation. Once again, he cites MacIntyre's description of a living tradition as an ongoing argument and declares paradoxically that Christian universities stand on the unifying center of a tradition that is inevitably conflictual. If participants can enter the fray with the conviction that "*conflict is good*", they are more likely to remain committed to the tensional dialogues that will occur.[151]

---

[147] Ibid., 130f.
[148] Ibid., 149f.
[149] See Hasker, "Faith-Learning Integration," 234–48.
[150] Harmon, *Towards Baptist Catholicity*, 181–83.
[151] Ibid., 184f. Emphasis added.

The final chapter of *Towards Baptist Catholicity* answers the question as to why Harmon remains a Baptist instead of migrating to denominations where the aspiration of catholicity is explicitly embraced. His significant reasons for remaining in place include the conviction that, having been formed in faith and theological education as a Baptist and by Baptists, he owes this tradition his continuing contribution, especially as an educator of future clergy. Furthermore, ecumenism would be hindered by the movement of persons between particular sections of the Christian Church as each only imperfectly realizes the fullness of God's will this side of the *eschaton*.[152] Choosing to sojourn among Baptists, many of whom will reject his proposals regarding a reconstructed communal identity built upon catholic retrieval, Harmon closes with an invitation for his fellow adherents to join in a "contested conversation" about the things that matter. In the end, the quest for greater catholicity can only succeed, and for Harmon only deserves to succeed, if it makes its case persuasively in the arena of Baptist *traditio*.

The comparison between Harmon and Coles's accounts of *traditio* demonstrates striking agreements. Both stress the polyvalent character of traditioning as remembering the community's inheritance and reconceiving it for new contexts. Both stress dialogical conflict as a vital component of practicing tradition, and that there are stable reference points by which to fix the conversation. The difference becomes one of emphasis that, yet again, reveals different prioritizations of the ateleological and the teleological. As referenced above, the practices of *traditio* named by Coles all have to do with cultivating receptivity to otherness above and beyond the received tradition. Harmon devotes the eighth chapter of *Towards Baptist Catholicity* to naming an ecology of practices as well. As Harmon's intent is for Baptists to retrieve a conscious awareness of their placement within the broader Christian tradition, the practices he proposes all aim at receptivity toward historical embodiments of the faith in corporate acts of worship.[153] Coles prods radical democrats to look outward, whereas Harmon encourages Baptists to be "radical" in their return to the roots of the Christian story. Nevertheless, he retains the posture of openness toward reconsideration and reconfiguration, but how are stewardship, interrogation,

---

[152] Ibid., 201f.
[153] Harmon, *Towards Baptist Catholicity*, 151–78.

and invention performed in Baptist ecclesiology and directed toward determinate if still fallible and contestable conclusions? How might *episkope* and *traditio* join together in the work of agonistic discernment?

Linking *Episkope* and *Traditio* in Communal Magisterium

Harmon further develops his catholic approach to Baptist theology in a subsequent book, *Baptist Identity and the Ecumenical Future*. Harmon notes the questions that have been raised in response to his previous work on Baptist catholicity, querying the necessity and validity of such a project. Should the answers he provides be deemed satisfactory, there still remains a fundamental question of means. "Where," Harmon opines, "is the magisterium that could reliably guide Baptists toward catholicity?"[154] In ecumenical Christian terminology, *magisterium* refers to the authority which establishes the teachings and practices a community must uphold. As he constructs his answer to this question, Harmon evinces his conviction that *episkope* and *traditio* are inextricably correlative practices for Baptist ecclesiology.

Harmon addresses the problem of locating this teaching authority in the seventh chapter, "Receiving the Gift of Magisterium." No community of Christians lacks some form of magisterium, even if it is not codified in formal structures. Baptists cannot escape the question of magisterium, for even criticism of the catholic turn is based on an assumed Baptist identity and implies a magisterial element to the tradition. Forming new generations of believers inevitably demands that some teaching be passed down, so how are the contours of that deposit assessed, validated, or revised?[155]

Three significant configurations of the magisterium have been advocated in the history of the Church. The first is expressed in the hierarchical communions which legitimate authority via the theory of apostolic succession: the Roman Catholic Church, the Eastern and Oriental Orthodox churches, and to a lesser extent the Anglican Communion. Harmon cites Cardinal Avery Dulles, who defines magisterium as the authority the bishops possess by virtue of their office to determine what is concordant or

---

[154] Harmon, *Baptist Identity and the Ecumenical Future*, 8.
[155] Ibid., 168f.

discordant with the body of Christian doctrine. In modern Roman Catholic teaching, this magisterium is sustained by the divine charism of infallibility, concretely realized in dogmatic papal pronouncements, that safeguards continuity with the faith as handed down from the apostles. Consultation with other voices—such as specialists, theologians, and practitioners—is viewed as a critical component of the discernment process, but the hierarchy maintains definitive and final authority.[156] The Protestant Reformers who first broke with the Roman church obviously could not affirm a theory of magisterium that disallowed their schism. Consequently, they prioritized locating magisterium in the true teaching of the gospel and only secondarily in the church leaders who transmit it. Pastors and theologians hold authority insofar as they preserve and proclaim the agreed-upon deposit of faith, but separation from and replacement of these leaders is necessary when they fall into heresy.[157]

Harmon elaborates the strengths and weaknesses of these two historically dominant authority patterns. The hierarchical vision, far from Protestant caricatures of papal despotism, preserves a strong impulse toward collegiality. Although formal authority is concentrated in the hands of a relatively small number—the clergy over against the body of the faithful—within that segment of the church personal opinions "must make way for communal discernment that seeks consensus under the lordship of Christ." But this college of teachers also sees itself to be the leadership of *the* true Church, which has been graced by God with the gift of infallibility. Harmon expresses a suitably Baptist concern that such institutional confidence results in an "overly realized eschatology" rather than the needed humility to receive correction both from within and without. Quite oppositely, the Protestant mainstream, committed to a vision of the Church *ever reforming*, possesses the strength of an adaptable magisterium. If one authority is found to be wanting, it can be rejected and others adopted or created. Still, there remains a weakness that arises from privileging certain voices. One's ecclesial community can become tied to particular teachers or to what Harmon calls the "paper magisterium" of select confessions. When these are made foundational to one's identity, change

[156] Ibid., 169–72.
[157] Ibid., 172–74.

becomes inherently problematic. Here, too, Harmon spots a similarly fore-shortened eschatology.[158] Ecclesial identity has been inextricably rooted in established soil, resistant to needed transplants.

While many Baptists or other Free Church Christians may not recognize that they possess their own form of magisterial authority, Harmon contends that this ecclesial tradition has embodied a third approach that incorporates some strengths of the other two while potentially avoiding their overdeterminations. After reviewing his proposal in *Towards Baptist Catholicity* that Baptists ascribe authority to the communion of saints extending across time and space, he asks how the arguments that make up the Church's living tradition should be decided, and how the many voices can be said to participate and influence the outcomes. In the Free Church model, the conclusive authority resides in the local, gathered church. Riffing on the traditional Baptist theme of the priesthood of all believers, Harmon denotes this principle as "the magisterium-hood of all believers."[159]

Certain qualifications prevent this magisterium from taking the form of parochialism or of simplistic anarchy. First, Baptists have acknowledged that a single congregation is not truly independent of connections with the wider Church and instead must be knit in association to the benefit of its health and mission. Discernment of Christ's will, therefore, should transcend the boundaries of each individual congregation, manifesting the interdependence of each on the other, as well as on the entirety of the Christian faith past and present. Second, drawing upon the work of British Baptist theologian Fiddes, Harmon contends that Baptist magisterial authority is realized in the interaction of two modes of *episkope*: that of the entire community and that of the ministerial leadership whom the community has appointed.[160] Fiddes declares that not all voices speak with equal power, for the pastor's voice "carries weight" to an extent surpassing the layperson's.[161] Ministerial *episkope* includes "equipping the members of the congregation with the resources they need from beyond the congregation for seeking the mind of Christ," such as the teaching and practices of

---

[158] Ibid., 174–76.
[159] Ibid., 176f.
[160] Ibid., 177–79.
[161] Fiddes, *Tracks and Traces*, 86.

THE CONTESTABLE CHURCH

other communities and Christian traditions.[162] This mediatory role is critical, for Harmon argues that a Free Church magisterial discipline should involve attending to the ancient creeds, historical confessions, liturgical texts, ecumenical statements, contextual theologies, and other elements of the ecumenical theological heritage.[163] Because this multitude of sources lacks uniformity, it is incumbent upon the gathered community to "weigh" them for their current validity and applicability. Baptists, Harmon says, can live into the fullness of catholicity if the contextual magisterium of the local church remains in conversation with the affirmations of other magisteria throughout the whole Church.

It has been shown that Harmon reiterates the symbiosis of pastoral and communal *episkope* in the process of discerning the mind of Christ for the present context. This complex arrangement arises from the Baptist view that Christian history is replete with closures against correction and failures of moral and theological imagination. The Church is ever vulnerable to corruption, misinterpretation, and deafness, and no authority of person, creed, or institution provides an impregnable resistance against the forces of human finitude. Although he does not explicitly refer to *traditio* in this chapter, Harmon continues to express this interactive approach to tradition that is both welcoming and questioning. He has made clear that ministerial overseers entwine *episkope* and *traditio* by bringing to bear the weight of time and of their own voices into the discernment conversation, but they themselves are not to suppress new insight.

What is needed, then, is to articulate how the church body performs the interplay of *episkope* and *traditio*. It must surely occur through what Coles identifies as an "ecology of practices" that sustain a democratic *ethos*.[164] But there is a specific practice that has a long history among Baptists and, if robustly renewed, may allow churches to better instantiate the vision of the faithfully contestable church. This practice was named in the *Baptist Manifesto* when the authors declared, "We affirm Bible Study in reading communities rather than relying on private interpretation or supposed "scientific" objectivity."[165] This is the practice of collective discernment through examining and discussing Scripture together, one that is

[162] Harmon, *Baptist Identity and the Ecumenical Future*, 179.
[163] Ibid., 180–88.
[164] Coles, *Beyond Gated Politics*, xxx.
[165] Freeman, "Can Baptist Theology be Revisioned?," 304.

208

radical in multiple senses of the word.[166]

Communal Hermeneutics
for the Contestable Church

The historical roots of communal Scriptural interpretation can be traced to the radical claims made by major Protestant Reformers early in their campaigns for a renewed Church. When Martin Luther appealed to the German nobility for support in 1520, he opined that the universal priesthood of believers entails the responsibility of every Christian—not merely the clergy—to judge the soundness of teaching by Scripture.[167] The Swiss reformer Huldrych Zwingli also initially believed that the interpretation of Scripture should be placed in the hands of the whole people of God, and put this conviction into practice by personally leading a study group and by encouraging lay gatherings throughout Zurich. Two members, Conrad Grebel and Felix Mantz, broke with Zwingli over disagreements regarding the pace and character of Zwingli's reform. They in turn founded the Swiss Brethren, a seminal Anabaptist sect.[168]

Zwingli also instituted the related, but public, practice of *prophezei* ("prophesying"), in which two or three clergy would exegete a text and another would deliver a sermon in the vernacular. Admission was open to all, but the aim was the instruction of future ministers. One participant was the Englishman John Hooper, who later returned to his home country and, while serving as a bishop under Edward VI, instituted prophesying there as a private, strictly clerical activity. A more populist model was imported by the Polish reformer Jan Łaski, who himself had spent time in Zurich and had known Zwingli personally. In Łaski's church of expatriates, every member would provide counsel or criticism regarding the teaching of the ministers.[169] For the most part, Elizabethan-era prophesying occupied the middle ground between these expressions, taking the form of public assemblies in which Puritan preachers honed their skills and their doctrine while also edifying a lay audience. Prophesying was followed by

---

[166] Besides the following, the reader should also note the discussion on communal hermeneutics or "reading in communion" in Freeman, *Contesting Catholicity*, 275–90.

[167] Luther, "To the Christian Nobility," 1:263–66, 269–72.

[168] For the preceding, see Snyder, "Swiss Anabaptism," 6:48–64.

[169] Collinson, Craig, and Usher, eds., *Conferences and Combinations*, 10:xxvii–xxix

THE CONTESTABLE CHURCH

closed-door conferences of the clergy wherein discussion, testimony, and censure proceeded.[170]

Although Elizabeth I suppressed prophesying, ministerial conferences were allowed to continue, and the exercise expanded to include gatherings of laity. Puritans encouraged heads of households to lead discussions of the minister's sermon during family meals, share the notes they had taken, and catechize family members directly from the Bible.[171] Unrelated "godly" parishioners could also hold meetings to study Scripture, admonish one another, and join in prayer. Given the reformers' emphasis on educated clergy, laypersons were counseled to heed closely to their sermon notes or learned writings as they read the Bible together.[172] However, the contents and contours of lay conferences would not always remain within the boundaries set by official authorities. Moreover, the practice of lay prophesying, which in essence was the exposition and preaching of biblical texts by multiple interpreters, was retained by some radical nonconformists as an element of congregational worship. Baptist movements arose in England and America in a context that nurtured participatory experimentalism in a manner far beyond the comfort of elite gatekeepers of religious and social propriety.[173]

At the outset of their history, New England Puritans could be counted among those who fostered methods of communal hermeneutics. Robinson, pastor to the Pilgrim colonists who was quoted at the beginning of the previous chapter, contended with clericalist Puritans over the right of laymen (but not women) to preach/prophesy as they felt the Spirit leading them.[174] Robinson actively encouraged the broad exercise of prophecy in his church, just as his colleague Smyth did in the community that became the first Baptists. When the Pilgrims migrated to Massachusetts, they lacked an ordained pastor for several years while lay elder William Brewster provided religious leadership. In this circumstance, communal prophesying flourished.[175] The settlers of the neighboring Massachusetts

[170] Jung, *Godly Conversation*, 34–37.

[171] Ibid., 137–42.

[172] Ibid., 142–44.

[173] For some examples from seventeenth-century England, see Hill, *World Turned Upside Down*, 104–106.

[174] Robinson, "Justification of Separation from the Church of England," 2:246–51.

[175] Hubbard, *General History of New England*, 65

210

Bay Colony also allowed prophesying in the early years before finally discouraging the practice.[176] John Cotton, pastor of the church in Boston ordered his worship services so that the formal sermon would be followed by the prophesying of elders and then, time permitting, prophesying by any layman. Finally, any male was allowed to address questions to the "prophets."[177]

The Baptist movement in America sprouted just as Puritan prophesying withered. John Clarke, a co-founder of Rhode Island, established America's second Baptist church in Newport during the 1640s. Clarke, who was never ordained, regularly encouraged other men to preach in Sunday worship. Open conversation did not take place in the service but Clarke, who was tolerant of some theological diversity, allowed vigorous discussion in separate church meetings.[178] His successor, Obadiah Holmes, apparently shifted from Clarke's moderate formalism back to greater spontaneity in worship services. Baptist historian Edwin Gaustad writes, "When Obadiah Holmes served the church, its worship was simple and extemporaneous. More didactic than ecstatic, the service allowed for the congregation and minister to engage in extensive dialogue."[179] Holmes outlined his vision of congregational hermeneutics in a letter written to the Newport church late in his life. The community must make space to "wait upon the Lord" that they may discover what gifts the Spirit is calling them to exercise in the gathering, including that of prophesy, which each member may produce.[180] Because no person will be an infallible interpreter, the congregants are to be diligent students of Scripture who charitably consider but also refute, if necessary, the readings that are publicly proclaimed.[181]

Organized Baptist witness in Massachusetts originated in a community of collective oversight and exhortation. Thomas Goold, a farmer and wagon maker in Charlestown, began to entertain private scruples about the legitimacy of infant baptism. With the encouragement of Baptist refugees from England, in 1663 Goold began hosting gatherings at his home.

---

[176] McLoughlin, *New England Dissent*, 1:56.
[177] Cotton, *True Constitution of a Particular Visible Church*, 6f.
[178] S. James, *John Clarke and His Legacies*, 22, 25, 39ff.
[179] Gaustad, ed., *Baptist Piety*, 106.
[180] Holmes, "To the Church," 109. See also Holmes, "Of My Faith," 91.
[181] Holmes, "To the Church," 109f.

THE CONTESTABLE CHURCH

The structure of the services fit the general pattern set by Puritan prophesyings of the previous century: a man with recognized gifts would read and preach from a Scripture passage and would be followed by lay exhortations. A second preacher might expound another passage, the Lord's Supper would be eaten on appointed days, and then the community would pray together to close the meeting.[182] At least one member would later testify to the authorities that he affiliated with the renegade conventicle because it retained the practice of lay prophecy.[183] It is also clear that many who joined Goold's fellowship reached their subversive convictions in the same manner as he did, by reading Scripture for themselves and drawing their own conclusions.[184] But in joining this participatory group, these persons intended to check such private judgment before the bar of communal discernment. These early Baptists retained their emphasis on collective hermeneutics even after they received a modicum of legitimacy from the Colonial government and moved to Boston to become a public, established church. The congregational confession, drafted to explain its stance in a hostile environment, included the stipulation that "they may all prophesie one by one that all may learne & all may be comforted."[185] It is worth noting that of the two express purposes of lay prophecy, learning is identified first and comfort second. The confession here demonstrates how Baptists had radicalized common exhortation beyond what their forebears had intended. Where before the Puritans had intended that lay conferences limit themselves to recall and reflect on the instruction given by clergy, the Baptist community in Boston insisted that sharing Scripture together opened to the possibility of novel understanding and commitment, and that this novelty could come by the inspiration of the Spirit through any given believer.

Baptists continued to support lay prophecy or exhortation in worship well into the eighteenth century.[186] This was primarily the case among the Separate Baptists who emerged from the Great Awakening. As discussed in chapter 1, the Separates were a moderately anti-clericalist movement,

[182] Pestana, *Quakers and Baptists in Colonial Massachusetts*, 45.

[183] McLoughlin, *New England Dissent*, 56.

[184] Pestana, *Quakers and Baptists in Colonial Massachusetts*, 66.

[185] See Wood, *History of the First Baptist Church of Boston*, 64–67, for the confession and its context. Wood, the church's minister, noted that the confession remained an official document at the time of his writing.

[186] Najar, *Evangelizing the South, 58.*

Authority and Tradition

suspicious of formal theological training and the concomitant concentration of authority in the hands of professional ministers. Over against these, the Separates rooted ecclesiological legitimacy in the work of the Holy Spirit; first, by making individuals fit for membership via the "new birth" conversion experience, and second, by empowering multiple persons to exercise spiritual gifts publicly for the edification of the community.[187] The Separates spread rapidly across the frontier and throughout the southern colonies, relying on lay exhortation and testimony as the substance of worship services in the many new churches that lacked called ministers. Spontaneity was the rule, for "[s]peakers rose when they felt the impression of the spirit."[188]

Lay prophesying in worship was a fading practice by the beginning of the nineteenth century. But even as Baptists professionalized the clergy and rendered unto them the prerogative of the pulpit, communal interpretation of Scripture lingered in secondary gatherings devoted to spiritual exercises. Multiple sources relate the nature of these alternate meetings, which were variously named conferences (thus retaining the Puritan designation), social meetings, or prayer meetings. A periodical of the Baptist Missionary Society of Massachusetts, for example, reproduces the diary entries of one Rev. Elisha Andrews who operated as an itinerant missionary across New England. On more than one occasion, Andrews records his participation in a conference. One particularly vivid account recalls his arrival in Hinsdale, New Hampshire on the evening of September 12, 1818. He depicts the conference as a "house crowded with worshippers; fervently praying, singing, and exhorting with singular pertinency and zeal."[189] Among many others, this particular community was conducting its conferences without relying on local pastoral leadership to provide guidance.

The writings of Baptist leaders demonstrate the role that such gatherings had in fostering lay proclamation well into the nineteenth century. In his *Notes on the Principles and Practices of Baptist Churches*, Wayland states, "In most churches there is an evening service once in the week,

[187] Lumpkin, *Baptist Foundations in the South*, 63; Goen, *Revivalism and Separatism in New England*, 174.

[188] Najar, "'More Striking…than the Loudest Preaching,'" 434, 438f. For a history of Separate Baptist expansion, see Lumpkin, *Baptist Foundations in the South*.

[189] *American Baptist Magazine and Missionary Intelligencer*, 2:29.

which is either occupied by the minister in a familiar discourse, or by the brethren for conference and prayer," or sometimes in combination. Lay-led conferences fulfill the Christian duty to edify one's fellows rather than merely receive the offering of others' gifts. Such a space also provides the opportunity to present "those views of truth" which one currently entertains, both to strengthen one's own conviction by presenting it and to offer new understandings of faithfulness to the hearers. Moreover, the communal exercise of gifts is especially useful for revealing those who possessed a talent for oratory; Wayland describes the conferences as "nurseries of the ministry."[190] Pendleton echoes this understanding of the conference as a proving ground for preachers. Ministerial leadership is discovered and forged in the fires of shared Scriptural interpretation.[191] Hiscocx's *The Baptist Directory* identifies exhortation as one of the key practices of Baptist worship, and a tool through which the Holy Spirit teaches the church. Every believer can speak of his or her own religious experience in "social worship" gatherings. It is not the lay exhorter's responsibility to expound the Bible, nor it is appropriate to speak in a preaching manner, but it is expected that Scripture will be frequently cited.[192]

Hiscocx's circumscription of the layperson's role in handling Scripture, which he means to clearly distinguish from that of the pastor, demonstrates a trajectory of compartmentalizing communal hermeneutics. For him, lay exhortation remains a constituent aspect of Baptist worship, but in a secondary and supportive manner to the main Sunday service. Nor does the layperson possess a similar authority to explain the meaning of the Bible, or to "expound" it. If the communal reading of Scripture occurs exclusively in the "social" gatherings, and no mechanism is provided for disseminating and discussing interpretations and applications of the text beyond these smaller subsets of a congregation, then it was inevitable that Baptists' earlier radicalism faded. Meanwhile, around the time that Hiscox was writing, the mid-nineteenth-century revivals swept across America. The revivals popularized the idea of a midweek prayer meeting, but one that gave less room for extemporaneous proclamation and conversation. From that period through much of the twentieth century, many Baptist churches structured these weekday services according to the pattern of a

---

[190] Wayland, *Notes on the Principles and Practices of Baptist Churches*, 330f.
[191] Pendleton, *Church Manual*, 152.
[192] Hiscox, *Baptist Directory*, 53–55.

brief pastoral sermon or other teaching, voicing of supplications and thanksgivings, and a period of common prayer.[193] With the demise of more conversational conferences, Baptist reading of the Bible has largely become a matter of either private interpretation, or mutual edification in Bible study groups, with minimal to no structure that enables churches to engage in discerning, public conversation based on the text.

This survey demonstrates that Baptists have a long if rather tenuous history of hermeneutical openness. At times they have stressed the right and responsibility of the whole community, and each of its individual members, to share their own insights into the meaning and significance of Scripture for the people of God in the here and now. Baptists have also held to the conviction that God has called pastors to the particular ministry of scriptural interpretation. Sometimes the dialogical character of lay interpretation has been encouraged, and at other times lay expression has been sublimated under pastoral guidance and limited to "testimony" or other such acts of a circumscribed piety. Southern baptist theologians, such as Harmon and Freeman, are beginning to recover communal study of the Bible and discernment of truth as a distinctive feature of the Baptist ecclesial *ethos*. Even if pastors have an especially "weighty" voice, it is one that sings within the chorus of collective *episkope*. This communal oversight necessarily engages in a contestable process of *traditio*. How might radical democracy help southern baptists sustain the interrelationship of these practices for congregations seeking the mind of Christ together?

Radicalizing Baptist *Episkope* and Centering Democratic *Traditio*

In seeking to answer the question about the nature of "democratic" authority, this review has demonstrated another set of convergences between the radical democracy of Coles and the ecclesiological themes expressed by southern baptists. First, the historical movement of Baptists through time exemplifies the tensions between ateleological and teleological dispositions, as was discussed in the previous chapter. What has been largely missing from Baptist self-awareness until recently, however, is the recognition of Christian communities as both traditioned and traditioning.

---

[193] Brackney, *Historical Dictionary of the Baptists*, 453f.; Reid, et al., *Concise Dictionary of Christianity in America*, 272.

Baptists have long assumed that they could simply read the Bible ahistorically according to the "plain sense," whether this was construed as an engagement with the immediacy of the text or, among some and more recently, as a historical-critical reconstruction of the realities that preceded the text. This hermeneutical presupposition has existed alongside a longstanding humility that welcomes new insights and criticisms from within and without the community. In recent decades, Bapto-Catholic scholars have begun to articulate a more coherent method of theological reasoning that accounts for the contingent and contextual nature of theological discourse. On the surface, critics read this project simply as an attempted imposition of creedal conformity on a riotously and necessarily diverse movement, but a close reading of Harmon demonstrates that he renders tradition in the register of *traditio* with all its implications for dissent, ambiguity, and tentativeness. In doing so, he, alongside other Bapto-Catholics, is making explicit what heretofore had been an inchoate intuition among Baptists.

Coles and southern baptists agree that the democratic process is not properly an anarchic free-for-all in which individuals emotively and chaotically express their desires without any guidance. Leadership is required, and so oversight is a task that somehow falls both on the shoulders of the whole community and those of particular figures as well. Good leaders in radically democratic organizations and in free churches have three main functions. First, they exemplify and elevate the virtues and skills for practice that are highly prized by the community. Second, they catalyze the development of these same virtues and skills throughout the whole of the membership. Finally, to prevent communal dissolution they preserve and pass along the *mythos*, or orienting story, which gives meaning to the body politic.

But now, with the assistance of Coles, southern baptists can take a step toward resolving the perennial conflict between the authority of the church as a whole and the authority of its pastors and elders. For Baptists, the ordained ministers have served as the tradents who communicate the tradition—that is, the Scripture as the divinely-inspired Word by way of accepted conventions of interpretation and through prayerful entreaties to the Holy Spirit for guidance. At the same time, "ordinary" believers have possessed the right to read Scripture themselves, engage in individual and collective discernment, and even challenge the pastor as necessary. Baptists have failed to adequately balance these forces because, in their ecclesial

Authority and Tradition

imaginary, the authority of the pastor and of the community are typically opposed such that one must impose upon the other. Does the pastor lead by providing a vision and proclaiming the meaning of Scripture? Do the people lead by exercising personal judgment and voting their opinions in church meetings?

In an ecclesiology oriented toward discernment through *traditio*, pastors exercise a process-oriented *episkope*. The oversight they provide is not a unidirectional passing down of what has been received to a passively receptive laity. Nor is it activating congregants' own habits of faith formation to the extent that they merely reproduce the same transfer of past deposit to future confession. Rather, what the pastor oversees in the contestable church is the ongoing, tensional, and uncertain dynamic of *traditio* in which all are invited to participate. At the heart of Baptist traditio is the *radical* return to Scripture, again and again, to prayerfully consider how the story contained therein is being retold, expanded, and reimagined by the people of God at this particular time and place. Through preaching and teaching, congregational ministers can model hermeneutical methods that open up the text in fresh ways. By virtue of their education and position as representatives of the unity and apostolicity of the faith, these leaders are especially suited to orient the congregation toward the wider Christian tradition and the convictions that have settled into the "common sense" of the body of Christ, which thus are deeply formative for Christians who seek both continuity and rupture with the saints who have gone before them.

That same heritage is replete with ruptures, so pastors who lead congregations to practice *traditio* must do so with a humble and holy willingness to let more such fissures open up. Or, more exactly, they must create the conditions that make the ruptures more likely to open. Equipping the laity means superintending opportunities through which persons build competencies for reading Scripture, engaging the practices of Christian life oriented toward the Spirit's presence among them, and develop the courage to speak a new word into the ongoing conversation as to the goods that define the journey of faith. Baptist congregations that best live out this convergence of *episkope* and *traditio* will recover and support a panoply of practices form Christians for communal discernment. Chief among these will be open conversations centered on shared reading of Scripture, itself a polyvalent text that exemplifies struggles to name and re-name the experience of God revealed in the story of Israel and of Jesus Christ.

THE CONTESTABLE CHURCH

Critics of this proposal can imagine multiple reasons why it is untenable or even dangerous. Such vulnerability in discernment has the potential to heighten fragmentation as individual congregations journey along wildly divergent theological paths unless denominations build similar toolkits for translocal discussion and discernment. Pastors who have been intensively educated in theological disciplines may fear the implications of empowering laity who, if they remain poorly formed themselves, will mistake prejudices and immediate intuitions for Spirit-led discernment, resulting in more chaotic exertions of self-possessive individualism. Attempts to resolve conversations toward determinate ends risk the accusation, accurate or otherwise, of arbitrary imposition upon the deliberative process and the liberty of persons to continue to speak what they sincerely believe is a prophetic utterance the church needs to hear.

No easy answer to these concerns exists. The fact remains that every organization of common life instantiates certain limitations and risks. A radically-democratic, pneumatologically-alert Baptist ecclesiology attempts to thread the needle in such a way to avoid, on the one hand, the temptations of institutional solidification that close off reform and, on the other hand, those of an anarchic personalism in which churches become arenas for emotive expressivism without intent or mechanism for *deciding* and *excluding*, however provisional any such conclusions must remain for a pilgrim people this side of the eschaton.

Despite his concerns about the self-confidence or jealousy of a tradition cutting off receptivity to new insights, Coles has his own concerns about preserving democratic cultures. As important a value as openness to the new may be, he understands the need for orientation as well, the teleological sharing ground with the ateleological. The critique from a Baptist perspective continues to be that Coles so emphasizes the latter that he does little to show how a community can *maintain* an identity as much as *reshape* it. Perhaps Coles's weakness here can be addressed by reworking the method by which a communal identity is forged. His concern has been creating opportunity for working the edges between traditions and movements so that sparks of energy may burst forth in the friction. Coles does not want those boundaries to become impermeable.

Coles has noticed that Yoder agrees with him, casting a vision of dialogical free churches that may choose to exclude voices from the community but never to exclude them from the conversation, holding that there are no firm barriers between the church and the world. Similarly, Harmon

218

Authority and Tradition

writes of the importance of listening to perspectives from all quarters, so that even those defined as "heretics" are recognized as contributors to and participants in the tradition. Both Yoder and Harmon, alongside the Baptist/Free Church tradition as a whole, have oriented the dialogue around a central confession of Jesus Christ as Lord and a central practice of unpacking the significance of this confession in the reading of Scripture together in particular communities and with awareness of the history of hermeneutics. What Baptists offer radical democrats, then, is an example of centering *traditio* on a common narrative rather than securely demarcating its limits. Coles explains how SNCC fell apart because the organization failed to retain its orientation toward its own center. Other radical democrats are subject to a similar jeopardy unless they develop more completely the teleological orientation. Perhaps they can do so through similar practices of rehearsing a shared story of democratic vision and struggle, knowing that with each retelling of the story the "text" of their common life will display new textures. Whether through Baptist faith in the infinity of God or radical-democratic faith in the wildness of being, no one need enter the story with the hubris that it is a complete picture of reality. It will be enough to know that in this story there is life, and life more abundantly than was known the last time it was told.

CONCLUSION

The preceding body of work has shown fruitful points of contact between the southern baptist tradition and radical democracy as it has been theorized by Romand Coles. I want to provide some pointers as how this theoretical exchange can be transposed into the practices of Baptist churches. First, though, I will devote some space to summarizing the convergences and divergences between Coles's account of radical democracy and the southern baptist ways of thinking and being church.

The first and primary element of convergence between the southern baptist tradition and radical democracy is that of respect for the constructive capacities of contestation. The chief principle of radical democracy is its positive appraisal of difference as a constitutive element of political practice. Certainly, all forms of democratic theory and practice acknowledge the experience of conflict in the social body and develop proposals for debate, compromise, and coexistence among opposing viewpoints. But radical democracy prioritizes hospitable exchange with one's others and its concomitant voicings of disagreement, rejecting attempts to minimize agonism by either the predetermined boundaries of "neutral reason" or a commitment to achieve consensus through "proper" modes of communication and deliberation.

Southern baptists have held to no singular valuation of conflict's role within the discernment processes of their churches and associational bodies. They have wrestled with the tension between two ideals: first, that of the "pure" church of regenerated believers who regulate themselves *through* disciplinary measures and *by* a shared set of doctrinal and moral standards; and second, that of a church *semper reformanda*, which expresses an alternative vigilance of openness to new conceptions of faithfulness as the pilgrim people of God journey through time and space. For the latter, conflict naturally arises as the gathering faithful discuss and evaluate proposals for reorientation. Baptist theologians consequently explain the significance of dissent for a polity that understands itself ultimately to be governed according to the will of God, from Harmon's macroscale practice of *traditio*, through which churches actively explore and reconsider their theological inheritance, to pastor-theologian Marney's microscale ecclesiology of face-to-face dialogue that disrupts the mythical closures of self-deception.

Conclusion

While it is not a programmatic principle for Baptists as it is for radical democrats, contestation does hold a significant place in the former's politics of discipleship.

A southern baptist ecclesiology reconceived in light of radical-democratic insights will not simply acknowledge the unavoidability but affirm the very essentiality of conflict as a positive good the fuels the process of mutual discernment. Baptists who explicitly value contestation will shape a way of being church that accentuates enhanced humility and a sense of provisionality regarding ecclesial judgments. Incorporating Colesian conceptions of the democratic *ethos* accentuates the pre-existent Baptist insistence to hear the Spirit speak through any and all voices. This stance of openness can be integrated with the other half of the Baptist spirit, the desire for a pure and regenerate church, through intentional processes of *traditio* that place all efforts at innovation within a context of conversational "looping back" to the received wisdom.

A second significant convergence between Coles and southern baptists is a rejection of overly individualistic accounts of democratic engagement. Both fault liberalism for a misconstrual of the person as an independent "sovereign" whose primary activity in the political sphere is the expressive assertion of one's rights over against others. For Coles, the self carries an intrinsic dependence upon the other for the crafting of its own identity. Baptists, meanwhile, have historically understood that faith formation of each Christian properly occurs in a communal context. It is in gathering together that the Bible is to be read and the Spirit heard, and it is the responsibility devolved on all believers to offer encouragement, instruction, accountability, and discipline to one another. Implicitly, therefore, Baptists have also recognized that the self grows into and refashions its identity through its interaction with others. Nevertheless, southern baptists experienced a shift in theory and practice toward heightened individualism, one that has been contested in recent decades by theologians seeking to recover the more holistic and communal vision expressed by early Baptists. Significant blame has been assigned to E. Y. Mullins because of his concept of soul competency. With the help of Coles, southern baptists may re-read soul competency as a developing function of the socially formed self that discovers God as both immediate presence and as mediated through the community. Radical democracy offers Baptists a path toward finding the elusive balance between individual conscience and personal faith experience, on the one hand, and the authority of the collective Body of Christ on the other.

The third major convergence is the agreement that the primary referent of the term "democracy" is a localized *ethos* of tending to commonalities and differences in the face-to-face interaction of persons accorded equal respect and dignity. Baptists are especially noted among the wider Christian tradition as emphasizing that the local church is fully Church, lacking in itself nothing essential because Christ directly leads his people "where two or three are gathered." In Marney's distinctive definition, the church exists in and as the encounter between persons who are willing to receive the constructive input that exposes the masks of self-deception. For Harmon, the local, gathered church enacts the magisterium, or teaching authority, acceded by Christ to the church as it reads Scripture and discerns its meaning for the present moment. Radical democrats like Coles conceive of democracy more a mode of existence than a method of government, one in which giving and receiving convictions, dispositions, habits and practices occurs within an atmosphere of generous contestation. Rethinking Baptist ecclesiology with the wisdom of radical democracy can assist current efforts among southern baptist theologians to recover the rich sense of the local church as a *polis*—that is, as a community that forms persons of a distinctive character as they discern the good and true and decide together on courses of action.

This study has not sought to strictly identify Baptist ecclesiology with radical democracy, however. Despite these points of agreement with the major themes of radical democracy, the Baptist vision of a spiritual polity maintains a critical distance due to its central convictions. The first and most obvious is the transcendent horizon of Baptist and Christian faith; in short, Baptists believe in God. Or rather, they worship God, and in doing so they trust that God is encountered in their midst as the ground and sustenance of their political life. This faith in the God who is revealed in Jesus, narrated in Scripture, and witnessed in the Church sets directional limits for the expression of contestability. In contrast to radical democrats, Baptists possess a greater stability of identity rooted in a common narrative. Whereas Coles and other theorists envision democracy as a practice of drawing connections and building coalitions across lines of extreme exterior difference, Baptist ecclesial "democracy" wrestles with differences that remain aimed at the unifying center of the gospel.

The singular narrative that defines Baptist identity results in another

Conclusion

critical distinction: the relationship between indeterminacy and determination, or what Coles terms the ateleological and the teleological. Coles sees these inclinations as two poles that must be endlessly juxtaposed, with neither one privileged, in the democratic processes of contestation and social change. Baptists can and should receive the gift of ateleological conflict as a vitalizing force that will renew their intrinsic affirmation of churches as spaces of contestation wherein the Spirit opens the eyes of God's people to new, as yet-unseen light. However, from the standpoint of faith the endless balance of the ateleological and teleological appears both illusory and hopeless. The Church is on pilgrimage, and thus accepts the relativity of its conclusions, but it is on pilgrimage toward an eschatological future that has proleptically appeared in the redemption its members now experience. The teleological conviction of a good future in God may foster an energetic and joyful embrace of ateleological contestation in the knowledge that our striving *does* have a destination. While Coles worries about the hubris of such claims, the trust that the *telos* is God's gift and not the Church's production can preserve the necessary humility to retain respectful dialogue. Baptists, in turn, may ask whether Coles and other radical democrats can receive the gift of teleology. Sometimes radical democrats raise his concern themselves. As Mouffe notes, there must remain some normative principles that, if questioned, put an end to democracy.[1] From a Baptist perspective, ateleological contestation necessarily occurs within a teleological frame. Agonism is productive because it reveals not the proclamation of different and disjunctive stories, but an ongoing conversation about what it means to live *this* story of who we are and where we are going.

How, then, might Baptists rethink the meaning of their democratic ecclesiology? I propose three answers derived from the theoretical work summarized above. First, the resolution of the dilemma between individual and community may be resolved by a renewal and re-interpretation of Mullins's soul competency concept, understanding it as a dynamic process rather than a static privilege. Baptists have affirmed, and may continue to

---

[1] Mouffe writes that agonistic politics entails struggle between adversaries who, despite disjunctive interpretations, hold in common a commitment to democratic principles. Even a robustly agonistic democracy is a "hegemonic order" that, even though it lacks "ultimate rational ground," must set certain limits and establish contingent formations of power (see Mouffe, *Agonistics*, 7, 14f., 130f).

affirm, that each individual Christian has direct access to God and can speak from one's personal religious experience. This experience, though, is but one ray of light onto the depths of Being and must seek further illumination as the self develops in relationship with others. This cognizance of the developing and interdependent self illuminates the need for belonging to a community of faith, but what shape shall that community take if contestability is to be accorded a prominent place? The community must be one defined by Coles's principle of receptive generosity or, in homologous terms, by Marney's notion of personhood born in vulnerable conversation with one another. The church is the place where persons *happen* as they discover the depths of themselves, each other, and the mystery of God precisely through their willingness to receive difference. Finally, southern baptist ecclesiology will be renewed by the realization that pastors and laity share the responsibility for *episkope* and *traditio*. For pastors, this entails a renewed emphasis on the equipping function of ordained ministry and a reordering of practices to prioritize this role. For laity, this entails a renewal of shared reading and discussion of Scripture so that persons are empowered to discuss and discern the shape of Baptist traditioning as disciples walk together in the journey of faith.

The possibilities for implementing this vision of the contestable church are manifold. I will limit myself to a set of tentative ideas that I hope may spark further creativity. I will group these suggestions in the categories of the three political practices or "arts" for democracy that Coles has drawn from the community organizing network Industrial Areas Foundation: listening, tabling, and traveling.[2]

The practice of *listening* names patient listening to the diversity of perspectives so that persons may learn each other's stories and experiences. The previous chapter already named communal hermeneutics as a historical Baptist exercise of listening to the word of God found in Scripture and interpreted in, through, and by the disciples who gather together. Communal hermeneutics may instantiate in spaces where biblical study is not beholden to singular clerical direction or the predetermined outlines of a curriculum. One example of sharing insights into the meaning of Scripture is that of group *lectio divina*, in which this personal practice of contemplative attention to the text becomes a collective work of prayerful reflection.[3]

[2] See Coles, *Beyond Gated Politics*, 217–33.
[3] See Prechtel, *Where Two or Three Are Gathered*, ch. 3.

Conclusion

I have also previously called attention to the "circle process" for small groups, which in my own experience I have found to be empowering for lay readers of Scripture to embrace their responsibility in the common magisterium.[4]

Listening need not be limited to small groups but can (and perhaps should) take its place in public Sunday worship, the central act of Christian community wherein believers rehearse the biblical narrative through song, prayer, reading, exposition, and the celebration of baptism and the Eucharist. Worship among Baptists reflects developments among Protestants more generally. The typical "options" for worship structure are the "traditional" service of hymns, prayers, and sermon, the "contemporary" or "praise and worship" plan of the extended song service followed by the sermon, and the "ecumenical" form inspired by the liturgical renewal movement and recovering longstanding practices such as the lectionary, psalm recitation, prayers of the people, and the standard pattern of Word and Table.[5] Much discussion of worship considers whether style and structure is biblically sound, spiritually formative, or richly reflective of theological conviction. There is concern for the participatory character of worship, but largely insofar as the lay majority demonstrates greater engagement with the service elements which have been planned in advanced by the clergy or lay leaders. Both early and contemporary Baptists and other Free Church Christians, influenced especially by Paul's description of worship in 1 Corinthians 14, have advocated for or even implemented more "spontaneous" patterns of worship in which contributions can be offered which have not been pre-planned.[6] *Listening* in worship may entail decentering the pastor's role as biblical exponent, giving way to the re-embrace of the personal testimony. Other practices of listening may include having multiple individuals present a brief message on the text, replacing the homiletical monologue with a dialogical conversation, and, in the spirit of the early Protestant conferences, creating spaces for ongoing discussion on the text beyond the service.

---

[4] Schelin, "Unbreaking the Circle," 19–32.

[5] See Ellis, *Gathering*, 56–64.

[6] A prominent popular-level example in the modern day would be the American author Frank Viola, an advocate for the house-church movement (see *Reimagining Church*, 49–72).

THE CONTESTABLE CHURCH

Tabling redirects the metaphor of the "table" or the established arrangements of power in a given society, as in the notion of political activism bringing once-marginalized persons "to the table." The verbal cognate names a process of re-orienting power dynamics; *tabling* is intentionally generative of contributions in the effort to ensure fuller participation. I see the practice of tabling as reconstituting the decision-making processes of a church with the goal of granting as much space and time as is needed for careful consideration of what the Spirit may be speaking through the contributions of all. One means of enacting this practice is to shape deliberation and decision-making with the goal of achieving consensus rather than a majority vote. Even when consensus is not achieved, the process that gives as much care to the means as it does to the ends may allow for churches to manage ongoing dissent in a peaceful manner. The Religious Society of Friends (Quakers) provides centuries of experience in this manner of decision-making, but another example would be the consensus methodologies adopted by the Evergreen Baptist Association of the American Baptist Churches, USA.[7]

The final practice is *traveling* or moving between different spaces to be transfigured by an encounter with others in new contexts. Traveling names the interdependence of a given congregation with wider associations of like-minded churches as well as the ecumenical diversity of Christianity and, finally, a willingness to learn from those who reside beyond the edges of the Church catholic, however defined. Moreover, traveling also names the grave moral responsibility of attending to differences in racial and ethnic identity or socioeconomic status. A contestable church embraces the challenge of fellowship with others whose testimony is discordant and even discomforting. Pastors usually travel most easily on behalf of their congregations by attending denominational gatherings and ministerial association meetings or supporting community organizing efforts. The benefit of receiving "more light" finds its greatest potential when the church as a whole travels to meet with others. Traveling may cross denominational and racial barriers through pulpit exchanges, shared worship to mark high points of the liturgical calendar, and collaborative efforts in tangible ministry. It may also include attending the services and meetings of other religious traditions or inviting guests into the church to represent the meaning and significance of their faith.

[7] See Sheeran, *Beyond Majority Rule*; Patton and Percival, *Sacred Decisions*.

Conclusion

The remarkable degree of overlap between Baptist ecclesiology and radical democracy has opened many avenues of reflection and, I hope, may ultimately foster many "real world" efforts to restore the dialogical character of discerning faith communities. It is my belief that God invites Christians to live into the reality of a contestable church as a Spirit-formed body that discovers an emergent unity in and through the vigorous exploration of difference as a gift and not as an obstacle. The history of the Church is replete with examples of imposing unity either by ignoring and minimizing the presence of difference or by suppressing it through the application of coercive, top-down power. Baptists, known as a tradition of dissent, bear the opportunity to provide an ecumenical witness to the Church universal. In the exercise of democratic discernment and decision-making, Baptists can exemplify a practiced faith that the Church is, truly one body with many members who, in their mutual dialogue, will grow together toward the fullness of Christ that is their eschatological hope.

BIBLIOGRAPHY

Adorno, Theodor. *Aesthetic Theory*. Translated by Christian Lenhardt. New York: Routledge and Kegan Paul, 1984.

———. *Negative Dialectics*. Translated by E. B. Ashton. New York: Continuum Publishing, 1973.

Adorno, Theodor, and Max Horkheimer. *Dialectic of Enlightenment*. Translated by John Cumming. New York: Seabury Press, 1972.

Allen, Diogenes, and Eric O. Springsted. *Philosophy for Understanding Theology*. 2nd edition. Louisville: Westminster John Knox Press, 2007.

Allen, William Lloyd. "Spiritual Discernment, the Community, and Baptists." In *Ties that Bind: Life Together in the Baptist Vision*, edited by Gary W. Furr and Curtis W. Freeman, 109–26. Macon: Smyth & Helwys, 1994.

Allen, Bob. "IMB drops ban on 'private prayer language.'" *Baptist News Global*. May 14, 2015. https://baptistnews.com/ministry/organiza-tions/item/30088-imb-drops-ban-on-private-prayer-language.

The American Baptist Magazine and Missionary Intelligencer. Vol. 2. Boston: James Loring and Lincoln & Edmands, 1819.

Ammerman, Nancy T. *Baptist Battles: Social Change and Religious Conflict in the Southern Baptist Convention*. New Brunswick: Rutgers University Press, 1990.

"Andrew Tribble." Thomas Jefferson Encyclopedia. August 31, 2011. Accessed August 17, 2023. https://www.monticello.org/research-education/thomas-jefferson-encyclopedia/andrew-tribble/.

Andrews, Charles R. "The Maine Wheele That Sets Us Awoke." *Foundations* 1/3 (July 1958): 28–41.

Anzaldúa, Gloria. *Borderlands/La Frontera: The New Mestiza*. San Francisco: Aunt Lute Books, 1987.

Axworthy, Michael. *Revolutionary Iran: A History of the Islamic Republic*. New York: Oxford University Press, 2013.

Baptist Press. "5-Point Statement on Ideals Released." August 24, 1963. Southern Baptist Historical Library and Archives, http://media.sbhla.org.s3.amazonaws.com/1780,24-Aug-1963.pdf.

Bebbington, David W. *Baptists through the Centuries: A History of a Global People*. Waco: Baylor University Press, 2010.

Bellah, Robert N., et al. *Habits of the Heart: Individualism and Commitment in American Life*. Berkeley: University of California Press, 1985.

Benson, Bruce Ellis. "Radical Democracy and Radical Christianity." *Political Theology* 10/2 (2009): 247–59.

Black, Anthony. "Communal Democracy and its History." *Political Studies* 45/1

(1997): 5–20.

Boersma, Hans. *Heavenly Participation: The Weaving of a Sacramental Tapestry.* Grand Rapids: Eerdmans, 2011.

Boswell, W. Benjamin. "Liturgy and Revolution Part I: Georgian Baptists and the Non-violent Struggle for Democracy." *Occasional Papers on Religion in Eastern Europe* 27/2 (2007): 48–71.

———. "Liturgy and Revolution Part II: Radical Christianity, Radical Democracy, and Revolution in Georgia." *Occasional Papers on Religion in Eastern Europe* 27/3 (2007): 15–31.

Brackney, William H. *Historical Dictionary of the Baptists.* 2nd ed. Historical Dictionaries of Religions, Philosophies, and Movements No. 94. Lanham: Scarecrow Press, 2009.

———. "Word Are Inadequate to Express Our Convictions: The Problem of the Autonomy of the Local Church." *American Baptist Quarterly* 38/1 (2019): 15–37.

Bronner, Stephen Eric. *Critical Theory: A Very Short Introduction.* Oxford: Oxford University Press, 2011.

Brown, J. Newton. *The Baptist Church Manual.* Philadelphia: American Baptist Publication Society, 1853.

Brown, Raymond E. "Unity and Diversity in New Testament Ecclesiology." *Novum Testamentum* 6 (1963): 298–308.

Bryant, Scott E. "An Early English Baptist Response to the Baptist Manifesto." *Perspectives in Religious Studies* 38/3 (2011): 237–48.

Calvin, John. *Institutes of the Christian Religion.* Christian Classics Ethereal Library. Accessed December 16, 2022. http://www.ccel.org/ccel/calvin/institutes.iv.xvi.html.

Canipe, Lee. *A Baptist Democracy: Separating God from Caesar in the Land of the Free.* Macon: Mercer University Press, 2011.

Carey, John J. *Carlyle Marney: A Pilgrim's Progress.* Macon: Mercer University Press, 1980.

Carter, J. Kameron. *Race: A Theological Account.* Oxford: Oxford University Press, 2008.

Cavanaugh, William T. "Killing for the Telephone Company: Why the Nation-State Is Not the Keeper of the Common Good." *Modern Theology* 20/2 (2004): 243–74.

Chilton, Amy L. Steven R. Harmon, eds., *Sources of Light: Resources for Baptist Churches Practicing Theology.* Perspectives on Baptist Identities. Macon: Mercer University Press, 2020.

Coles, Romand. *Beyond Gated Politics: Reflections for the Possibility of Democracy.* Minneapolis: University of Minnesota Press, 2005.

———. *Rethinking Generosity: Critical Theory and the Politics of Caritas.* Ithaca: Cornell University Press, 1997.

Conclusion

———. *Self/Power/Other: Political Theory and Dialogical Ethics*. Ithaca: Cornell University Press, 1992.

———. "Storied Others and Possibilities of *Caritas*: Milbank and Neo-Nietzschean Ethics." *Modern Theology* 8/4 (October 1992): 331–51.

———. *Visionary Pragmatism: Radical and Ecological Democracy in Neoliberal Times*. Durham: Duke University Press, 2016.

———. "The Wild Patience of Radical Democracy: Beyond Žižek's Lack." In *Radical Democracy: Politics between Abundance and Lack*, edited by Lars Tønder and Lasse Thomassen, 68–85. Manchester: Manchester University Press, 2005.

Collinson, Patrick, John Craig, and Brett Usher, eds. *Conferences and Combinations Lectures in the Elizabethan Church: Dedham and Bury St. Edmunds 1582–1590*. Church of England Record Society Vol. 10. Woodbridge: Boydell Press, 2003.

Colwell, John E. *Promise and Presence: An Exploration of Sacramental Theology*. Milton Keynes, UK: Paternoster, 2005.

"Comparison Chart." Southern Baptist Convention. Accessed 16 December 2022. https://bfm.sbc.net/comparison-chart/.

Conner, W. T. *Christian Doctrine*. Nashville: Broadman Press, 1937.

Connolly, William E. *Identity/Difference: Democratic Notions of Political Paradox*. Expanded edition. Minneapolis: University of Minnesota Press, 2002.

———. *Pluralism*. Durham: Duke University Press, 2005.

———. *The Terms of Political Discourse*. 3rd ed. Oxford: Blackwell, 1993.

———. *Why I Am Not a Secularist*. Minneapolis: University of Minnesota Press, 1999.

Corrigan, John, and Winthrop S. Hudson. *Religion in America: An Historical Account of the Development of American Religious Life*. 7th ed. Upper Saddle River: Pearson Education, Inc., 2004.

Cothen, Grady C. *What Happened to the Southern Baptist Convention? A Memoir of the Controversy*. Macon: Smyth & Helwys, 1993.

Cotton, John. *The True Constitution of a Particular Visible Church, Proved by Scripture*. London: Samuel Satterthwaite, 1642.

Critchley, Simon. *Continental Philosophy: A Very Short Introduction*. Oxford: Oxford University Press, 2001.

Dagg, John Leadley. *Manual of Theology, Second Part: A Treatise on Church Order*. Charleston: Southern Baptist Publication Society, 1859.

Davis, Andrew. "Practical Issues in Elder Ministry." In *Baptist Foundations: Church Government for an Anti-Institutional Age*, edited by Mark Dever and Jonathan Leeman, 291–310. Nashville: Broadman & Holman Academic, 2015.

Dever, Mark. "Baptist Polity and Elders." *Journal for Baptist Theology and Ministry* 3/1 (2005): 5–37.

———. "Elders and Deacons in History." In *Baptist Foundations: Church Government for an Anti-Institutional Age*, edited by Mark ʃDever and Jonathan Leeman, 229–42. Nashville: Broadman & Holman Academic, 2015.

———, ed. *Polity: Biblical Arguments on How to Conduct Church Life*. Washington: Center for Church Reform, 2001.

DeWeese, Charles W. *Baptist Church Covenants*. Nashville: Broadman Press, 1990.

Dilday, Russell. "Mullins the Theologian: Between the Extremes." *Review & Expositor* 96/1 (1999):75–86.

———. "The Significance of E. Y. Mullins' *The Axioms of Religion*." *Baptist History & Heritage* 43/1 (2008): 83–93.

Downing, Lisa. *The Cambridge Introduction to Michel Foucault*. Cambridge: Cambridge University Press, 2008.

Dunn, James. "Church, State, and Soul Competency." *Review & Expositor* 96/1 (1999): 61–73.

Durnbaugh, Donald F. *The Believers' Church: The History and Character of Radical Protestantism*. Eugene: Wipf and Stock Publishers: [1968] 2003.

Durso, Pam. "Baptist Women in America, 1638–1800." In *Distinctively Baptist: Essays on Baptist History. A Festschrift in Honor of Walter B. Shurden*, edited by Marc A. Jolley and John D. Pierce, 193–218. Macon: Mercer University Press, 2005.

Dykstra, Craig, and Dorothy C. Bass. "Times of Yearning, Practices of Faith." In *Practicing Our Faith: A Way of Life for a Searching People*, edited by Dorothy C. Bass, 1–12. San Francisco: Jossey-Bass Publishers, 1997.

Ellis, Christopher J. *Gathering: A Theology and Spirituality of Worship in Free Church Tradition*. London: SCM Press, 2004.

Emerson, Matthew Y., and R. Lucas Stamps, eds. *Baptists and the Christian Tradition: Toward an Evangelical Baptist Catholicity*. Nashville: Broadman & Holman Academic, 2020.

Fiddes, Paul S. *Tracks and Traces: Baptist Identity in Church and Theology*. Studies in Baptist History and Thought. Vol. 13. Milton Keynes, UK: Paternoster, 2003.

Freeman, Curtis W. "Can Baptist Theology Be Revisioned?" *Perspectives in Religious Studies* 24/3 (1997): 273–310.

———. "A Confession for Catholic Baptists." In *Ties That Bind: Life Together in the Baptist Vision*, edited by Gary A. Furr and Curtis W. Freeman, 83–98. Macon: Smyth & Helwys, 1994.

———. *Contesting Catholicity: Theology for Other Baptists*. Waco: Baylor University Press, 2014.

———. "E. Y. Mullins and the Siren Songs of Modernity." *Review & Expositor*

96/1 (1999): 23–42.

———. "Roger Williams, American Democracy, and the Baptists." *Perspectives in Religious Studies* 34/3 (2007): 267–86.

Freeman, Curtis, W., et al., eds. *Baptist Roots: A Reader in the Theology of a Christian People*. Valley Forge: Judson Press, 1999.

Foucault, Michel. "On the Genealogy of Ethics: An Overview of Work in Progress." In *Michel Foucault: Beyond Structuralism and Hermeneutics*. 2nd ed, edited by Hubert L. Dreyfus and Paul Rabinow, 229–52. Chicago: University of Chicago Press, 1983.

Garrett, James Leo, Jr. "An Affirmation of Congregational Polity." *Journal of Baptist Theology and Ministry* 3/1 (2005): 38–55.

Garrett, James Leo, Jr. *Baptist Theology: A Four-Century Study*. Macon: Mercer University Press, 2009.

Gaustad, Edwin S. "The Backus-Leland Tradition." In *Baptist Concepts of the Church: A Survey of the Historical and Theological Issues which have Produced Changes in Church Order*, edited by Winthrop S. Hudson, 106–34. Philadelphia: Judson Press, 1959.

Gaustad, Edwin S., ed. *Baptist Piety: The Last Will and Testament of Obadiah Holmes*. Grand Rapids: Christian University Press, 1978.

George, Timothy. "The Priesthood of All Believers and the Quest for Theological Integrity." *Criswell Theological Review* 3/2 (1989): 283–94.

Gentry, Weston. "As Baptists Prepare to Meet, Calvinism Debate Shifts to Heresy Accusation." *Christianity Today*, June 18, 2012. http://www.christianitytoday.com/ct/2012/juneweb-only/baptists-calvinism-heresy.html.

Glasser, Arthur F. "Church Growth at Fuller." *Missiology* 14/4 (1986): 401–20.

Goen, C. C. *Revivalism and Separatism in New England, 1750–1800*. Middletown: Wesleyan University Press, 1987.

Goossen, Rachel Waltner. "'Defanging the Beast': Mennonite Responses to John Howard Yoder's Sexual Abuse." *Mennonite Quarterly Review* 89/1 (2015): 7–80.

Grantham, Thomas. *Christianismus Primitivus*. London: Francis Smith, 1678.

Grenz, Stanley J. *The Baptist Congregation: A Guide to Baptist Belief and Practice*. Valley Forge: Judson Press, 1985.

———. *Theology for the Community of God*. Grand Rapids: Eerdmans, 2000.

Grenz, Stanley J., and John R. Franke. *Beyond Foundationalism: Shaping Theology in a Postmodern Context*. Louisville: Westminster John Knox Press, 2001.

Griffith, Benjamin. "A Short Treatise Concerning a True and Orderly Gospel Church." In *Polity: Biblical Arguments on How to Conduct Church Life*, edited by Mark Dever, 95–114. Washington: Center for Church Reform, 2001.

Guth, Karen. "Doing Justice to the Complex Legacy of John Howard Yoder:

Restorative Justice Resources in Witness and Feminist Ethics." *Journal of the Society of Christian Ethics* 35/2 (2015): 119–39.

Gutmann, Amy, and Dennis Thompson. *Why Deliberative Democracy?* Princeton: Princeton University Press, 2004.

Habermas, Jürgen. *Moral Consciousness and Communicative Action.* Translated by Christian Lenhardt and Shierry Weber Nicholsen. Cambridge: MIT Press, 1990.

Hammett, John S. *Biblical Foundations for Baptist Churches: A Contemporary Ecclesiology.* Grand Rapids: Kregel, 2005.

———. "From Church Competence to Soul Competence: The Devolution of Baptist Ecclesiology." *Journal of Baptist Theology and Ministry* 3/1 (2005): 145–63.

Harmon, Steven R. *Baptist Identity and the Ecumenical Future: Story, Tradition, and the Recovery of Community.* Waco: Baylor University Press, 2016.

———. *Towards Baptist Catholicity: Essays on Tradition and the Baptist Vision.* Studies in Baptist History and Thought. Vol. 27. Milton Keynes, UK: Paternoster, 2006.

Harrell, David Edwin, Jr. "The Evolution of Plain-Folk Religion in the South, 1835–1920." In *Varieties of Southern Religious Experience*, edited by Samuel S. Hill, 24–51. Baton Rouge: Louisiana State University Press, 1988.

Harvey, Barry. "Where, Then, Do We Stand? Baptists, History, and Authority." *Perspectives in Religious Studies* 29/4 (2002): 359–80.

Hasker, William. "Faith-Learning Integration: An Overview." *Christian Scholar's Review* 21/3 (1992): 234–48.

Hatch, Nathan O. *The Democratization of American Christianity.* New Haven: Yale University Press, 1989.

Hauerwas, Stanley, and Romand Coles. *Christianity, Democracy, and the Radical Ordinary: Conversations Between a Radical Democrat and a Christian.* Eugene: Cascade Books, 2008.

Haykin, Michael A. G. "Some Historical Roots of Congregationalism," In *Baptist Foundations: Church Government for an Anti-Institutional Age*, edited by Mark Dever and Jonathan Leeman, 27–46. Nashville: Broadman & Holman Academic, 2015.

Haymes, Brian, Ruth Gouldbourne, and Anthony R. Cross. *On Being the Church: Revisioning Baptist Identity.* Eugene: Wipf & Stock, 2009.

Haynes, Dudley C. *The Baptist Denomination: Its History, Doctrines and Ordinances.* New York: Sheldon, Blakeman & Co., 1856.

Held, David. *Introduction to Critical Theory: Horkheimer to Habermas.* Berkeley: University of California Press, 1980.

Helwys, Thomas. *The Mystery of Iniquity.* Edited by Richard Groves. Macon: Mercer University Press, 1998.

Heyrman, Christine Lee. *Southern Cross: The Beginnings of the Bible Belt.* New

York: Alfred A. Knopf, 1997.

Hill, Christopher. *The World Turned Upside Down: Radical Ideas During the English Revolution*. London: Penguin Books, 1975.

Hinson, E. Glenn. "The Baptist Experience in the United States." *Review & Expositor* 79/2 (1982): 217–30.

———. "E. Y. Mullins as Interpreter of the Baptist Tradition." *Review & Expositor* 96/1 (1999): 109–22.

———. "Oh Baptists, How Your Corporation Has Grown!" In *Distinctively Baptist: Essays on Baptist History*, edited by Marc A. Jolley and John D. Pierce, 17–34. Macon: Mercer University Press, 2005.

Hiscox, Edward T. *The Baptist Church Directory: A Guide to the Doctrines and Practices of Baptist Churches*. New York: Sheldon & Co., 1859.

———. *The New Directory for Baptist Churches*. Philadelphia: American Baptist Publication Society, 1894.

Hobbs, Herschell H. *The Baptist Faith and Message*. Rev. ed. Nashville: Convention Press, 1971.

Hoelzl, Michael, and Graham Ward. *The New Visibility of Religion: Studies in Religion and Cultural Hermeneutics*. New York: Continuum, 2008.

Holmes, Stephen R. *Listening to the Past: The Place of Tradition in Christian Theology*. Grand Rapids: Baker Academic, 2002.

Honig, Bonnie. *Political Theory and the Displacement of Politics*. Ithaca: Cornell University Press, 1993.

Hovey, Alvah. *Manual of Systematic Theology and Christian Ethics*. Boston: Henry A. Young & Co., 1877.

Hubbard, William. *A General History of New England from the Discovery to MDCLXXX*. 2nd ed. Boston: Charles C. Little and James Brown, 1848.

Hudson, Winthrop S. *Baptists in Transition: Individualism and Christian Responsibility*. Valley Forge: Judson Press, 1979.

———. "By Way of Perspective." In *Baptist Concepts of the Church: A Survey of the Historical and Theological Issues which have Produced Changes in Church Order*, edited by Winthrop S. Hudson, 11–29. Philadelphia: Judson Press, 1959.

Humphreys, Fisher. *The Way We Were: How Southern Baptist Theology Has Changed and What It Means to Us All*. Rev. ed. Macon: Smyth & Helwys, 2002.

Ignatius of Antioch. "To the Magnesians." In *The Apostolic Fathers, Volume I*. Edited and translated by Bart D. Ehrman, 241–55. Loeb Classical Library 24. Cambridge: Harvard University Press, 2003.

James, Larry. "'In the world but not but not of the world': Church Discipline in Antebellum Mississippi and Louisiana Baptist Churches." *Restoration Quarterly* 25/2 (1982): 82–101.

James, Sydney V. *John Clarke and His Legacies: Religion and Law in Colonial*

Rhode Island 1638–1750. Edited by Theodore Dwight Bozeman. University Park: Pennsylvania State University Press, 1999.

Jardine, Murray. *The Making and Unmaking of Technological Society: How Christianity Can Save Modernity from Itself.* Grand Rapids: Brazos Press, 2004.

James Jenkins, "The African American Baptist Pastor and Church Government: The Myth of the Dictator," *Journal for Baptist Theology and Ministry* 2/1 (2004): 74-86.

Johnson, W. B. "The Gospel Developed through the Government and Order of the Churches of Jesus Christ." In *Polity: Biblical Arguments on How to Conduct Church Life,* edited by Mark Dever, 161–248. Washington: Center for Church Reform, 2001.

Jones, Robert P. "Revision-ing Baptist Identity from a Theocentric Perspective." *Perspectives in Religious Studies* 26/1 (1999): 35–58.

Jones, Samuel. "A Treatise of Church Discipline and a Directory." In *Polity: Biblical Arguments on How to Conduct Church Life,* edited by Mark Dever, 137–60. Washington: Center for Church Reform, 2001.

Jung, Joanne J. *Godly Conversation: Rediscovering the Puritan Practice of Conference.* Grand Rapids: Reformation Heritage Books, 2011.

Kapoor, Ilan. "Deliberative Democracy or Agonistic Pluralism? The Relevance of the Habermas-Mouffean Debate for Third World Politics." *Alternatives* 27 (2002): 459–66.

Käsemann, Ernst. "Unity and Diversity in New Testament Ecclesiology." *Novum Testamentum* 6 (1963): 290–97.

Keach, Benjamin. "The Glory of a True Church and Its Discipline Displayed." In *Polity: Biblical Arguments on How to Conduct Church Life,* edited by Mark Dever, 63–94. Washington: Center for Church Reform, 2001.

Keener, Craig S. *The Gospel of John: A Commentary.* 2 vols. Grand Rapids: Baker Academic, 2003.

Keep, Jack. *What is a Baptist Association?* Shaumburg: Regular Baptist Press, 1989.

Koyzis, David T. *Political Visions and Illusions: A Survey and Christian Critique of Contemporary Ideologies.* Downers Grove: InterVarsity Press, 2003.

Laclau, Ernesto, and Chantal Mouffe. *Hegemony and Socialist Strategy: Towards a Radical Democratic Politics.* London: Verso Books, 1985.

Land, Richard, and Ralph H. Langley. "Pastoral Leadership: Authoritarian or Persuasive?" *Theological Educator* 37 (1988): 75–92.

Leeman, Jonathan. *Church Discipline: How the Church Protects the Name of Jesus.* Wheaton: Crossway Books, 2012.

Leland, John. "Advertisement—Great Reward Offered." In *The Writings of the Late Elder John Leland,* edited by L. F. Greene, 680–82. New York: G.Wx. Wood, 1845.

———. "The Government of Christ a Christocracy." In *The Writings of the Late*

Elder John Leland, edited by L. F. Greene, 273–82. New York: G. W. Wood, 1845.

———. "Letter to Thomas Bingham, esq., July 1833." In *The Writings of the Late Elder John Leland,* edited by L.F. Greene, 642–43. New York: G. W. Wood, 1845.

———. "The Rights of Conscience Inalienable." In *The Writings of the Late Elder John Leland,* edited by L. F. Greene, 179–92. New York: G. W. Wood, 1845.

———. "The Virginia Chronicle." In *The Writings of the Late Elder John Leland.,* edited by L. F. Greene, 92–124. New York: G. W. Wood, 1845.

Lemke, Steve W. "History or Revisionist History? How Calvinistic Were the Overwhelming Majority of Baptists and Their Confessions in the South until the Twentieth Century?" *Southwestern Journal of Theology* 57/2 (2015): 227–54.

Leonard, Bill J. *Baptist Ways: A History.* Valley Forge: Judson Press, 2003.

———. *The Challenge of Being Baptist: Owning a Scandalous Past and an Uncertain Future.* Waco: Baylor University Press, 2010.

———. "In Search of the One, True Church: Ecclesiology in *The Baptist Faith and Message* (1963)." In *Sacred Mandates of Conscience: Interpretations of The Baptist Faith and Message,* edited by Jeff B. Pool, 161–72. Macon: Smyth & Helwys, 1997.

———. "Southern Baptists and the Laity." *Review & Expositor* 84/4 (1987): 633–47.

———. "Types of Confessional Documents among Baptists." *Review & Expositor* 76/1 (1979): 29–42.

———. *God's Last and Only Hope: The Fragmentation of the Southern Baptist Convention.* Grand Rapids: Eerdmans, 1990.

Lloyd, Moya, and Adrian Little. "Introduction." In *The Politics of Radical Democracy,* edited by Moya Lloyd and Adrian Little, 1–12. Edinburgh: Edinburgh University Press, 2009.

Locke, John. "A Letter Concerning Toleration." 1689. Translated by William Popple. Constitution Society. http://www.constitution.org/jl/tolerati.htm.

Lovejoy, Arthur O. *The Great Chain of Being: A Study of the History of an Idea.* Cambridge: Harvard University Press, 1936.

Lumpkin, William L. *Baptist Confessions of Faith.* Rev. ed. Valley Forge: Judson Press, 1969.

———. *Baptist Foundations in the South: Tracing through the Separates the Influence of the Great Awakening, 1754–1787.* Nashville: Broadman Press, 1961.

———. "The Role of Women in Eighteenth Century Virginia Baptist Life." *Baptist History & Heritage* 8/3 (1973): 158–67.

Luther, Martin. "To the Christian Nobility of the German Nation Concerning the Reform of the Christian Estate, 1520." In *Selected Writings of Martin*

Luther. 4 vols., edited by Theodore G. Tappert, 251–353. Minneapolis: Fortress Press, 2007.

MacArthur, Robert Stuart. *The Baptists: Their Principle, Their Progress, Their Prospect*. Philadelphia: American Baptist Publication Society, 1911.

MacIntyre, Alasdair. *After Virtue: A Study in Moral Theory*. 2nd ed. Notre Dame: University of Notre Dame Press, 1984.

Madison, Jessica. *In Subjection: Church Discipline in the Early American South, 1760–1830*. Macon: Mercer University Press, 2014.

Madkins, Jerry B. "The Leadership Crisis in the Black Church: The Search for the Right Pastor." *The Journal of the Interdenominational Theological Center* 19/1–2 (1991–1992): 102–12.

Manoussakis, Jon Panteleimon. *After God: Richard Kearney and the Religious Turn in Continental Philosophy*. Perspectives in Continental Philosophy 49. New York: Fordham University Press, 2006.

Maring, Norman H. "The Individualism of Francis Wayland." In *Baptist Concepts of the Church: A Survey of the Historical and Theological Issues which have Produced Changes in Church Order*, edited by Winthrop S. Hudson, 135–69. Philadelphia: Judson Press, 1959.

———, and Winthrop S. Hudson. *A Baptist Manual of Polity and Practice*. 2nd rev. ed., edited by David Gregg. Valley Forge: Judson Press, 2012.

Marney, Carlyle. *The Coming Faith*. Nashville: Abingdon Press, 1970.

———. *Faith in Conflict*. Nashville: Abingdon Press, 1957.

———. *Priests to Each Other*. Macon: Smyth & Helwys, [1974] 1991.

———. *The Recovery of the Person*. Nashville: Abingdon Press, 1969.

Marsh, Charles. *The Beloved Community: How Faith Shapes Social Justice, From the Civil Rights Movement to Today*. New York: Basic Books, 2005.

Marshall, Molly T. "Exercising Liberty of Conscience: Freedom in Private Interpretation." In *Baptists in the Balance: The Tension between Freedomf and Responsibility*, edited by Everett C. Goodwin, 141–50. Valley Forge: Judson Press, 1997.

Maston, T. B. *Isaac Backus: Pioneer of Religious Liberty*. Rochester: American Baptist Historical Society, 1962.

Mathews, Donald G. *Religion in the Old South*. Chicago: University of Chicago Press, 1977.

McBeth, H. Leon. *The Baptist Heritage*. Nashville: Broadman Press, 1983.

McClendon, James William, Jr. *Ethics: Systematic Theology Volume I*. Rev. ed. Nashville: Abingdon Press, 2002.

———. *Doctrine: Systematic Theology Volume II*. Nashville: Abingdon Press, 1994.

McGrath, Alister E. *Christian Theology: An Introduction*. 5th edition. Oxford: Wiley-Blackwell, 2011.

McLoughlin, William G. *New England Dissent, 1630–1833*. 2 vols. Cambridge:

Harvard University Press, 1971.

McLoughlin, William G., and Martha Whiting Davidson. "The Baptist Debate of April 14–15, 1668." *Proceedings of the Massachusetts Historical Society* 76 (1964): 91–133.

McNutt, William Roy. *Polity and Practice in Baptist Churches.* Philadelphia: Judson Press, 1935.

McSwain, Larry. "A Critical Appraisal of the Church Growth Movement." *Review & Expositor* 77/4 (1980): 521–38.

Medley, Mark S. "Catholics, Baptists, and the Normativity of Tradition." *Perspectives in Religious Studies* 22/2 (1995): 119–29.

———. "Stewards, Interrogators, and Inventors: Toward a Practice of Tradition." *Pro Ecclesia* 18/1 (2009): 69–92.

Mell, P. H. "Corrective Church Discipline: With a Development of the Scriptural Principles upon which it is Based." In *Polity: Biblical Arguments on How to Conduct Church Life*, edited by Mark Dever, 409–78. Washington: Center for Church Reform, 2001.

Merleau-Ponty, Maurice. *The Visible and the Invisible.* Translated by Alphonso Lingis. Evanston: Northwestern University Press, 1968.

Merkle, Benjamin L. "The Biblical Role of Elders." In *Baptist Foundations: Church Government for an Anti-Institutional Age*, edited by Mark Dever and Jonathan Leeman, 271–90. Nashville: Broadman & Holman Academic, 2015.

———. "The Scriptural Basis for Elders." In *Baptist Foundations: Church Government for an Anti-Institutional Age*, edited by Mark Dever and Jonathan Leeman, 243–52. Nashville: Broadman & Holman Academic, 2015.

Miller, David. *Political Philosophy: A Very Short Introduction.* Oxford: Oxford University Press, 2003.

Mohler, R. Albert, Jr. "Baptist Theology at the Crossroads: The Legacy of E. Y. Mullins." *Southern Baptist Journal of Theology* 3/4 (1999): 4–22.

———. "Discipline: The Missing Mark." In *Polity: Biblical Arguments on How to Conduct Church Life*, edited by Mark Dever, 43–62. Washington: Center for Church Reform, 2001.

Moore, Scott H. *The Limits of Liberal Democracy: Politics and Religion at the End of Modernity.* Downers Grove: InterVarsity Press, 2009.

Mouffe, Chantal. *Agonistics: Thinking the World Politically.* London: Verso Books, 2013.

Mullins, E. Y. *The Axioms of Religion: A New Interpretation of the Baptist Faith.* Philadelphia: Judson Press, 1908.

———. *Baptist Beliefs.* Valley Forge: Judson Press, 1925.

———. *The Christian Religion in its Doctrinal Expression.* New York: Roger Williams Press, 1917.

———. *Freedom and Authority in Religion.* Philadelphia: Griffith & Rowland

Press, 1913.

Murphy, Nancey. *Beyond Liberalism and Fundamentalism: How Modern and Postmodern Philosophy Set the Theological Agenda*. New York: Trinity Press International, 2007.

Najar, Monica. *Evangelizing the South: A Social History of Church and State in Early America*. New York: Oxford University Press, 2008.

———. "'Meddling with Emancipation': Baptists, Authority, and the Rift over Slavery in the Upper South." *Journal of the Early Republic* 25 (2005): 157–86.

———. "'More Striking...than the Loudest Preaching': Baptist Women's Testimony in the Early Evangelical South." *Perspectives in Religious Studies* 36/4 (2009): 433–43.

Newson, Ryan Andrew. *Radical Friendship: The Politics of Communal Discernment*. Minneapolis: Fortress Press, 2017.

Patton, Marcia J., and Nora J. Percival. *Sacred Decisions: Consensus in Faith Communities*. Valley Forge: Judson Press, 2021.

Pearse, Meic. *The Great Restoration: The Religious Radicals of the 16th and 17th Centuries*. Carlisle: Paternoster Press, 1998.

Pendleton, James Madison. *Church Manual*. Philadelphia: American Baptist Publication Society, 1867.

Pestana, Carla G. *Quakers and Baptists in Colonial Massachusetts*. Cambridge: Cambridge University Press, 1991.

Porter, Fran. "Facing Harm: What to Do with the Theology of John Howard Yoder?" *Anabaptism Today* 4/1 (2022): 1–13. Available at https://anabaptismtoday.co.uk/index.php/home/article/view/194.

Prechtel, Daniel L. *Where Two or Three Are Gathered: Spiritual Direction for Small Groups*. Kindle edition. New York: Morehouse Publishing, 2012.

Pressler, Paul. *A Hill on Which to Die: One Southern Baptist's Journey*. Nashville: Broadman & Holman, 1999.

Rainer, Thom S. *The Book of Church Growth: History, Theology, and Principles*. Nashville: Broadman Press, 1993.

Ransby, Barbara. *Ella Baker and the Black Freedom Movement: A Radical Democratic Vision*. Chapel Hill: University of North Carolina Press, 2003.

Rawls, John. *A Theory of Justice*. Cambridge: Belknap Press, 1971.

Reid, Daniel G., et al. *Concise Dictionary of Christianity in America*. Eugene: Wipf & Stock, [1995] 2002.

Reynolds, J. L. "Church Polity: Or the Kingdom of Christ, in Its Internal and External Development." In *Polity: Biblical Arguments on How to Conduct Church Life*, edited by Mark Dever, 295–408. Washington: Center for Church Reform, 2001.

Robinson, John. *The Works of John Robinson: Pastor of the Pilgrim Fathers*. 2 vols. Edited by Robert Ashton. London: John Snow, 1851.

Saint Augustine. *Confessions*. Translated by Henry Chadwick. Oxford: Oxford University Press, 1991.

Sandel, Michael. *Liberalism and the Limits of Justice*. Cambridge: Cambridge University Press, 1982.

Schelin, Christopher. "'In a Congregational Way': The Baptist Possibility of Sacramental and Radical Democracy." *Journal of European Baptist Studies* 10/3 (2010): 22–36.

———. "Unbreaking the Circle: Conversational Hermeneutics and Intra-Congregational Difference." *Journal of European Baptist Studies* 16/2 (2016): 19–32.

Schlesinger, Arthur, Jr. *The Disuniting of America: Reflections on a Multicultural Society*. New York: Norton, 1993.

———. *The Vital Center: The Politics of Freedom*. Boston: Houghton Mifflin, 1949.

Scholer, David M. "The Authority of the Bible and Private Interpretation: A Dilemma of Baptist Freedom." In *Baptists in the Balance: The Tension between Freedom and Responsibility*, edited by Everett C. Goodwin, 174–93. Valley Forge: Judson Press, 1997.

Scruton, Roger. *Kant: A Very Short Introduction*. Oxford: Oxford University Press, 2001.

Sheeran, Michael J. *Beyond Majority Rule: Voteless Decisions in the Religious Society of Friends*. Denver: Regis College, 1983.

Sherratt, Yvonne. *Adorno's Positive Dialectic*. Cambridge: Cambridge University Press, 2002.

Shurden, Walter B. *Associationalism Among Baptists in America: 1707–1814*. New York: ArnoPress, 1980.

———. *The Baptist Identity: Four Fragile Freedoms*. Macon: Smyth & Helwys, 1993.

———. "The Baptist Identity and the Baptist *Manifesto*." *Perspectives in Religious Studies* 25/4 (1998): 321–40.

———. *Not an Easy Journey: Some Transitions in Baptist Life*. Macon: Mercer University Press, 2005.

———. "The Priesthood of All Believers and Pastoral Authority in Baptist Thought." In *Proclaiming the Baptist Vision: The Priesthood of All Believers*, edited by Walter B. Shurden, 131–54. Macon: Smyth & Helwys, 1993.

———. "Southern Baptist Responses to their Confessional Statements." *Review & Expositor* 76/1 (1979): 69–84.

———. "The Struggle for the Soul of the SBC: Reflections and Interpretations." In *The Struggle for the Soul of the SBC: Moderate Responses to a Fundamentalist Movement*, edited by Walter B. Shurden, 275–90. Macon: Mercer University Press, 1993.

Smith, James K. A. *Who's Afraid of Postmodernism? Taking Derrida, Lyotard, and*

Foucault to Church. Grand Rapids: Baker Academic, 2006.

Smith, John E. "Freedom as Self-Determination." In *On Freedom*. Vol. 10 of Boston University Studies in Philosophy and Religion, edited by Leroy S. Rouner, 79–95. Notre Dame: University of Notre Dame Press, 1989.

Smyth, John. "Parallels, Censures, Observations." In vol. 2 of *The Works of John Smyth*, edited by W. T. Whitley, 327–562. Cambridge: Cambridge University Press, 1915.

———. "Principles and Inferences Concerning the Visible Church." In vol. 2 of *The Works of John Smyth*, edited by W. T. Whitley, 249–68. Cambridge: Cambridge University Press, 1915.

Snyder, C. Arnold. "Swiss Anabaptism: The Beginnings, 1523–1525." In *A Companion to Anabaptism and Spiritualism, 1521–1700*. Vol. 6 of Brill's Companions to the Christian Tradition, edited by John D. Roth and James M. Stayer, 48–64. Leiden: Brill Publishers, 2007.

Solomon, Robert C., and Kathleen M. Higgins. *What Nietzsche Really Said*. New York: Schocken Books, 2000.

Sorabji, Richard. *Self: Ancient and Modern Insights about Individuality, Life and Death*. Oxford: Clarendon Press, 2006.

Spangler, Jewel. "Democratic Religion Revisited: Early Baptists in the American South." In *Through a Glass Darkly: Contested Notions of Baptist Identity*, edited by Keith Harper, 30–50. Tuscaloosa: University of Alabama Press, 2012.

Sparks, John. *The Roots of Appalachian Christianity: The Life and Legacy of Elder Shubal Stearns*. Lexington: University Press of Kentucky, 2001.

Stewart, Howard R. *Baptists and Local Autonomy: The Development, Distortions, Decline and New Directions of Local Autonomy in Baptist Churches*. Hicksville: Exposition Press, 1974.

Stout, Jeffrey. *Democracy and Tradition*. Princeton: Princeton University Press, 2004.

Strong, Augustus H. *Systematic Theology*. 3 vols. Philadelphia: American Baptist Publication Society, 1907–1909.

Taylor, Charles. *Sources of the Self: The Making of Modern Identity*. Cambridge: Cambridge University Press, 1989.

Thompson, David M. "Conscience, Private Judgment and the Community of Faith." *Mid-Stream* 40/1 (2001): 1–20.

Thompson, James J., Jr. *Tried as by Fire: Southern Baptists and the Religious Controversies of the 1920s*. Macon: Mercer University Press, 1982.

Tillich, Paul. *The Protestant Era*. Translated by James Luther Adams. Chicago: University of Chicago Press, 1948.

Tønder, Lars, and Lasse Thomassen. "Introduction: rethinking radical democracy between abundance and lack." In *Radical Democracy: Politics between*

Abundance and Lack, edited by Lars Tønder and Lasse Thomassen, 1–13. Manchester: Manchester University Press, 2005.

Torbet, Robert G. "Landmarkism." In *Baptist Concepts of the Church: A Survey of the Historical and Theological Issues which have Produced Changes in Church Order*, edited by Winthrop S. Hudson, 170–95. Philadelphia: Judson Press, 1959.

Towns, Elmer, C. Peter Wagner, and Thom S. Rainer. *The Everychurch Guide to Growth: How Any Plateaued Church Can Grow*. Nashville: Broadman & Holman, 1998.

Viola, Frank. *Reimagining Church: Pursuing the Dream of Organic Christianity*. Colorado Springs: David C. Cook, 2008.

Walker, Williston. *The Creeds and Platforms of Congregationalism*. Boston: The Pilgrim Press, [1893] 1960.

Ward, Bruce K. *Redeeming the Enlightenment: Christianity and the Liberal Virtues*. Grand Rapids: Eerdmans, 2010.

Ward, Graham. *The Politics of Discipleship: Becoming Postmaterial Citizens*. Grand Rapids: Baker Academic, 2009.

Wayland, Francis. *The Limitations of Human Responsibility*. Boston: Gould, Kendall, and Lincoln, 1838.

———. *Notes on the Principles and Practices of Baptist Churches*. New York: Sheldon & Co, [1856] 1867.

Weaver, C. Douglas. "The Baptist Ecclesiology of E. Y. Mullins: Individualism and the New Testament Church." *Baptist History & Heritage* 43/1 (2008): 18–34.

———. "Early English Baptists: Individual Conscience and Eschatological Ecclesiology." *Perspectives in Religious Studies* 38/2 (2011): 141–58.

———. *In Search of the New Testament Church: The Baptist Story*. Macon: Mercer University Press, 2008.

———. Review of *Towards Baptist Catholicity*, by Steven R. Harmon. *Baptist History & Heritage* 43/3 (2008): 105–107.

———. "Second Baptist Church, Atlanta: A Paradigm of Southern Baptist Identity in the Nineteenth Century." In *Distinctively Baptist: Essays on Baptist History*, edited by Marc A. Jolley and John D. Pierce, 75–98. Macon: Mercer University Press, 2005.

Wellum, Stephen J., and Kirk Wellum. "The Biblical and Theological Case for Congregationalism." In *Baptist Foundations: Church Government for an Anti-Institutional Age*, edited by Mark Dever and Jonathan Leeman, 47–77. Nashville: Broadman & Holman Academic, 2015.

West, Cornel. *Democracy Matters: Winning the Fight against Imperialism*. New York: Penguin Books, 2004.

White, Thomas. "The Why, How, and When of Church Discipline." In *Baptist*

Foundations: Church Government for an Anti-Institutional Age, edited by Mark Dever and Jonathan Leeman, 199–226. Nashville: Broadman & Holman Academic, 2015.

Wilentz, Sean. *The Rise of American Democracy: Jefferson to Lincoln*. New York: W. W. Norton, 2005.

Williams, D. H. *Evangelicals and Tradition: The Formative Influence of the Early Church*. Grand Rapids: Baker Academic, 2005.

———. *Retrieving the Tradition and Renewing Evangelicalism: A Primer for Suspicious Protestants*. Grand Rapids: Eerdmans, 1999.

Wills, Gregory A. *Democratic Religion: Freedom, Authority, and Church Discipline in the Baptist South, 1785–1900*. New York: Oxford University Press, 1997.

Wolin, Sheldon. *Democracy Incorporated: Managed Democracy and the Specter of Inverted Totalitarianism*. Princeton: Princeton University Press, 2008.

———. "Fugitive Democracy." In *Democracy and Difference: Contesting the Boundaries of the Political*, edited by Seyla Benhabib, 31–45. Princeton: Princeton University Press, 1996.

———. *Politics and Vision: Continuity and Innovation in Western Political Thought*. Expanded edition. Princeton: Princeton University Press, 2004.

———. *The Presence of the Past: Essays on the State and the Constitution*. Baltimore: Johns Hopkins University Press, 1989.

Wood, Nathan E. *The History of the First Baptist Church of Boston (1665–1899)*. Philadelphia: American Baptist Publication Society, 1899.

"The Word of God in the Life of the Church: A Report of International Conversations between the Catholic Church and the Baptist World Alliance 2006–2010." *American Baptist Quarterly* 31/1 (2012): 28–122.

Wright, Nigel G. *Free Church, Free State: The Positive Baptist Vision*. Milton Keynes, UK: Paternoster Press, 2005.

Wring, Robert. "Elder Rule and Southern Baptist Church Polity." *Journal for Baptist Theology and Ministry* 3/1 (2005): 188–212.

Yarnell, Malcolm, III. "Changing Baptist Concepts of Royal Priesthood: John Smyth and Edgar Young Mullins." In *The Rise of the Laity in Evangelical Protestantism*, edited by Deryck W. Lovegrove, 236–52. London: Routledge, 2002.

———. "Democratic Congregationalism: A Seventh Baptist Distinctive in Peril." SBC Today Print Resources. Available at Internet Archive. Accessed December 16, 2022. https://web.archive.org/web/20130116085132/http://whub21.webhostinghub.com/~sbctod5/wp-content/uploads/2011/04/democraticcongregationalism.pdf.

INDEX

Adorno, Theodor, 23, 84, 114, 135, 140-149, 151, 152, 161, 163
Alliance of Baptists, 12, 20, 69, 127, 164
Ammerman, Nancy, 118, 176
Anzaldúa, Gloria, 194-196
anthropology, 22-23, 64, 72-112, 160-161
Aquinas, Thomas, 151
Arendt, Hannah, 187-188
Arminius, Jacobus, 85
associations, 31-32, 37, 49, 52, 53-55, 60, 61, 63, 65, 68, 69-70, 86, 175, 179, 226
Augustine of Hippo, 22, 74-75, 76-84, 85, 105-106, 108, 111, 134-135, 135n80, 152, 161
authority (*episkope*), 1-2, 4, 9, 12, 20, 23, 38, 41, 43, 45-46, 50, 93-94, 97, 119, 124, 127-129, 133, 167-190, 192-193, 205-209, 215-219, 224
autonomy, church, 1, 26, 32, 34-35, 43, 46, 61-62, 64
Backus, Isaac, 59-60, 64, 122
Baker, Ella, 184-185, 187
Baptist Faith and Message, 1, 25, 42-43, 62, 86, 119, 123-124, 124-126
Baptist Manifesto, 69, 99, 124, 130-131, 132, 133, 199, 202, 208
Baptist World Alliance, 96, 119, 182
Bapto-Catholics, 69, 131, 170, 197-200, 198n120, 216
Barth, Karl, 157, 201-203
Benson, Bruce Ellis, 18n62
Boswell, W. Benjamin, 19
Boyce, James Petigru, 125
Broadus, John, 125
Brown, John Newton, 62, 116
Browne, Robert, 3
Bryant, Scott, 128
Buber, Martin, 157

Calvin, John, 90-91
Calvinism, 20-21, 45, 63, 65-66, 85-87, 115, 119-120, 123
Canipe, Lee, 47n96, 101, 102
Christocracy, 26-29, 44
Church Growth Movement, 176-177
Clake, John, 211
confessions of faith, 1, 25, 28n10, 62, 86-87, 89, 91-93, 116, 121n29, 122-127, 151n167, 183, 198, 206-207, 208, 212
Conner, Walter T., 41
Connolly, William E., 15, 16, 17
communal hermeneutics, 169, 172, 209-215, 224-225
conflict and dissent, 2, 11-12, 13-14, 16, 19, 23, 24 26, 36-37, 44, 47, 58, 64, 69-70, 111, 112, 113-115, 116, 117n10, 118-120, 127-128, 133-134, 144, 146, 149-150, 162, 163-165, 177, 190, 192-193, 199, 202-204, 220-221, 223,
congregationalism, 1-5, 9-12, 27-30, 32-35, 37-39, 42-47, 48-51, 53, 63, 71, 72-73, 85, 89-90, 93-95, 103-105, 106-107, 113, 167-168, 172, 173-174, 176, 179-180, 182-183, 210
consensus, 5, 9, 13, 16, 31n23, 36-37, 44, 54, 58, 58n149, 114, 116, 123, 140, 144, 145-146, 148-149, 149-150, 187, 192, 201, 206, 220, 226
Cooperative Baptist Fellowship, 12, 20, 69, 119, 127n50, 164
Cotton, John, 211
covenants, church, 52, 121-122, 162, 179, 180-181, 183
Criswell, W.A., 176
critical theory, 13, 140-141, 145
Cross, Anthony R., 2
Dagg, J.L., 116, 174-175

democracy, 1-3, 5-7, 9-12, 13, 15, 16-17, 22, 25-48, 58, 70-71, 72, 81, 84, 101, 145, 167-168, 187, 190, 222, 223
Dever, Mark, 68
discipline, church, 31n23, 32, 35, 36, 37, 49, 50-53, 54, 55, 57-58, 61, 63, 65-70, 102, 116-117, 172, 173, 179, 181, 221
Dobbins, Gaines, 67
Draper, James T., 119n20
Drinker, Edward, 129
Dulles, Avery, 205-206
Edwards, Morgan, 175
egalitarianism, 1, 6, 27-28, 29, 30, 34, 35-37, 38, 42, 45-46, 49, 50-53, 55, 56-58, 65, 69, 72, 95, 106-107, 175-176, 187-188, 207
eschatology, 109, 115, 144, 160, 162-163, 164-165, 193, 200, 202, 204, 206-207, 218, 223, 227
Fiddes, Paul, 2, 182, 198n120, 207
Foucault, Michel, 22, 74-75, 77-79, 80, 81-84, 105, 107, 111
Freeman, Curtis W., 60n158, 102-103, 127n50, 130-132, 182n57, 198, 209n166, 215
Garrett, James Leo, Jr., 99, 125n41, 180
Gaustad, Edwin, 211
George, Timothy, 100, 182n57
Goold, Thomas, 211-212
Gouldbourne, Ruth, 2
Grantham, Thomas, 123
Grebel, Conrad, 209
Grenz, Stanley, 43-44, 45, 45n93, 46, 87-89, 173
Griffith, Benjamin, 49, 54, 175-176, 178-179
Habermas, Jürgen, 13, 23, 84, 114, 135, 142, 145-149
Harmon, Steven R., 131-132, 170-171, 178n37, 182, 198-209, 215, 216, 218-219, 220, 222
Harvey, Barry, 115
Hauerwas, Stanley, 13n42, 18, 184

Haymes, Brian, 2
Haynes, Dudley, 33-35, 40, 46
Hegel, G.W.F., 140
Helwys, Thomas, 11, 59, 59n153, 86, 92, 128-129
Hiscox, Edward T., 30-32, 34-35, 37, 47, 62, 116, 174n13, 174n16, 214
Hobbs, Herschell H., 42-43
Horkheimer, Max, 142, 145
Hudson, Winthrop S., 56, 63, 68, 68n197, 70, 99
Holmes, Obadiah, 211
Honig, Bonnie, 16n55
Hooper, John, 209
Hovey, Alvah, 94
Hume, David, 74, 135-136
Ignatius of Antioch, 169
individualism, 7-9, 10-11, 16, 22-23, 34, 36, 38-39, 42, 43, 46, 47-48, 56, 58-62, 64, 65-71, 96, 99-100, 102-105, 111-112, 113, 115n1, 130, 131, 132, 134, 156, 160, 164, 218, 221-222
Industrial Areas Foundation, 187-188, 196-197, 224
Irenaeus of Lyons, 157n187
James, William, 102-103
Jefferson, Thomas, 33-34, 56, 58
Johnson, W.B., 28-30, 29n15, 33, 41, 47, 93n101, 174
Jones, Robert P., 199
Kant, Immanuel, 23, 114, 134-140, 147, 149
King, Martin Luther, Jr., 185
Koyzis, David, 6-7, 7n20, 26n1
Laclau, Ernesto, 14
Land, Richard, 177
Landmarkism, 30, 32, 63-64, 65, 69
Łaski, Jan, 209
Lawton, J.S., 66
Leland, John, 26-28, 28n10, 30, 33, 38, 42, 46, 48, 59-60, 64, 94, 126
Leonard, Bill J., 11, 42, 120n24, 176
liberalism, 7-9, 13, 16, 17, 18, 18n62, 25, 26n1, 32, 34, 41, 64, 66, 68, 71, 75, 137, 194-195, 197, 221

Index

Little, Adrian, 12-13
Lloyd, Moya, 12-13
Locke, John, 59, 131, 132
Lumpkin, William, 125, 213n188
Luther, Martin, 161, 209
MacIntyre, Alasdair, 17-18, 191-193,
   201, 203
Madison, Jessica, 51
magisterium, 133, 178n37, 181, 205-
   208, 222, 225
Mantz, Felix, 209
Marney, Carlyle, 23, 114-115, 134,
   150, 153-165, 220, 222, 224
Marshall, Molly, 130
McBeth, Leon, 175
McClendon, James William, Jr., 3-4,
   4n12, 99n124, 133, 165n213,
   168n2
McNutt, William Roy, 117
Medley, Mark, 199-200
Mell, P.H., 116-117
Mercer, Jesse, 28, 46-47, 58
Merleau-Ponty, Maurice, 22, 74-75,
   79-84, 105, 107, 111
Milbank, John, 135n80
Mohler, R. Albert, Jr., 99
Mouffe, Chantal, 14, 223
Mullins, E.Y., 22-23, 37-41, 42, 44,
   46-47, 73, 95-112, 113, 117-118,
   130, 160, 179, 221, 223-224
Murphy, Nancey, 96n113
mutability principle, 23, 113, 120-127,
   149
Najar, Monica, 53
Newson, Ryan Andrew, 19
Oden, Thomas, 201
Pendleton, J.M., 30, 32, 34, 47, 62, 63-
   64, 115-116, 214
Pilgrims, 120, 210
priesthood of believers, 45, 94, 114,
   119, 133-134, 158-164, 183, 207,
   209
private judgment, 11, 34-35, 35-36, 42,
   46, 60-61, 71, 113-114, 127-134,
   149, 163-164, 212
Puritans, 3, 28n10, 129, 175, 209-213

radical democracy, 12-19, 24, 47-48,
   69-70, 73, 85, 90, 111-112, 114-
   115, 153, 164-166, 167-169, 194,
   220-223
Rainer, Thom, 176-177
Rawls, John, 75-76
receptive generosity, 15-16, 23, 114,
   133-135, 141, 143, 144-145, 149-
   153, 160, 164, 165, 184, 194, 224
revivalism, 63, 64, 66, 117, 214
Reynolds, J.L., 29-30, 47, 93-94, 174,
   176, 179, 181
Ricoeur, Paul, 201-202
Robinson, John, 120-121, 210
Sandel, Michael, 75-76
Schleiermacher, Friedrich, 157
Schlesinger, Jr., Arthur, 195
Scholer, David, 132-133
self, 22, 73-84, 88, 89, 100, 105-112,
   114, 134-135, 139, 142-143, 146-
   147, 156, 160-161, 221
Separate Baptists, 11, 20-21, 49, 51,
   58n149, 60, 126, 212-213
Separatists, 3, 72, 91-92, 120, 172,
   173, 175
Shurden, Walter B., 44-45, 46, 53-55,
   120n23, 125-126, 132-133
Smyth, John, 11, 86, 92, 120n25, 173-
   174, 210
soul competency, 22-23, 38-41, 42,
   44n88, 73, 96-106, 109, 111-112,
   124, 130, 179, 221, 223-224
Southern Baptist Convention, 1, 11-
   12, 20-21, 28, 44, 62, 66-68, 96,
   99, 118-119, 123-127, 164, 174,
   176-177, 180, 198
Stout, Jeffrey, 6n15, 7
Strong, Augustus H., 35-38, 41-42, 44,
   47, 87, 88-89, 94-95, 130, 180
Student Nonviolent Coordinating
   Committee, 170, 184-187, 219
Sutton, Jerry, 176
Taylor, Charles, 74, 109-110, 152
teleological and ateleological, 24, 48,
   90, 114-115, 150, 151, 153, 162-
   163, 164-166, 167, 169, 170, 171,

190, 191, 192-194, 196, 197, 204, 215, 218-219, 222-223
Thiel, John, 199-200
Thomassen, Lasse, 14
Thompson, David M., 131n68
Tilley, Terrence, 199-200
Tillich, Paul, 127
Tønder, Lars, 14
tradition (*traditio*), 23, 24, 131-132, 168-171, 183, 190-205, 208, 215-219, 220-221, 224
triple office (*munus triplex*), 22, 73, 90-96, 98, 104
Turner, William, 129
unity, 2, 23, 36-37, 39, 55, 58, 78, 112, 113, 115-120, 149, 164-165, 184, 198, 199, 202, 227
Wagner, C. Peter, 177n32
Ward, Graham, 6
Wayland, Francis, 34, 60-65, 94, 128, 129-130, 213-214
Weaver, C. Douglas, 66, 128, 199
Wellum, Steven J. and Kirk, 4, 179
West, Cornel, 15n55
Williams, D.H., 131-132
Williams, Rowan, 84, 151n167
Wills, Gregory, 57-58, 63, 65, 66, 71
Wittgenstein, Ludwig, 165n213
Wolin, Sheldon S., 14-15, 17
The Word of God in the Life of the Church, 182-184
Wright, Nigel G., 1-2
Yarnell, III, Malcolm, 45-46, 100
Yoder, John Howard, 17-18, 191, 193-194, 218-219
Zwingli, Huldrych, 209